F. E. PEACOCK PUBLISHERS, INC.   Itasca, Illinois

DEVELOPMENTAL EFFORTS IN

individualized

LEARNING

Edited by

ROBERT A. WEISGERBER

American Institutes for Research, Palo Alto

Contents

vi

Foreword

The art of progress
is to preserve order amid change,
and to preserve change amid order.
          ALFRED NORTH WHITEHEAD

The tenor of our times is one of change. In every facet of society we are constantly reminded of the fact that the techniques and methods of the past no longer are apt to be unchallenged, even when they may have served quite adequately to meet past needs. Indeed, the current emphasis on change has brought with it a kind of jargon that is semantically loaded. For instance, the lexicon of "revolution," "overthrow," "upheaval," and similar words implies drastic change with *no* inherent guarantee that the new offers any improvement over the old. But in contrast, "breakthrough," "advance," "innovation," and similar words we *assume* not only change but an inherent improvement. The use of these terms and the dynamics they represent are now as much a part of the educational system as they are in any other facet of our society.

It was fashionable, for quite a long time, to cite education as taking 50 years to assimilate a new development. Over the years numerous projects have been undertaken in order to disseminate educational information and to promote strategies for introducing change per se into what was viewed as essentially a static system.

Since the early 1960's, the momentum of change in education has been steadily increasing and today, partially in response to strong pressures from students, the whole framework of educational goals, curriculum, methods, and evaluation is undergoing "instant" revision—but *not* necessarily improvement.

In a trend that reflects our contemporary times, the emphasis is shifting from concern with the group norm toward concern for the individual, including his needs, his capabilities and his personal preferences. Though this trend is readily perceptible it is not equally clear just what *form* this individualization of teaching and learning should take, nor in what *contexts* it is most appropriately used. Interestingly enough, the very individuality of educators tends to make them view the subject of individualized learning from their unique perspectives. As a natural consequence there has been a proliferation of approaches.

ix

It is *not* the purpose of the companion books *Perspectives in Individualized Learning* and *Developmental Efforts in Individualized Learning* to provide an exhaustive coverage of all the efforts to individualize education that are under way today, for that would be as elusive a task as chasing change itself. Nor are they intended to answer the question of which approach is optimal, for that would be expected to vary with time and place, according to the educational purpose and within the constraints of locally available resources and personnel. Instead, these books are meant to provide some insight into the *process* of individualization through a selection of papers that represent both *principles and practice.*

Hopefully, the reader of *Perspectives in Individualized Learning* will develop a better understanding of some of the assumptions that underlie the concept of individualized learning, such as the determination of student need, specification of learning goals, and measurement of outcomes. The reader may also develop a better understanding of how these assumptions influence the functional roles of various components in the individualized setting, such as the teacher, technology and facilities.

Developmental Efforts in Individualized Learning should provide the reader with an understanding of how the underlying assumptions and operational components are being applied in major developmental projects presently under way across the country. The reader will also become aware of the diversity of practice that presently characterizes individualized learning at the local school level and in higher education.

Papers have been grouped within each book to facilitate the reader's choice of which papers he reads and the order in which he reads them. Each group of papers has been prefaced with an overview page which relates each paper to the topic. In spite of this effort at grouping papers on a basis of their presumed commonality, the reader will no doubt discover that certain papers have relevance to more than one of the topical groupings. It is hoped that the overview page will be a shortcut by which the reader can readily select those papers which are most relevant to his individual interests.

Observers of the movement toward individualization in recent years will no doubt note that some of the leaders of the movement, some of the pioneering school districts, and some of the more widely published papers have not been featured in either book. This is neither an oversight nor a denial of their importance, for the work of men such as Frederic Burk, and Robert Anderson, to name two, and the pioneering of schools like Winnetka and Duluth have helped to lead the way in a very real sense. Instead, these books, to the extent that space permits, will try to provide a balance between some familiar authors and some relatively new ones. An attempt will be made to give recognition to modest experiments in local schools as well as to larger, better known projects. As a result of presenting a variety of views, the reader may better be able to recognize and adopt those evolving ideas and approaches that seem to be pertinent to his *own* individual needs.

As suggested by Alfred North Whitehead's statement, cited previously, commitment to change per se is not sufficient. For educational change to be an improvement rather than simply a replacement of the old routine, Whitehead suggests that the change should be orderly rather than chaotic. If, in the broadest sense, the experimental, analytic studies of researchers and the iterative, pragmatic tryouts of educators can be interrelated through these companion books (i.e., seen as parts of a larger process of evolution in learning), then a measure of order may be introduced to optimize the sweeping changes which are already underway in education.

Lest it be overlooked, the effect to be achieved through the symbiotic interplay of change and order, according to Whitehead, is *progress*. This progress, it seems to this writer, cannot be simply equated to the lowering of costs, to simplifying the tasks of educators, or to a regeneration of school spirit that can result whenever there is appreciable break from routine. Rather, *progress should be measured by the extent to which the individualization of education can be demonstrated to have an observable and salutary effect on the learners themselves and on the process of learning.*

Acknowledgments

The companion books *Perspectives in Individualized Learning* and *Developmental Efforts in Individualized Learning* have resulted less from the vision of their editor than from the vision and leadership of John C. Flanagan. His conviction that learners should be recognized as individuals grows not from armchair reasoning but from decades of empiric research and development culminating in Project TALENT, a longitudinal study of 440,000 high school graduates who were the products of our educational system at the start of the sixties. His perceptiveness in recognizing that education's failure to meet the great diversity of needs in that student population was *not* an irreversible phenomenon led to his undertaking Project PLAN, described elsewhere in this book. In a very real sense, my association with John Flanagan in Project PLAN has educated *me* to the possibilities inherent in the individualization of education and to an awareness of the many diverse forms that individualization can take.

The editing of these books on an "off-duty" basis would have been immeasurably more difficult to achieve had not the organizational resources of the American Institutes for Research, particularly its library, been made available to me. Miss Laura Christopher and Mrs. Alice Grundy, Research Librarians, were most helpful. Similarly, the professional staff have been instrumental in providing me with intellectual inputs regarding the important parameters of individualized learning and in adding to my knowledge of persons and places active in the area. Thanks are due to Dr. William Shanner, Dr. Malcolm Danoff, Dr. Albert Chalupsky, Dr. H. J. A. Goodman, Dr. Richard Bell, and Dr. Charles Bollman for their counsel.

In compiling this selection of readings a concerted effort was made to contact schools where work was reported to be underway, regardless of whether any written report had already emanated from those locations. Numerous suggestions were received in response to these inquiries and this led to further correspondence seeking specific summaries of local effort. Finally, authors of published articles, as well as selected speakers whose papers seemed relevant, were contacted. The size of the stack of correspondence which resulted attests to the number of educators around the country to whom I owe thanks for their cooperation and for the materials they sent. For those who consented to have their papers used I owe a double measure of gratitude. I regret that space limitations precluded my using more of them.

My wife, Adrienne, was truly my helpmate during the course of the manuscript preparation. She not only served as corresponding secretary but in more relaxed moments helped me keep a sense of proportion as the

xiii

study in our house reached a state of constant overflow and disarray. Finally, she has shared with me the unique learning that has been ours to enjoy through long observation of two rather special individual learners—our children, Laraine and Scott, to whom these companion books are dedicated.

Part A

Individualized Programs at the National Level: The Project PLAN System

Introduction

Thirteen school districts from California, Massachusetts, New York, Pennsylvania and West Virginia joined with the American Institutes for Research and Westinghouse Learning Corporation in February, 1967, to begin the four year development of Project PLAN (Program for Learning in Accordance with Needs). The focus of their efforts was to be an individualized learning system spanning grades 1 through 12 in the subject areas of Language Arts, Science, Social Studies, and Mathematics. In subsequent years, related developmental support has come from the U.S. Office of Education relative to the areas of Guidance and Teacher Training. Beginning in 1969, at primary levels, the system was extended to certain additional school districts across the country on an economically self-supporting basis.

Project PLAN has been built on the premise that the long range goals of individual learners vary considerably, just as do their abilities and levels of achievement, and that this variation can be accommodated by a systematic reorganization of currently available learning materials into modular form so that educational experiences become more meaningful and learners become more self-motivated.

In each of the formative years three "grade levels" of teaching-learning units were developed, and then refined in the subsequent year. The initial years of tryout have made it abundantly clear that the original system design is workable. Revision cycles, to eliminate errors in the teaching-learning units and to introduce efficiencies in the classroom, are expected to continue (as recurring events) in the evolution of the system.

The six papers which follow deal with the philosophy and goals of Project PLAN (Chapter 1, John Flanagan); the underlying principles of guiding students through an appropriate curriculum according to their needs

(Chapter 2, James Dunn); the techniques by which learners are given options in learning materials and activities within a structured system of modules, each comprising alternative teaching-learning units (Chapter 3, Robert Weisgerber and Harold Rahmlow); the method for analyzing student performance as a criterion for revising and improving the teaching-learning units (Chapter 4, Harold Rahmlow); the mood and the look of an operational PLAN school (Chapter 5, Norman Carter); and the provision for teacher in-service training which is built into the system (Chapter 6, Margaret Steen).

The basic research and development for Project PLAN as undertaken by the American Institutes for Research had been completed by 1970 and the full individualized system had become reality in the four disciplines at all twelve grade levels. PLAN subsequently entered an expansion phase (Westinghouse Learning Corporation is the marketing organization) and by the end of 1970 was in active use in some 72 sites. Over 15,000 students were registered and approximately 21,000 module tests, as well as more than 1000 achievement and placement tests, were being taken during a given week. It is expected that the number of registered students will continue to expand at a rapid rate.

Chapter 1. THE GOALS OF
PROJECT *PLAN*

INDIVIDUALIZING EDUCATION

John C. Flanagan

In the early 1900's, Thorndike (1907) and other American educational psychologists (Ayres, 1909) studied what was happening to students entering American public schools. They found that, of those entering the first grade, less than 10% completed high school. Many students were held back year after year because of their failure to attain the high standards set by the classical curriculum. About this time a series of research studies designed to test the theory of mental faculties and the doctrine of mental discipline was carried out by Woodworth and Thorndike (1901). The important research programs that followed, provided a wide variety of new courses for the public schools. These course changes plus other factors during the past 50 years have made it possible for more than 70% of the students entering the first grade to graduate from high school.

The change from 10% to 70% certainly represents progress. However, in today's affluent society, 70% is definitely not good enough. America's

SOURCE: Reprinted from an invited address presented to Division 15, American Psychological Association, San Francisco, September, 1968. Published in *Education*, Vol. 90, No. 3 (February-March, 1970), pp. 191-206. Reprinted by permission of author and publisher.

educational program must be improved for the 30% who are now drop-outs and also for the middle 40% who are in many cases getting a watered-down college preparatory course rather than the types of education which would be of most value to them.

A major failure of American education is that many of our students are being taught the wrong things. Another deficiency shown by the recent Project TALENT survey (1964) is that the present instructional programs are not enabling students to achieve the levels in reading comprehension that are essential for effective participation in a democracy. For example, only 7% of 9th grade students and 25% of 12th grade students were able to answer correctly half of the questions based on typical paragraphs discussing national issues in *Time Magazine*. These results suggest that today's high school graduates are ill-equipped to evaluate the evidence and make wise decisions and choices with respect to important national issues.

That some of this failure to develop skill in reading comprehension is due to the assignment of inappropriate material is suggested by the fact that about 34% of both the boys and girls in the 12th grade stated (Flanagan, Dailey, Davis, Goldberg, Neyman, Orr, and Shaycoft, 1964) that about half the time or more frequently "I read material over and over again without really understanding what I have read."

Psychologists, by applying the methods of science and technology, can assist the nation in taking a major step in the improvement of the educational system. In 1967, while he was Secretary of Health, Education, and Welfare, a very distinguished psychologist, John W. Gardner (1967), stated that one of the major tasks facing our society is that: "We must redouble our efforts to create an educational system that will provide the maximum individual fulfillment for each American (p. 39)."

In the discussion of ways to improve education, there is frequent reference to individualizing instruction. To quote from a few experts:

> The desirability of individualizing instruction is no longer questioned by anyone. The objections to it are concerned chiefly with the application of the theory to classroom conditions. Among the many partial solutions offered to the problem is that of differentiated requirements, or the practice of varying the amount of work to be accomplished in accordance with the ability of the individual pupils of a group. While differentiating requirements makes possible a high degree of individualization, its successful administration in the classroom presupposes on the part of the teacher (1) knowledge of the educational status of his pupils as individuals, (2) organization of the materials of instruction so as to permit flexible assignments, and (3) the adoption of a technique of instruction which will enable the

teacher to use a large share of his teaching time in directing work rather than hearing lessons.

> The classroom then becomes a workshop in which the instructor is the director . . . individuals advance at their own rate and the instructor assigns to each the amount of assimilative material which in his judgment is needed to insure the understanding desired.

Or, to quote another expert in the same publication,

> Under the old regime in the effort to give different children the same subject matter in the same length of time, the quality of the children's work, the degree of their mastery, varied from poor to excellent, as attested by their report cards. But under the new technique of individual education, instead of quality varying, time varies: a child may take as much time as he needs to master a unit of work, but master it he must. The common essentials, by definition, are those knowledges and skills needed by everyone. To allow many children, therefore, to pass through school with hazy and inadequate grasp of them, as one must under the class lock-step scheme, is to fail in one of the functions of the school.

These quotes may have a contemporary ring but they are statements made by Reavis (p. 49, 1925) of the University of Chicago High School and Washburne (p. 79, 1925) of the Winnetka Public Schools in the 1925 Yearbook of the National Society for the Study of Education entitled, *Adapting the Schools to Individual Differences.* The same yearbook describes how San Francisco State College installed in 1913 what was then called "the individual system" of Burk. This system was used with all 700 children in the training school.

In the 1962 Yearbook of the same group entitled, *Individualizing Instruction,* Wilhelms (1962) says analysis of various systems including the Winnetka plan,

> . . . reveals a disappointing amount of true individualization. In both schemes there has been far too much tendency to individualize with respect to little more than *rate of progress.* . . . And one must have a meager conception of individualization to settle for students merely being able to do these same things at a different pace. Such "individualization" largely fails to come to grips with the fundamental differences among students—differences in their interests and purposes, their personal needs, and their whole modes of thinking and learning (p. 65).

Thus, in the 1960's, as 50 years ago, educational leaders see a very great need for the individualization of instruction because of individual differences among our students. Many groups are giving thought at the present time to how education can be improved. An excellent statement has just been published by the Committee for Economic Development (1968) under the title, *Innovation in Education: New Directions for the American School*. In a recently published discussion, Carter (1968) presented seven points drawn from a variety of studies and experiences, relating to using knowledge in attacking major contemporary problems. In a recent paper Flanagan (1967) presented 11 points on using research and development to improve education. All of these discussions emphasize the need for extensive research, experiment, development, and evaluation in education. They emphasize the importance of evaluation, both in a formative and summative sense. They also emphasize the importance of a comprehensive program as contrasted with fragmentary, small local efforts.

What efforts have been made in the last 50 years to adapt education to individual differences and what are the important considerations educational psychologists must keep in mind in approaching this problem? To adapt for individual differences, four aspects of the educational program have been varied. Perhaps the most common type of adaptation to individual differences has been in terms of differentiated assignments. Students have been asked to read different books, to write about topics of their own choosing and related to their own interests, and to do projects and papers related to their specific abilities and interests. These types of differentiated assignments, under the name of enrichment or adaptation, have been the hallmark of the master teacher for many years. The second type of adaptation to individual differences is with respect to rate of learning. Although the recent surveys of Goodlad and Anderson (1963) suggest that this is not as prevalent as the frequency of reference to ungraded schools might suggest, it is clearly the next most popular way of handling individual differences. The third procedure for varying instruction is in terms of methods and media.

In the past, these types of adaptation have been mainly confined to the primary levels to help children learn to read and to acquire the other fundamental skills. Teachers have varied their approach to fit the particular child's needs. Although teachers have done a good deal of improvising and adapting, there is almost no adequately verified knowledge regarding the matching of methods, media and materials to learning styles, but many psychologists and educators are convinced that research in this area will be very rewarding in improving the efficiency of instruction.

The last and most important of the methods of adapting education to individual differences is with respect to the goals of the educational program. In the typical elementary school today there is very little variation in goals. The secondary schools, by offering a choice of courses and a choice of electives, are providing some opportunity for variation of this type. However, there is a definite need for more flexibility and more adaptation of the educational program to the goals of the individual at both the elementary and the secondary level.

Before proceeding to a discussion of the problems and research opportunities confronting educational psychologists it is important to make a distinction between the title of this paper, "individualizing education," and the more commonly used term "individualizing instruction." The distinction made here is that a program of instruction is one which imparts knowledge and skills with respect to specific well-defined goals. A program of education includes, in addition to instruction, assisting the student to become acquainted with the many opportunities, roles and activities which life offers and assisting the student to gradually develop convictions as to the relation of his own unique talents, interests, and values to these possible roles. In simpler terms, individualized education includes guidance and individual planning. Individualized instruction does not include such a formulation of goals and plans.

An effective program for individualizing education must be based on extensive additional psychological research and development work in at least five areas. In the discussion which follows, it will become very clear that each of these five areas represents a major challenge to psychologists. The accumulation of verified building blocks in any one area will require not only a number of years, but also a substantial effort in terms of both cost and quality of research and development staff. Only by demonstrating significant progress in each of these five areas can psychologists hope to obtain the type of support essential for carrying out their role with respect to the most important mission facing society today—the education of our young.

EDUCATIONAL OBJECTIVES: FORMULATING THE FUNCTIONS OF AN EDUCATIONAL SYSTEM

The topic of educational objectives raises many questions of philosophy and values. However, in present-day American society, there is substantial agreement on the general purposes of American education as shown by the reports of many committees and commissions who have studied the functions of the schools in the past several decades. Although each group expresses their educational goals in slightly different terms, the central theme, with great consistency, is the maximum individual fulfillment for each American. See, for example, the statement in *Goals for Americans* (1960). Included in individual fulfillment is, of necessity, the development of an environment in terms of a social and civic order which will make this possible. Similarly, individual fulfillment can be thought of as having two major components; fulfillment in work or a career, and fulfillment in leisure time, cultural, and recreational pursuits.

It is believed that the educational system of the future should be able to take for granted the satisfaction of such primitive drives as Maslow's (1954) physiological and safety or security requirements. This would make it possible to concentrate on the higher order drives in his hierarchy including affiliation or close affective relations and achievement and esteem. The desired condition would be to enable each person to focus primarily on his highest level drive, self-actualization, involving the full development of his potential in terms of skills, abilities, and appreciation.

In the complex society of the present day, with the great diversity of individual talents, interests, and values, it is obvious that only by individualizing the goals of education can we hope to achieve full and satisfying lives for each of our citizens.

Granted these desirable general goals for the educational system, how do we determine for a particular child, the nature and sequence of achievement of educational goals which will make it possible for him to obtain individual fulfillment?

Typically, the solution to this problem has been sought in terms of a colossal over-simplification of the nature and scope of the investigation required to provide meaningful statements of educational objectives. The first over-simplification has been to establish only one set of goals for all the nation's children for the elementary schools. For example, the recent goals set for education in Pennsylvania (1965) could be cited. Even at the secondary school level, the number of separate sets of goals which has been established has been very limited. What is needed is a unique set of goals for each individual. Thus from the universe of all educational objectives deemed acceptable by whatever developmental procedure is utilized, one can select a unique set in terms of the educational requirements for each individual. These goals must be formulated in terms of his particular pattern of talents, interests, and values, and the relation of these to the opportunities, roles, and activities for which he wishes to prepare.

The second serious over-simplification in establishing goals is the assumption that a group of 10, 20, or 100 adults, even though very wise and experienced, has the necessary background and information to formulate, using their memories and judgment, a comprehensive set of educational objectives to be offered to the students. The most extensive effort of this type in recent years has been that of the efforts at national assessment under the auspices of the Exploratory Committee on Assessment of Progress in Education (Tyler, 1966). There seems no adequate substitute for wise and experienced committees, but these committees must be supplied with much more detailed information about the skills and abilities possessed by the students at various levels of development, their needs at the next levels, and particularly, the requirements for effective participation in the roles and activities which are likely to be open to them.

There are many ways to collect the detailed information about requirements in terms of knowledge, abilities, and appreciations which are essential for successful performance in specific roles. A leading expert in this field, Ralph W. Tyler (1951) suggests studies of learners, studies of the demands of life outside the school, the views of subject-matter scholars and philosophers, and studies of the psychology of learning as sources of the required information. As examples, two types of information-gathering procedures are proposed here. The first of these consists in the collection at several levels, such as 4th grade, 8th grade, and 12th grade and 5 years and 10 years after graduation, of intensive longitudinal case studies of individual development. It is believed that following these individuals through time with relatively complete information about their initial status and their progress would provide a basis for a much better understanding of the achievements required at a particular level to insure success in the appropriate activities at the next level. Experience has shown (Flanagan, 1966) that it is quite difficult to say what would be the best experience this year for a fourth-grade class. It is much easier for competent observers to agree on a specific program for a particular boy, given the detailed facts about his background, abilities, interests, values, and recent experiences. The facts usually point quite clearly to what the school can best do for his development during the next year.

The second type of information to be collected for the committees would be the analysis and summarization of several thousand critical incidents (Flanagan, 1954) on specific behaviors observed by teachers, parents, and other observers. These incidents would involve specific observed behaviors which indicated a particular student deficiency. Here again it has been found that there is little difficulty in getting two observers of a specific behavior on the part of a child to indicate that either this is something which should be encouraged or it is something which should be corrected and improved for the child's effective growth and development. These specific observations would also be of very great value in contributing to the judgments of appropriately established committees. Such committees should include lay citizens, teachers, educational administrators, subject-matter specialists, and scholars in philosophy, human learning, and development.

In recent years there has been considerable controversy over the form in which educational objectives should be presented to the teacher and to the student. The recent stress on terminal objectives and specific behavioral objectives (Mager, 1962) has revealed the undue emphasis in current education on trivial aspects of subject fields as compared with objectives more likely to be relevant in the achievement of important goals. There is also little doubt that there is need for caution against accepting the more easily specified objectives as Atkin (1968) and Travers (1968) have noted. Outcomes such as creative originality in art or undesirable, unplanned effects such as the dislike of the field of mathematics, could as easily be overlooked by a zealous curriculum builder bent on "stamping out non-behavioral objectives" as by those who build their curriculum on the basis of broad goals such as these and fail to formulate specific definitions of what is meant by these goals.

The appropriate procedure certainly must include providing as much objectivity, specificity, and relevance as possible in the definition of educational objectives. However, if we cannot specify any set of judgments by any group of persons which will establish that Exhibit A shows more creative originality in art than Exhibit B, it may be just as well for us to drop this as an objective for our Art Department.

A basic skill, such as reading comprehension, which takes many years to develop to a reasonable adult level is much more important than any group of easily specified behavioral objectives. However, there are many who would argue that reading comprehension consists of a very comprehensive and complicated use of an extraordinarily large number of behavioral elements. If these can be identified and taught in such a way as to improve the reading comprehension of our 12th-grade students this will certainly be an important development.

Other long-range objectives are such items as learning how to learn, taking responsibility for learning, and learning to manage one's own learning program.

The effort required to develop a comprehensive set of educational objectives which includes appropriate sub-sets for each of our young people, will be of very great scope. Furthermore, the changing society and technological and scientific advances together with the expected increase in understanding of human learning processes should require that these objectives be in a constant state of revision and modification. The point to be emphasized is that the present stage of development in terms of deriving objectives for individual students is somewhere between pre-primitive and primitive and a very major effort will be required in the next few years to obtain a clear picture of the goals of American education.

LEARNING METHODS AND MATERIALS: ACHIEVING THE INDIVIDUAL'S EDUCATIONAL GOALS

Once the objectives have been established, the only criterion for evaluating the quality of instruction is efficiency. This statement, of course, assumes that the list of desired objectives is complete and precise. Both Carroll (1968) and Gagné, as reported by Lange (1968), after acknowledging the serious limitations of our present knowledge regarding the conditions of learning in the classroom, point out that presently available instructional material does not make use of the many well-established principles of learning. Recent experience suggests that perhaps this discrepancy between well-established psychological knowledge and current instructional materials may not be as important as it might appear.

For example, two teams of psychologists, one headed by Markle, and the other by Short, both of the American Institutes for Research, recently undertook the development of specific instructional programs in which one of the major goals was efficiency in attaining a high level of mastery. In both instances it was found that the major gains in efficiency in the program came not from insights and applications of psychological principles, but from repeated empirical tryouts and feedback as to the effectiveness of the initial attempts to assist the student to learn. The very dramatic improvement obtained in these courses as a result of a series of empirical tryouts emphasizes the great inadequacy of our present knowledge regarding learning. In Markle's study (1967) the procedures of empirical tryout and revision resulted in a program which enabled the least apt student using the new instructional materials and methods to learn as much as the most apt student using the earlier materials. In Short's study (1968), using a somewhat similar procedure, a high level of mastery of all important objectives was obtained in a fraction of the time required by the programs previously in use.

Certainly progress is being made toward understanding classroom learning. Gagné's conditions of learning (1965), Briggs' monographs (1967, 1968) on instructional media and sequencing of instruction, and Carroll's recent article (1968) on learning from being told appear to point the way toward better understanding of what is happening in the classroom. Another promising approach to understanding the apparent changes in the quality of performance in age-related stages of development as noted by Piaget and others is Gagné's recent article (1968) proposing that behavioral development results from the cumulative effects of learning rather than from simple maturation or the acquisition of a basically different ability to deal with logical processes.

In adapting learning methods and materials to a specific individual, the concept of "quality of instruction" can be easily extended to indicate the degree to which the task to be learned is structured or organized in such a way that it is optimally efficient for the specific learner. In discussing this problem, Cronbach (1967) includes four procedures for adapting instruction to individual differences. The first and simplest of these is, given a fixed set of instructional materials, simply vary the time given the student for completion. The second type of adaptation discussed by Cronbach is matching goals to the individual. Cronbach points out a number of limitations and possible dangers of too much emphasis on dropping goals for individuals because of their difficulty in attaining them. The third type of adaptation he mentions is by erasing individual differences. The suggestion here is that if a requisite ability has not been adequately developed that attention be given to the development of the ability prior to initiating work with the instructional materials. The last of the methods mentioned is adaptation to individual differences by altering instructional methods. Such items are discussed as interactions between learning abilities and performance. There is also a discussion of designing alternative treatments to interact with variables which seem likely to show differential results. The final point discussed is adaptation to take advantage of the interaction between such attitudes as willingness to take risks, confidence, and motivation for achievement.

In his discussion of Cronbach's points, Carroll (1967) suggests that psychologists must do a great deal of research before we can be sure that the achievement of all pupils seeking a given educational goal will be optimal and significantly better than if we had used a single best method to teach all of them. Significant findings in the search for individual learning styles have been reported by Beard (1967), Kropp (1967), and Tallmadge (1968), among others. Because of the very great number of patterns of individual differences, an enormous amount of research needs to be done to even approach being able to prescribe the optimal instructional materials and methods for each student to learn each type of educational objective. The recent surveys by Briggs suggest that sequencing and the selection of the most appropriate media may be of great importance in achieving efficiency in instructional programs.

EVALUATION: MONITORING THE INDIVIDUAL'S PROGRESS

A basic requirement in developing any system of education is to be able to assess its outcomes. Much of the evaluation of school programs done in the past decades has been in terms of the analysis and description of the school's facilities and organization for education. Accreditation of schools and similar types of evaluation have been done in terms of such variables as the assessment of the quality of the educational building, the equipment of the classrooms, the number of books in the library, the pupil/teacher ratio, the amount of training of the teachers, and similar factors. Elaborate systems have been established for conducting this type of evaluation and teams regularly carry on school evaluations of this type throughout the country. It need hardly be added that most of the variables studied have been shown to have no relation to the quality of instruction received by the students.

In recent years, considerable attention has been given to the process of instruction. Observations have been made of teacher behaviors and student behaviors in classrooms. These have been classified, and more recently, studies have been made of the relation of various types of teacher behaviors to student learning. Certainly the study of process is important in education and work along this line will be discussed more fully in a later section on teacher development.

The trend at the present time is very strongly in the direction of evaluating the product of education in terms of the preparation and development of students. Most of the present evaluation programs suffer from two serious defects. First, only a limited number of the basic skills and types of knowledge included in the educational program are sampled in the testing programs. Second, there is a tendency to give all students all of the various measures whether they are relevant to that particular student's developmental program or not.

An effective program for evaluating the effectiveness of the education provided an individual must be very comprehensive in scope so as to include all of the objectives planned by this student. The student must receive detailed feedback regarding the success of his learning activities in the past week or two. Periodically there must be measures of his progress with respect to such long-range abilities as reading comprehension, vocabulary knowledge, and problem-solving. It is especially important that the assessment procedures for the more important long-range objectives include estimates of progress with respect to such very important, but very difficult to measure objectives, as originality, effectiveness of written expression, and various attitudes and appreciations. It is also important that the comprehensive assessment program include provisions for evaluating the presence of any unplanned effects resulting from the educational program of either a desirable or undesirable nature.

To communicate to the individual his progress with respect to his educational program, it is especially important to be able to report the progress in meaningful terms. For example, it is much more useful to be able to report to the student that he has learned the English equivalents of 5,000 French words and is able to read stories designed for elementary school children, but will have difficulty with a typical Paris newspaper, than to report that he has reached the 86th percentile in terms of second-year norms for high school French.

Some progress has been made in developing assessment procedures for the most difficult objectives, but it will take a large effort over quite a long period of years before very satisfactory procedures are available for assessing all of the outcomes of elementary and secondary education.

A second function of the evaluation program is to determine the effectiveness of the instructional methods and materials. The importance of empirical feedback for improving programs of this type was mentioned in the previous section. In recent years, research and development workers in education and psychology have adopted the words "formative" and "summative" evaluation to differentiate the evaluation used to improve the instructional materials while they are in the process of development from the terminal evaluation of the final product. If instructional materials and methods are to be improved substantially in the next few years, much formative evaluation will have to be done.

The final type of evaluation to be mentioned is in terms of the effectiveness of the educational program in preparing the student for the roles, opportunities, and activities which he engages in as an adult. This type of evaluation is of great relevance and many more studies involving long-range follow-up should be carried out. Insofar as possible, in this, as in all other types of evaluation, systematic efforts should be made to relate specific instructional methods and materials and their objectives with the more ultimate outcomes in terms of effectiveness in the adult role. Only in this way can the educational system anticipate continued improvement in terms of known effectiveness.

GUIDANCE AND INDIVIDUAL PLANNING: FORMULATING GOALS AND PLANNING INDIVIDUAL DEVELOPMENT

In a recent survey of students one year and five years after they graduated from high school, these students were asked to evaluate their high school experience in this study by Flanagan (1966). One item asked them to complete the sentence, "The main thing I believe I needed which was not provided by this high school was _____." Approximately 25% of the students in each class indicated that "guidance and counseling" was the most important unfilled need in their high school education. This was by far the most frequent response in both classes. The only other comment which was made by an appreciable proportion of the students was "assistance in learning how to study." The other replies were scattered over a wide variety of needs.

Some of the basis for this dissatisfaction with the school's guidance program was shown in the report on the one-year follow-up studies of Project TALENT. In that report by Flanagan and Cooley (1966) it was found, for example, that only 19% of the boys who indicated in the 10th grade they were planning one of 30 occupations as a career reported they had the same plans three years later. Some persons have interpreted the results of these and related studies to indicate that secondary school students are "too young to choose." This implies that counselors, parents, teachers, or others must make their decisions for them. Other writers (Cicourel and Kitsuse, 1963) deplore the fact that the adolescent is forced to make decisions and to declare choices from a range of alternatives he can hardly be expected to know. These writers suggest that school personnel now have control of the access of students to the curricula and therefore over their major life decisions.

In a recent rejoinder to some of these comments and discussion, McDaniels (1968) states, "Youth are not too young to choose, only too poorly prepared to make choices (p. 242)." Although one can sympathize with the 45-year-old businessman looking back on his life with some dissatisfaction and regrets who said, "Who gave that 18-year-old boy the authority to determine my life?" His quarrel is not primarily that someone else should have made the decision for him, but principally that nobody prepared him in terms of information and skills to make that decision.

In this field also psychologists are embarrassed by the lack of sound principles and data to provide the basis for an effective program. Students are not receiving adequate assistance at the present time even for the relatively limited decisions permitted by the lock-step conventional school organization. The need for choices, decisions, and plans becomes very much greater in a system of individualized education. The research findings required to set up an effective program of guidance and individual planning in an individualized educational system include three types of data:

1.   The first type of finding required includes the data essential to assist the student to formulate his life goals. These goals would refer to various possible adult roles and activities with respect to a career, leisure pursuits, and social and citizenship responsibilities. It is assumed that these goals would be in the nature of general directions and would be in a continuous state of development rather than pin-pointed and fixed.

2.   The second type of information needed is that required to develop a program for helping the student take responsibility for and plan a developmental program which will enable him to achieve his goals. It is important that he develop skill in planning and decision-making, and that these plans and decisions be based on sound information regarding the alternatives and probabilities that he can successfully achieve specific objectives included in his plans. The five-year follow-up data from Project TALENT supply some of the required data. However, little information is available as to how to assist a young person to develop skill in making wise decisions and choices using these data and other relevant information.

3.   The third area in which information is needed is how to assist students to manage and achieve their planned developmental program. The studies of Skinner (1953), Homme (1966), and Bandura (1964), suggest that it may be possible to assist students to manage their developmental programs by using techniques of reinforcement or contingency management. Although confirmed research findings with respect to the application of some of these techniques to problems of student development are even more limited than in some of the other areas mentioned, the promise is great and the rewards for an effective program would be of very fundamental importance.

As support for these major functions of an effective program of guidance and individual planning, a number of additional types of information must be obtained. One of these is information on how to communicate an understanding of his personal characteristics including his abilities, interests, and values to an individual in such a way that they provide a sound basis for formulating goals and plans. A discussion of some of the factors involved in transmitting this type of information is given by Berdie (1969). He emphasizes the need for much more specific and experimentally established information in this area.

One of the greatest deficiencies in present educational programs, as pointed out by McDaniels (1968), is the failure to transmit to the student a comprehensive understanding of opportunities, roles, and activities which provide the alternatives from which he must choose. The other specific need is for procedures based on extensive research and development work establishing a program for developing the ability to make sound decisions and plans. Krumboltz (1965), Thoresen (1967), and Tiedeman (1961), have all contributed to defining this area and indicating its importance, but only a beginning has been made on establishing the relations necessary to develop an effective program in this area.

The values of goals and plans in which the individual firmly believes have been repeatedly demonstrated. There are few contributions which psychologists could make to the next generation which would have a greater impact than enabling them to develop realistic plans for individual fulfillment in careers, in leisure activities, and in social and civic responsibilities.

TEACHER DEVELOPMENT: PREPARING THE TEACHER FOR INDIVIDUALIZING EDUCATION

In any system of education the focus should be on the individual student. The primary responsibility for helping him set goals, assume responsibility, identify appropriate instructional materials and methods, and monitor his progress is the teacher's. No program for individualizing education can succeed without adequately preparing the teachers for their roles. An excellent discussion of this preparation is provided by Swenson (1962). She stresses the importance of giving teachers an understanding of individual differences and the importance of the teacher's role in guiding learning and controlling the environment for learning.

The preparation of most teachers has included some of the knowledges and understandings required to deal with children as individuals. However, because of the lack of adequate support procedures and appropriate programs, most of the teachers have had very little opportunity to individualize their educational programs in more than a superficial way. Some insights into the research and development problems facing those responsible for the training of teachers for individualizing instruction may be gained from a recent discussion by Gage (1968).

In his discussion of the development of technical skills in teachers through such new procedures as micro-teaching, he listed nine technical skills. These include: *(a)* establishing set; *(b)* establishing appropriate frames of reference; *(c)* achieving closure; *(d)* using questions; *(e)* recognizing and obtaining attending behavior; *(f)* control of participation; *(g)* providing feedback; *(h)* employing rewards and punishment; and, *(i)* setting a model. Although some of these technical skills will apply equally whether the teacher is working in an individualized program or in a conventional classroom setting, there are several of them which would not be appropriate in the individualized setting and there are several others not included in the list which become of great importance in the individualized instruction setting.

Considerable attention has been devoted to teacher selection, training, and supervision. There are very few published research findings regarding the identification of effective practices in either individualizing instruction or in the usual classroom situation. In the article mentioned, Gage reports the preliminary identification of two specific types of activity which seem to discriminate on cross-validation between teachers who are effective and teachers who are less effective in assisting students to learn the same sets of materials. He terms these two activities, "explaining links" or providing the how, why, or effect of something, and the "rule-example-rule" presentation which involves stating a generalization, giving examples, and summarizing a series of illustrations at a higher level of generality than used in the illustrations. Much more research of this type will be required before we can be confident that we are preparing teachers who will be of maximum assistance to the students in an individualized education program. This is emphasized by recent findings of Popham (1967) and others that untrained college students and housewives were as effective as teachers in assisting students to learn a specific lesson.

PROJECT *PLAN:* INDIVIDUALIZING EDUCATION USING THE KNOWLEDGE NOW AVAILABLE

The foregoing listing of the needs for research and development to plan and carry out an effective program for individualizing education are somewhat staggering. Certainly the things we do not know seem to very greatly exceed those that we do know. However, it does appear that we do know how to assist students to learn better than the programs exemplified by current practice in schools. Therefore, a number of psychologists and educators have joined with a learning corporation and a number of school districts in a developmental program to attempt to move one step up the ladder toward the type of individualized educational program that appears possible.

This program, known as Project PLAN (Program for Learning in Accordance with Needs), was tried out in three grades, 1, 5, and 9, with the assistance of 14 cooperating school districts during the past academic year with 2,000 students. This year 4,000 students in grades 1, 2, 5, 6, 9, and 10 will be participating in Project PLAN. Having recited all of the things we don't know about individualizing education, it may be useful to review briefly the preliminary decisions made in establishing this program. As an introduction to these points, the major strategy in initiating the program will be summarized. First, we chose to work within the school setting and closely with school personnel. Second, a comprehensive, rather than a piecemeal approach to the problem was selected. Third, only those school districts who were sufficiently interested and committed to make a substantial contribution in time and funds were included. Fourth, a team of behavioral scientists with long experience in the application of research and development to practical problems was assembled. Fifth, plans for the program from the outset included the evaluation of each aspect of the program in terms of the assessment of the results with the students. And sixth, the developmental program was scheduled over a several year period with a clear indication at the outset that initial progress could be expected to be slow and difficult.

The major decisions made with respect to the five points discussed above including educational objectives, learning methods and materials, evaluation, guidance and individual planning, and teacher development are reported briefly below.

1. *Educational Objectives.* With respect to educational objectives, Project PLAN has developed comprehensive lists for grades 1 to 12 which reflect current thought and practice. These lists have been prepared in the four subject-matter areas of language arts, social studies, science, and mathematics. They are based on the reports of various committees which have been studying the curriculum in connection with new government-sponsored developmental programs in these areas and on the available instructional materials.

It is intended that each Project PLAN student select his own educational objectives with the help of his teacher. For the present these are restricted to objectives for which instructional materials are available. It is expected that as better information becomes available about the educational objectives of most value to students with specific ambitions in terms of life goals and activities, it will be possible to develop new instructional materials to permit the student to achieve these objectives efficiently.

In Project PLAN about five objectives are grouped together in a module. Each of the objectives is intended to require two to three hours to achieve, and thus the module is intended as approximately a two-week segment of instruction.

2. *Learning Methods and Materials.* As indicated above, it was decided that Project PLAN should begin with available instructional materials and media. To provide the necessary flexibility for individualizing education, several teaching-learning units are provided for each module. A teaching-learning unit is a four-page guide which lists each objective along with the materials to be used by the student in attaining this objective. An effort has been made to provide for individual differences in terms of interests and learning styles by presenting several alternate routes to achieve the same

objectives. The various teaching-learning units make varying use of audio-visual media and capitalize on such differences as there are in the instructional methods used by different authors and publishers.

An important aspect of this program is the evaluation of the effectiveness of the various instructional methods and materials in terms of learners with known characteristics. By dividing the instructional program into manageable segments of these types, it is possible to vary the time spent on objectives. A person might complete as few as 12 modules, or as many as 24 modules in a year in a particular subject. Also, the procedure makes possible at least a limited adaptation of the individual's learning style to an available instructional program. Finally, the modules permit tailoring the curriculum for each student to his short-range and long-range objectives and requirements.

3. *Evaluation.* The program of monitoring and evaluating Project PLAN is accomplished with two main types of assessment materials. The first type includes specific test questions focused on the achievement of the objectives in a particular module. These questions, or alternate forms of them, are also used in placement and survey tests. They are intended to indicate mastery of the stated objective.

The second type of assessment procedure is designed to measure a long-term objective. An example of one of the most important objectives of this type is reading comprehension. Other objectives of this type would include attitudes, appreciations, originality, and other important skills and abilities which require more than two weeks to develop.

Procedures other than pencil and paper tests are used, particularly to assess some of the long-term objectives of the program.

4. *Guidance and Individual Planning.* The guidance and individual planning program of Project PLAN represents a major developmental effort in this educational system. Two factors have led to this emphasis: First, the conviction that individual planning must be a central function in a program for individualizing education; and, second, the newly available data from Project TALENT students given a comprehensive set of tests and followed-up five years after they had completed their high school courses. These data provide a solid foundation on which to build a career planning program. The Project PLAN program is focused on assisting each student to formulate his goals in terms of adult opportunities, roles, and activities; to take responsibility for and plan a developmental program to achieve these goals; and to learn to manage his own developmental program to carry out these plans.

The Project PLAN guidance and individual planning program consists of four major components. The first two are primarily related to information and concepts and their interpretation. And the second two are more specific skills and abilities for planning and carrying out the individual's development based on the knowledge presented in the first two components.

(a)   The first component is a program for acquainting each individual with the status of his development with respect to abilities, interests, physical and social characteristics and values in the areas of education, vocations, social behaviors, citizenship, and the use of leisure time. This program should include developing an understanding of individual differences during childhood, adolescence, and maturity and the basic principles of learning. In this program it is proposed to substitute for the concepts of intelligence and aptitudes, the slightly different concept of developed abilities. The concepts of aptitude and intelligence connote abilities which are too fixed and unchangeable. The concept of developed abilities is given a much more controllable quality. The individual would be informed of the level of development of his abilities in statements having direct meaning such as the number of words he understands from among those listed in *Webster's Collegiate Dictionary*. Or, his ability to read might be reported in terms of the types of materials he can read with a defined level of comprehension, for example, the type of text book or newspaper or news magazine which he understands.

In interpreting the student's score on reading comprehension the student would be told that the average gain in reading comprehension on this particular test of developed ability in reading comprehension was 6 points. It could be pointed out that his chances of being admitted to an engineering program in a university and completing this program would be less than 10 in 100 if his gain during the next three years was only 6 points. On the other hand, if he were able to increase this gain to 12 points, his chances of success would be increased to 50 in 100. Information could also be supplied to the student on the frequency with which gains of this size have occurred. This type of interpretation will be discussed in terms of planning and decision-making skills.

(b)   The second component consists of a program to familiarize the student with the variety of opportunities, roles, and activities in the world of work, in social and civic relations, and in cultural, recreational, and other leisure time pursuits. This information includes the educational requirements for various occupations, the competencies in terms of developed abilities required for admission and success in these occupations, and the conditions and importance of each of the various roles. Similar types of information would be provided with respect to the other types of adult activities for which the student might wish to prepare himself.

(c)   The third component is a program to assist each student to formulate his long-term goals and to take the responsibility for and plan a developmental program to achieve these goals. Each individual would be assisted in relating his personal potentials for developing abilities, his interests, and his values with opportunities likely to be available to him. The

program would include substantial training in decision-making and problem-solving. One procedure which will be used extensively is to give the student practice in making decisions and plans for other students on the basis of their Project TALENT information. The decisions and plans made for the student would then be compared with the experience of this student in real life. This training is being formalized in a career game which would ask the student to make a series of decisions for a specific person with known characteristics. These decisions would cover a period of 10 or 15 years in the life of the hypothetical person whose career was being planned, but would be made on the basis of periodic feedback in just a few weeks by the person being trained in planning and decision-making. Feedback would be provided based on Project TALENT data in the same way as in the usual simulation and business games. Only after the individual has shown considerable competence in making plans for these other students which are appropriate and in accordance with their goals and abilities would he be asked to make decisions having to do with his own development.

(d) The last component in the guidance program is a set of procedures designed to assist the student in learning to manage his own development. This development would be defined in terms of his goals and plans. It is proposed that one of the inputs to this program would be the record of critical incidents observed by the teacher which defines certain areas needing improvement in behavior. It is anticipated that at least some students will be able to carry out a program of reinforcement of desirable behaviors which will correct their behavioral patterns in those areas in which improvement is needed. Other students will require more direct assistance from teachers, counselors, and parents in managing their development programs.

5. *Teacher Development.* The teacher development program of Project PLAN consists of two parts. The first part is a three day individualized program which uses modules, teaching-learning units, objectives, and tests. To achieve these objectives, extensive use is made of motion pictures and video tapes. In using the motion pictures and video tapes, there is considerable emphasis on modeling for the teacher and actual practice by the teacher of the skills found to be most important in individualizing education along the lines of Project PLAN. This practice is recorded on video tape and critiqued to improve the teacher's performance. The second phase of the teacher development program is the in-service training program. This consists of the identification of problems, the discussion and development of solutions, and the additional use of modeling and practice techniques to develop effective behavior patterns during the school year.

CONCLUSION

In concluding this discussion, it seems appropriate to mention that we do use a computer in Project PLAN. The function of the computer is simply to perform clerical and statistical activities of a teacher-support nature. These activities include test scoring, preparing records, filing, matching characteristics, and estimating probabilities. The program could function without a computer, but it would be more expensive and less responsive. The Project PLAN system is an adaptive system in the sense that the response of the system is modified by the nature of the input. In Project PLAN, in any given subject, inputs and adaptive responses occur at only two-week intervals in any subject. It is the belief of the group working on Project PLAN that an adaptive system is essential, but that modification of the instructional program at two-week intervals probably provides sufficient external monitoring. The teacher and student, of course, are expected to be responsive in an adaptive way to student behavior in the interim period.

Comparing the modest objectives of Project PLAN with the enormous task facing psychologists in improving education on the basis of valid research evidence, it seems like a small beginning. To succeed in the major task will require the active participation of many hundreds of psychological researchers. It is hoped that both the trained psychologists and the required support can be found to make the needed rapid progress on this very important problem in the next few years.

REFERENCES

ATKIN, J. M.   "Behavioral Objectives in Curriculum Design: A Cautionary Note," *The Science Teacher,* Vol. 35, No. 5 (1968), pp. 27-30.

AYRES, L. P.   *Laggards in Our Schools, A Study of Retardation and Elimination in City School Systems.* New York: Russell Sage Foundation, 1909.

BANDURA, A., and KUPERS, C. J.   "Transmission of Patterns of Self-reinforcement through Modeling," *Journal of Abnormal and Social Psychology,* Vol. 69 (1964), pp. 1-9.

BEARD, J. G.   "Adapting Instruction to Student Characteristics," paper presented at the Conference of Directors of State Testing Programs, Princeton, N.J., October 1967.

BERDIE, R. F.   "The Uses of Evaluation in Guidance," in National Society for the Study of Education, *Yearbook,* Vol. 68, Part 2 (1969), pp. 51-80.

BRIGGS, L. J.   "Sequencing of Instruction in Relation to Hierarchies of Competence," *American Institutes for Research Monograph,* No. 3 (1968).

BRIGGS, L. J., CAMPEAU, P. L., GAGNÉ, R. M., and MAY, M. A.   "Instructional Media: A Procedure for the Design of Multi-media Instruction, a Critical Review of Research, and Suggestions for Future Research," *American Institutes for Research Monograph,* No. 2 (1967).

CARROLL, J. B.   "Instructional Methods and Individual Differences," in R. M. Gagné (ed.), *Learning and Individual Differences.* Columbus, Ohio: Charles E. Merrill Books, Inc., 1967.

CARROLL, J. B. "On Learning from Being Told," *Educational Psychologist,* Vol. 5, No. 2 (1968), pp. 1, 5-10.

CARTER, L. F. "Knowledge Production and Utilization in Contemporary Organizations," in T. L. Eidell and J. M. Kitchel (eds.), *Knowledge Production and Utilization in Educational Administration.* Eugene, Ore.: University of Oregon, Center for the Advanced Study of Educational Administration, 1968.

CICOUREL, A. V., and KITSUSE, J. I. *The Educational Decision-Makers.* Indianapolis: The Bobbs-Merrill Co., Inc., 1963.

COMMITTEE FOR ECONOMIC DEVELOPMENT, RESEARCH AND POLICY COMMITTEE. *Innovation in Education: New Directions for the American School.* New York: CED, 1968.

CRONBACH, L. J. "How Can Instruction Be Adapted to Individual Differences," in R. M. Gagné (ed.), *Learning and Individual Differences.* Columbus, Ohio: Charles E. Merrill Books, Inc., 1967.

DYER, H. S., and HEMPHILL, J. K. "A Plan for Evaluating the Quality of Educational Programs in Pennsylvania," a report from Educational Testing Service to the State Board of Education, June 30, 1965. Princeton, N.J.: Educational Testing Service, 1965.

FLANAGAN, J. C. "The Critical Incident Technique," *Psychological Bulletin,* Vol. 51 (1954), pp. 327-58.

FLANAGAN, J. C. *A Survey of the Educational Program of the Hicksville Public Schools.* Pittsburgh: American Institutes for Research, 1966.

FLANAGAN, J. C. "Using Research and Development to Improve Education," paper presented at the meeting of the American Educational Research Association, New York, 1967.

FLANAGAN, J. C., and COOLEY, W. W. "Project TALENT One-Year Follow-up Studies," Cooperative Research Project No. 2333, U.S. Office of Education. Pittsburgh: University of Pittsburgh, 1966.

FLANAGAN, J. C., DAILEY, J. T., DAVIS, F. B., GOLDBERG, I., NEYMAN, C. A., JR., ORR, D. B., and SHAYCOFT, M. F. "The American High-School Student," Cooperative Research Project No. 635, U.S. Office of Education. Pittsburgh: University of Pittsburgh, 1964.

GAGE, N. L. "An Analytical Approach to Research on Instructional Methods," *Phi Delta Kappan,* Vol. 49 (1968), pp. 601-06.

GAGNÉ, R. M. *Conditions of Learning.* New York: Holt, Rinehart & Winston, Inc., 1965.

GAGNÉ, R. M. "Contributions of Learning to Human Development," *Psychological Review,* Vol. 75 (1968), pp. 177-91.

GARDNER, J. W. "The Ten Commitments," *Saturday Review,* Vol. 50, No. 26 (1967), pp. 39-40.

GOODLAD, J. I., and ANDERSON, R. H. *The Nongraded Elementary School.* Rev. ed. New York: Harcourt, Brace & World, Inc., 1963.

HOMME, L. "Contingency Management," *Newsletter of the Section on Clinical Child Psychology*, Division of Clinical Psychology, American Psychological Association, Vol. 5, No. 4 (1966).

KROPP, R. P., and OTHERS. "Identification and Definition of Subject-Matter Content Variables Related to Human Aptitudes," Cooperative Research Project No. 2914-1, January, 1967, Florida State University, Contract OEC-5-10-297, U.S. Office of Education.

KRUMBOLTZ, J. D. "Behavioral Counseling: Rationale and Research," *Personnel and Guidance Journal*, Vol. 44 (1965), pp. 383-87.

LANGE, P. C. "Media and the Learning Process," *Audiovisual Instruction*, Vol. 13 (1968), pp. 554-57.

MAGER, R. F. *Preparing Instructional Objectives*. Palo Alto, Calif.: Fearon Publishers, Inc., 1962.

MARKLE, D. G. *The Development of the Bell System First Aid and Personal Safety Course*. Palo Alto, Calif.: American Institutes for Research, 1967.

MASLOW, A. H. *Motivation and Personality*. New York: Harper & Row, Publishers, 1954.

McDANIELS, C. "Youth: Too Young to Choose?" *Vocational Guidance Quarterly*, Vol. 16 (1968), pp. 242-49.

POPHAM, W. J. "Development of a Performance Test of Teaching Proficiency," Final Report No. BR-5-0566, August, 1967, University of California, Los Angeles, Contract OEC-6-10-254, U.S. Office of Education.

REAVIS, W. C. "Differentiated Requirements in the University of Chicago High School," in National Society for the Study of Education, "Adapting the Schools to Individual Differences," *Twenty-fourth Yearbook*, Part II (1925), pp. 49-52.

SCRIVEN, M. "The Methodology of Evaluation," in R. W. Tyler, R. M. Gagné, and M. Scriven, *Perspectives of Curriculum Evaluation*. American Educational Research Association Monograph Series on Curriculum Evaluation, No. 1. Chicago: Rand McNally & Co., 1967.

SHORT, J., GAREE, M. K., KRESS, G. C., JR., and O'BRIEN, R. K. *A Study of a Training System for Advanced AT&T Salesmen*. Pittsburgh: American Institutes for Research, 1968.

SKINNER, B. F. *Science and Human Behavior*. New York: The Macmillan Co., 1953.

SWENSON, E. J. "Teacher Preparation," in National Society for the Study of Education, "Individualizing Instruction," *Sixty-first Yearbook*, Part I (1962), pp. 287-304.

TALLMADGE, G. K., SHEARER, J. W., and GREENBERG, A. M. "Study of Training Equipment and Individual Differences: The Effects of Subject Matter Variables," Technical Report NAVTRADEVCEN 67-C-0114-1, May, 1968, American Institutes for Research, Contract No. N61339-67-C-0114, U.S. Naval Training Device Center.

THORESEN, C. E., and MEHRENS, W. A. "Decision Theory and Vocational Counseling: Important Concepts and Questions," *Personnel and Guidance Journal,* Vol. 46 (1967), pp. 165-72.

THORNDIKE, E. L. "The Elimination of Pupils from School," U.S. Bureau of Education. *Bulletin,* No. 4 (1907).

TIEDEMAN, D. V. "Decision and Vocational Development: A Paradigm and Its Implications," *Personnel and Guidance Journal,* Vol. 40 (1961), pp. 15-21.

TRAVERS, R. M. W. "Models of Education and Their Implications for the Conduct of Evaluation Studies," Paper presented at the meeting of the American Educational Research Association, Chicago, February, 1968.

TYLER, R. W. "The Functions of Measurement in Improving Instruction," in E. F. Lindquist (ed.), *Educational Measurement.* Washington, D.C.: American Council on Education, 1951.

TYLER, R. W. "The Objectives and Plans for a National Assessment of Educational Progress," *Journal of Educational Measurement,* Vol. 3 (1966), pp. 1-4.

U.S. PRESIDENT'S COMMISSION ON NATIONAL GOALS. *Goals for Americans: Programs for Action in the Sixties.* Englewood Cliffs, N.J.: Prentice-Hall, Inc., 1960.

WASHBURNE, C. W. "Burk's Individual System as Developed at Winnetka," in National Society for the Study of Education, "Adapting the Schools to Individual Differences," *Twenty-fourth Yearbook,* Part II (1925), pp. 77-82.

WILHELMS, F. T. "The Curriculum and Individual Differences," in National Society for the Study of Education, "Individualizing Instruction," *Sixty-first Yearbook,* Part I (1962), pp. 62-74.

WOODWORTH, R. S., and THORNDIKE, E. L. "The Influence of Improvement in One Mental Function upon the Efficiency of Other Functions," *Psychological Review,* Vol. 8 (1901), pp. 247-61, 394-95, 553-64.

Chapter 2. GUIDING STUDENTS THROUGH APPROPRIATE CURRICULUM IN *PLAN*

THE ACCOMMODATION OF INDIVIDUAL DIFFERENCES IN THE DEVELOPMENT OF PERSONAL PROGRAMS OF STUDY

James A. Dunn

It has long been the goal of education to make educational programs more fully fit the needs of individual learners. It is in this area that the next major step forward in the improvement of education must take place. And it is toward this goal that Project PLAN is working. It is hoped that PLAN will be able to mobilize the resources of contemporary education toward the satisfaction of the specific needs of individual children. The purpose of this paper is to describe one aspect of the PLAN enterprise; namely, the process by which individualized Programs of Study are generated for PLAN students.

There are two distinct, but interconnected, curriculum problems to be considered in dealing with the question of individualized Programs of

SOURCE: Adapted from a presentation at the 1969 APA Symposium, Washington, D.C., by permission of the author.

27

Study. They are: (1) how the curriculum should be *defined;* and (2) how the curriculum should be *implemented.* Both are essential. The former involves not only *what* should be learned but also *how much* should be learned; and *when* it should be learned; and *how fast* it should be learned. While the present paper is concerned primarily with how the curriculum should be implemented, it would be well to put the issues in perspective.

HOW THE CURRICULUM SHOULD BE DEFINED

Our society has traditionally been, and is, a pragmatic one. Interest in education in our society has always been on its practical implication. Even though there has often been disagreement as to what was most practical, it is reasonably accurate to state that the curriculum effort of the late nineteenth and early twentieth centuries was based fundamentally on the acceptance of Herbert Spencer's 1859 argument that what a child most needed to learn was that which would be most useful to him as an adult (Kearney and Cook, 1960).

On the one hand were those theorists who emphasized the importance of mastery of formal disciplines. They did so not so much because of the intrinsic value of the material *per se,* but rather because they considered sound disciplinary training the best preparation for the demands of adulthood. On the other hand were those who challenged the theory of formal discipline and who argued that one should base curriculum considerations on more explicit, empirically demonstrable, considerations.

The underlying differences between the disciplinists and empiricists came to the fore in 1895 with the recommendations of the Committee of Fifteen. The Committee of Fifteen had been concerned with establishing a set of guidelines which would be to elementary education what the recommendations of the better known Committee of Ten (1893) were for secondary education; i.e., the standardization of the format of elementary education. Instead of achieving their goal they succeeded only in polarizing the views of the educational community and in precipitating what Drost (1967) has described as the "Great Curriculum Debate." At the heart of the debate was the question of whether content should be selected for its direct utilitarian value, or its contribution to the maintenance and/or enhancement of the integrity of a given subject field. The debate continues to this day. On one side, Bruner (1960), concerned with the exponential explosion of information, has suggested reorganization of the educational curriculum even to the point of eliminating such traditional fields as history. On the other side, the trend of the various curriculum projects such as Harvard Project Physics, the School Mathematics Study Group (SMSG), the Biological Sciences Curriculum Study (BSCS), and the like, has been to create more and more intensive, and elegant, disciplinary programs, with apparently little regard to how much of the field is necessary for practical living, or even what proportion of public school students will want, or be able to complete, their various programs. (Bellack, 1969; McNeil, 1969.)

HOW THE CURRICULUM SHOULD BE IMPLEMENTED

The Committee of Ten had earlier (1893) wrestled with the problem of how best to implement a more individualized secondary school program. Their solution was very simple; and, with only slight modification in 1918, it set the mode of secondary education for half a century (Sizer, 1964). In essence, the recommendations called for the establishment, and standardization, of a set of core courses which would comprise the educational base of all students. Collateral with these basic requirements would be an array of "elective" courses which could then be selected by the student on the basis of his interest. This paradigm still has clear contemporary relevance and remains the standard educational pattern.

The Committee of Ten individualized programs by permitting differential content exposure. The unit of content exposure, however, was the "course." Later elaborations of the paradigm involved the identification of various sub-programs such as vocational, business, general, and college preparatory, while still preserving the student elective option. Responsibility for "tracking" students into these various programs was, for the most part, retained by the schools, however.

More recently, programmed instruction and various forms of modern instructional technology have skirted the issue of *what* is to be studied. And since they generally require content mastery, these procedures individualize instruction by allowing variability in the *amount of exposure* that the content gets. In this way individual differences in learning *rate* are allowed to operate.

If one is to be serious about the individualization, however, in addition to individualization based on *what* is to be learned, and individualization based on *amount of exposure* to that which is to be learned, individualization must also be based on *how* one will learn, i.e., on learning style, on the various ways in which the content to be learned may be studied. Contemporary individualized educational programs, if they are to lay claim to that title, must begin to accept some responsibility *vis-à-vis* the differential selection of the material from which the student is to learn.

In particular, individualization of educational programs must consider among other things:

1. What the student needs to know
2. What the student would like to know
3. What the student already knows
4. The rate at which the selected content should be presented
5. The sequence in which that content should be presented

6. The size of the steps in the sequence of that content
7. The mode of presentation of that content
8. The amount, type, and schedule of feedback associated with the presentation
9. The difficulty level of the learning materials used to teach the content
10. The meaningfulness of the content to the individual learner
11. The nature of the physical and social context in which the teaching-learning takes place
12. The contemporary affect state, including the motivational state, of the learner at the time of learning
13. The amount of teacher supervision—media richness—technology involved
14. The amount of variation provided for in the learning program
15. The amount of overlearning, and/or periodic review built into the program, and so forth.

To do this the necessity for moving toward an ungraded program, toward individualized rather than group testing, and toward criterion normed rather than group normed tests should be obvious. This of course imposes problems on administration. And evaluation of the program cannot rest on such simple and traditional criteria as significant differences in the mean achievement scores of experimental and control groups because standardized testing is based on the assumption of *fixed* exposure to a *common* content.

In addition, if one insists that the curriculum should be relevant, one must know relevant for what. That is, one must know what *goals* the child has set for himself so that one may decide whether or not the content to be assigned is in fact relevant.

Such individualized education, then, obviously imposes a massive monitoring task; a task that cannot be done without the aid of computer-support services. These services are available in PLAN and with those services we are attempting to accomplish as much of the preceding as possible.

PLAN PROCEDURES FOR 1969

In 1969, approximately 9,000 PLAN students in 61 different school buildings in 17 different school systems will be entering school. Waiting for them should be 9,000 individualized Programs of Study. We do not offer these programs as ideal, but they are at least real, and they represent, as far as can be ascertained, the largest such effort at purposeful individualization in education to date.

I would like to summarize briefly for you the paradigm for the development of a PLAN Program of Studies. I shall describe the paradigm in its most complex form—that used at the secondary school level. The procedure is scaled down for use at the lower grades where some of the more complex variables such as long-range vocational goals, educational aspirations, and the like, lose relevance.

Instructional Resources. First, we have in PLAN over 1,000 lessons (or modules) divided across our nine operating grades and four subject-matter areas. At the secondary level we have approximately 85 modules per subject area. This would yield, on the average, approximately 170 weeks of instruction distributed across grades 9, 10, and 11. The typical student in the typical secondary school, which operates an average of 38 weeks in the school year, would have, excluding final examination periods, special vacations and the like, an average of 110 weeks available for formal instruction. So, for the hypothetical student we can offer a Program of Studies derived from a lesson bank containing over half again as much work as he could reasonably be expected to accomplish. In addition, each of these modules is offered, on the average, in two different forms called teaching-learning units (TLU).

It is not enough to simply have an extremely rich lesson bank, however. For individualized education, the lesson bank must be coded so that specific lessons can be retrieved for the specific needs of specific students. Each of the more than 1,000 modules and 1,700 TLU's in the PLAN system were coded along a variety of dimensions.

Each module was coded as to whether or not it was a part of a state or local requirement, essential for a given educational or occupational area, highly desirable for that area, essential for minimal functioning as a citizen, highly desirable for all citizens to know, or would make the individual a particularly well-informed citizen.

Each teaching-learning unit was coded as to its reading difficulty, the degree to which it required teacher supervision, its media richness characteristic, the degree to which it required social involvement and/or group learning activities, the amount of reading involved, and the variety of activities inherent in the unit.

The Individual Data Base. In order to use this cross-reference lesson bank for the development of individualized Programs of Study, it is also necessary to have information about the needs, interests, abilities and aspirations of the individual for whom the Program of Study is to be generated. To this end, data on the following variables were collected:

1. Parent and student educational goal;
2. Parent and student vocational aspiration;
3. Student's vocational interests;
4. Student's level of achievement;
5. Student's level of developed abilities (on such dimensions as reading comprehension, arithmetic reasoning, and the like);

6.   The student's recall of past studies;
7.   And the student's learning style.

Learning style, for the time being, was defined as: (*a*) need for teacher supervision; (*b*) need for social involvement; (*c*) need for media richness; (*d*) need for variety of learning activities; and (*e*) preference for reading.

Data on parent-student vocational and educational aspirations were collected via parent-student questionnaires. This information was used to identify parent-student long-range goals. Student interests, achievement levels, and developed abilities are obtained from the Expressed Interests Inventory, the PLAN Achievement Tests and the Developed Abilities Performance Tests. Information regarding the student's optimum learning style was obtained from a series of student ratings made by his teacher.

From information about the student's developed abilities a second long-range vocational goal was generated for the student, using TALENT-based regression equations. This "data-suggested" goal was used to supplement the parent-student planning so as to have as many realistic options open for the student as possible. The student's two long-range goal (LRG) categories plus his expressed interests carry a major role in determining what content will be recommended for him. His level of tested achievement, plus his record of past studies in Project PLAN determine his placement and quota of modules.

Module Assignment.   The process in generating what lessons are to be recommended for a student is as follows: given information about a student's long-range goals, his expressed interests, citizenship requirements, and state and local school requirements, the computer generates a three-year list of recommended modules arranged in the following order: (1) state requirements; (2) local requirements; (3) essential citizenship requirements; (4) parent-student long-range goal requirements; (5) parent-student long-range goal highly desirable modules; (6) data-suggested LRG requirements; and (7) data-suggested highly desired experiences. This list is then followed by modules selected alternately on the basis of (first) probable interest and (second) citizenship. This alternating selection process is continued until the student's quota is filled. His quota is based on the measured level of the student's developed abilities plus data on the number of modules he completed in PLAN the preceding year.

This process gives a three-year list which is then broken into annual increments. Each increment is composed of one-third of the requirements identified above plus one-third of the highly desirable modules identified above plus one-third of the iterative process modules described above. Now placement becomes an issue. On the basis of the individual's tested achievement plus his record of past studies in PLAN, the child is given credit for that material he already knows. If there is material for which he cannot demonstrate mastery and which is considered prerequisite to modules to which he is assigned, the prerequisite material is also assigned.

TLU Selection.   At this point, specific TLU assignment takes place. Up to now the consideration has only been of identification of the content to be studied, i.e., which lessons, how many lessons, and in what sequence the lessons should be taken. Now we are faced with the question of learning style, i.e., what particular TLU's the student should take to study the assigned lessons so as to maximize the likelihood of his mastering the content as quickly as possible. It is at this point that the computer, from a complex set of decision rules, matches the student with specific TLU's.

The results of these decisions are then printed as a formal Program of Study for the student. It is printed in two copies, one for school record keeping, and the other for teacher-student classroom use. Figure 2-1 shows a sample of the POS format.

COMPLETION CODE	MODULE NUMBER	MODULE NAME	DATE FINISHED

Take <u>all</u> of the following modules.

    40-775   Introduction to Historical Inquiry
    40-759   Introduction to Economics
    40-772   The Research Paper

Choose <u>five</u> of the following modules. The modules are grouped into clusters. It is suggested that once a student chooses a module from a particular cluster, he choose the remaining modules in that cluster.

    40-754   Economic Problems I
    40-755   Economic Problems II

    40-756   Conflict-Wars
    40-763   Conflict-Minorities

    40-757   Compromise and Adjustment-Foreign Affairs
    40-769   Compromise and Adjustment-Legislative-Executive I
    40-778   Compromise and Adjustment-Legislative-Executive II

    40-758   Social Change-Women
    40-761   Social Change-Role of Blacks
    40-777   Social Change-The Progressive Movement

Choose <u>twelve</u> of the following modules. These modules may be sequenced in a number of ways. You may want to consult the Teacher Supplement for suggestions to aid in sequencing.

    43-643   European Monarchism
    43-644   Development of Democracy in England

FIGURE 2-1

POS FORMAT

The POS module assignment and TLU matching rules are not best fit rules however, since one wants a student's program to stretch the student a little, to broaden his interests and strain his intellectual ability a little, and lead him a little further down the educational road than he might ordinarily go. Best fit is called for in only an arbitrary percentage of the time, e.g., 90 percent. One of the big unanswered questions is what this value should be. Clearly from the need-achievement/fear-of-failure research, and other motivation research, this should be a variable. And in time, given experience with POS operation, this value will be individualized as well as any of the other factors.

Conclusion.   In conclusion, it may be said that a student's recommended POS is not an inviolate entity. The teacher can add or delete modules to the POS with considerable ease; and if she chooses she can even totally revise the recommended Program of Studies. A formal change in the POS can be made by simply indicating the number of the module she would like to delete or add. Barring this, the teacher can even effect a change in the POS by simply having the student study a module or TLU not on his POS. Then, when the student's Status Card is filed with the computer terminal, the computer notes that the module or TLU is different from any on the student's recommended POS and asks the teacher to verify that a coding mistake on the Status Card has not been made, i.e., that the new selection is in fact a deliberate selection. Upon confirmation, the computer adds the new selection to the student's Program of Studies file automatically and from that point forward it is carried in his record.

As one might expect, with programs of the complexity we are describing, and given the current state of sophistication with regard to the requisite data necessary for sophisticated individualization, a large number of arbitrary, interim decisions have had to be made. As was indicated, the 1969 PLAN POS procedure is not offered as a finished model. It is not the best of all possible procedures; it is, rather, a first operating prototype. As additional sophistication is achieved in the identification of specific student needs, the identification of those aspects of currently available instructional materials that are relevant to the needs of youth, and ways to further accommodate individual differences in learning style, the POS procedures will be modified accordingly.

It is important to say, however, that a procedure such as this offers research capability of uncommon proportions. Some of the specific questions being asked of this year's POS data are: (1) how similar are student-parent long-range goals to the "best fit" goals suggested by the level and pattern of the student's developed abilities; (2) what proportion of a typical school curriculum is in fact relevant to the long-range vocational goals of youth; (3) to what long-range educational and vocational goals do youth currently aspire, and the like. By this time next year, empirical data on the effectiveness and the specific operating characteristics of this model will be available and a second-generation procedure will be in use on a sample of approximately 40,000 students.

REFERENCES

BELLACK, A. A. "History of Curriculum Thought and Practice," *Review of Educational Research,* Vol. 39, No. 3 (1969), pp. 283-91.

BRUNER, J. S. *The Process of Education.* Cambridge, Mass.: Harvard University Press, 1960.

DROST, W. H. "The Immortal Day in Cleveland—The Report of the Committee of Fifteen," *Educational Theory,* Vol. 17 (1967), pp. 178-91.

KEARNEY, N. C., and COOK, W. W. "Curriculum," in *Encyclopaedia of Educational Research.* 3rd ed. New York: The Macmillan Co., 1960.

MCNEIL. J. D. "Forces Influencing Curriculum," *Review of Educational Research,* Vol. 39, No. 3, 1969, pp. 293-318.

SIZER, T. R. *Secondary Schools at the Turn of the Century.* New Haven, Conn.: Yale University Press, 1964.

Chapter 3. THE PROCESS OF LEARNING IN *PLAN*

STRATEGIES FOR LEARNING IN *PLAN*

Robert A. Weisgerber and Harold F. Rahmlow

PLAN is a system of individualized education built on a data-base of instructional objectives, learning materials, performance tests, and personalized programs of study in social studies, language arts, science, and mathematics. The system is adaptive to widely varying school facilities and to school budgets. In addition, PLAN emphasizes the counseling and classroom management skills of the existing instructional staff.

OVERVIEW OF THE INSTRUCTIONAL SYSTEM

PLAN instructional objectives are derived from an overall curriculum developed by PLAN staff and teachers from the cooperating research and development schools, in consultation with national curriculum authorities. The objectives are then organized into study modules for use by students. Often about five or six objectives constitute a module of study. Ultimately, a

This article was prepared especially for publication in this volume.

program of studies is developed to assist the student in selecting modules appropriate to his needs and interests.

In PLAN, the module is defined as a unit of work lasting approximately two weeks for an "average student." These units may or may not be organized around a single topic, for example, the Civil War. Alternatively, topical organization might be based on closely related objectives dealing with such activities as handwriting, spelling, and speaking. In the former case it makes sense to organize by topics since a two-week study of the Civil War has intrinsic benefit. In the latter case, it is desirable for motivational reasons to intersperse activities of a diverse nature over a two-week period of study.

Actually, the PLAN module is an organizational unit comprising two or more interrelated documents: one for the pupil, called the teaching-learning unit (TLU), and the document for the teacher, called the teacher's supplement.

Typically, alternative TLU's are available to students who have been assigned to a given module, and all the alternative TLU's cover the same instructional objectives. Teaching-learning units are based upon different assumed[1] learning styles of students and are guided by a philosophy of education (Flanagan, 1967), and a theory of learning (Gagné, 1965).

In general, the teaching-learning unit is begun with the statement of an instructional objective. This is followed by an example of the concept or the behavior criterion. The objective and example provide a mechanism for directing the student's thoughts toward the activities he will pursue and provide a reference point against which he can check his progress. At the primary level, objectives tend to be used in an inductive sense and, contrary to the upper grades, are placed at the end of the teaching-learning unit.

Figure 3-1 shows two objectives and an example from a PLAN module. Before beginning work on the learning activities, the student reads the objective and example to see what is expected of him. If he can do what the example asks and feels he can accomplish the objective in its entirety, he should by-pass the learning activities for this objective and proceed to the next. On the other hand, if the student cannot perform what the example asks or feels he is not competent in the objective as a whole, he would proceed with the learning activities until he feels he can master the objective. After he feels he has achieved satisfactory performance on *all* objectives of the module, he will be given an evaluation exercise to measure his progress. As can be seen, *the emphasis is not on activity, but rather on what the student can do as a result of some activity.*

TYPES OF TEACHING-LEARNING UNITS

In PLAN, two types of teaching-learning units are developed: (1) the *materials-general* TLU, which specifies learning activities but generalizes

Step 3.   OBJECTIVE:
6213   Given the total sales and the amount of commission, compute the net
           proceeds.

           Example: If the commission on sales of $438.00 amounts to $22.50,
                     what are the net proceeds?

Step 1.   OBJECTIVE:
7941   Identify the major sources of environmental pollution and the methods
           of preventing and controlling pollution.

           Example: All of the following contribute significantly to the pollution
                     of water except

                            A. industrial waste
                            B. sewage
                            C. insecticides
                            D. automobile exhaust.

FIGURE 3-1

SELECTED OBJECTIVES

about the materials the student should use in order to accomplish the
objectives, and (2) the *materials-specific* TLU, which specifies learning
activities *and* the resources a student should use in accomplishing the
objectives.

Materials-General TLU.   The intent of this generic approach to materials
is twofold. First, it is meant to provide a challenging opportunity for the self-
directing learner. Second, it is meant to be highly adaptable for schools
having widely varying instructional materials resources.

In the materials-general TLU there are "assists" given to the student so
that he can facilitate his search for relevant material. For example, a student
may be told to collect certain information about the Gettysburg Address but
would not be told on which pages of what books this information would be
found. However, to help the student locate the information, "key words" are

provided. These key words can be used as a reference point for the student to enter the resources he chooses. The materials-general TLU provides a place for the student to record the specific resources he is using in the accomplishment of the objectives.

To be more concrete, an illustration of one objective in a materials-general TLU is provided in Figure 3-2. It can be seen that the student is given the objective, "Distinguish between characteristics which describe individuals and those which describe populations." The student is then asked a question relating to the objective. Assuming he could not do or did not understand what the example asked for, he would continue on to the learning activities. He is told to get pictures, models, etc., then list descriptive characteristics of them. He is given suggestions to assist him in organizing categories. Next he is asked to define words related to the objective he is studying. As can be seen from Figure 3-2, he is led through a series of exercises by which he has practice in differentiating those characteristics which describe individuals and those which describe populations. As he works, he can use the specific resources column for keeping track of those resources which were particularly useful to him.

After working on the objective for a suitable time, the student should be able to do what is called for in the objective. When he feels confident, he moves on to the next objective (not shown on Figure 3-2). After completing and reviewing all objectives in the TLU, he will have the opportunity to check himself on a performance test. As a result of his performance on the test, he will either move forward to new objectives in a new module or do additional work on objectives not mastered.

In review, it can be seen that in a materials-general TLU the student is given a variety of activities to pursue and considerable latitude in the materials he uses. Often these materials involve the use of technological media, and PLAN students readily accept the responsibility for operating the equipment themselves. The materials-general TLU thus provides a maximum of student-initiated behavior and allows for great flexibility in resource utilization that may be indigenous to his school.

Materials-Specific TLU. The characteristic feature of the materials-specific TLU is that it references specific materials for the student to utilize in his pursuit of the objective. The intent of the specification of materials is also twofold. First, it provides a structured approach which can lead many students through an orderly set of selected experiences. Second, because different combinations of learning activities and technology can be specified, it is possible for PLAN personnel to generate other teaching-learning units which, upon empirical tryout and revision, can be said to meet the needs of different students. Eventually, following research, it is hoped that these alternatives in learning activities and materials can be consciously selected for their known relevance to individual differences among PLAN students.

31-643-1   CHARACTERISTICS OF INDIVIDUALS AND POPULATIONS   (0,00)
                                                                          69-70 Ed.

Step 1.   Objective: DISTINGUISH BETWEEN CHARACTERISTICS WHICH DESCRIBE INDIVIDUALS
(7609)   AND THOSE WHICH DESCRIBE POPULATIONS.

          Example: Population density, natality, and mortality are among the charac-
                    teristics that ecologists investigate when they want to conduct
                    a study of _____. (an individual, a population)

LEARNING ACTIVITIES	KEY WORDS	SPECIFIC RESOURCES
(a) Get a picture, model, or live specimen of a small animal (fish, frog, lizard, bird, cat, etc.) 1. List at least ten descriptive, not inferential, characteristics of that animal. (Descriptive characteristic: the cat is thin; inferential characteristic: the cat is hungry.) 2. Use the following categories of descriptive characteristics as a guide for your list: (1) color, (2) weight (approx.), (3) height or length, (4) number of eyes, (5) number and type of appendages, (6) skin texture, plus four more. 3. Save this list for later use. (b) Write brief definitions for each Key Word. (c) Read about individuals and populations in a science book. (d) Write a brief sketch of Malthus' theory. (e) Which of the words in the Key Words column might be used to describe characteristics of populations? Give an example illustrating the use of each of the words you chose. (f) Consider a population, perhaps a herd of elk or a pack of wolves, and describe the effects of any changes in its density due to mortality, natality, emigration, or immigration. (g) How do these characteristics differ from the descriptive characteristics of a single animal?	*characteristic* *description* *inference* *population density* *population* *rate* *genetic pool* *natality* *immigration* *emigration* *mortality* *area* *metabolism* *Thomas Robert Malthus*	

FIGURE 3-2

As in the materials-general TLU, the student who uses a materials-specific TLU is provided with the objective and an example, but from here on the format of the two TLU's differs. In the materials-specific TLU, there is a "Use" column and a "Do" column. The "Use" column lists for the student specific resources to use and the "Do" column indicates what the student should do with these resources. In the primary grades, the student is also provided with a "Done" column which he can use to note or self-monitor his own progress.

To illustrate the materials-specific TLU and to provide a comparison with the materials-general TLU just examined, an illustration is provided in Figure 3-3. It will be noted that the objective and example for this TLU are identical with that in Figure 3-2 although the remainder of the format is distinct. After studying the objective and example, the student begins working with the first specific resource. In the "Do" column, the student is told to "Read 'Individuals and Populations,' p. 22 to the top of p. 30," and the material to be used in connection with this activity is given in the "Use" column. The student would continue working through the activities mentioned and after completing them would be expected to be able to perform the objective. He would then go on to the next objective, shown at the bottom of Figure 3-3. It is important that the instructions in the "Do" column should be clear enough that the student will not have to rely on the teacher for procedural help but rather can look to the teacher for professional assistance.

It should be clear that the teaching-learning units illustrated in Figures 3-2 and 3-3 are both drawn from the same module; that is, both represent alternative methods of accomplishing the same set of objectives. All students taking *either* the materials-general or the materials-specific TLU will be given the *same* test and both will be evaluated on their ability to demonstrate mastery of the objectives. The results of the tests are added to the computer data base and become a part of the student's progress record.

INSTRUCTIONAL GUIDES

Although in PLAN the teaching-learning unit is a reference document and not an instructional material itself, there are occasions when it is necessary to provide further detailed information for the student. In such cases, an instructional guide is developed. Instructional guides can be divided into two general categories: those which provide direct instruction to the student when such instruction is not available through the normal commercially available sources, and those which contain work sheets for the student to practice a skill he is attempting to develop. Figure 3-4 provides an example of one type of instructional guide that may be contained in a PLAN teaching-learning unit. This instructional guide is related to the objective, "Given two states of matter, tell whether heat must be added or taken away to go from the first state to the second, and give the name of the process."

31-643-2   CHARACTERISTICS OF INDIVIDUALS AND POPULATIONS   (0,00)
                                                                        69-70 Ed.

Step 1.   Objective: DISTINGUISH BETWEEN CHARACTERISTICS WHICH DESCRIBE INDIVIDUALS
(7609)   AND THOSE WHICH DESCRIBE POPULATIONS.

          Example: Density, natality, and mortality are among the characteristics
                    that ecologists investigate when they want to conduct a study
                    of _____. (an individual, a population)

USE	DO
High School Biology: BSCS Green Version (Sixth Printing, June,1966), Biological Science Curriculum Study. (Rand McNally & Company: 1963)	(a) Read "Individuals" and "Populations," p. 22 to the top of p. 30. (b) Answer questions in Figures 2.4 and 2.5 on p. 26. (c) Answer questions 2, 5, and 6, pp. 48-49.
Biological Science: Molecules to Man, (BSCS Blue Version), (Revised Edition, 1968), Biological Sciences Curriculum Study. (Houghton Mifflin Company: 1963)	(d) Read 27-1, p. 679. (Omit Investigation 27-2. Your teacher may assign it later.) (e) Read 27-3 through 27-5, pp. 682-687. (f) Do Investigation 27-6, p. 688. Answer questions 1-6, p. 688.
High School Biology: BSCS Green Version, Student's Manual, (Third Printing, October, 1964), Biological Sciences Curriculum Study. (Rand McNally & Company: 1963)	(g) Optional: Perform Exercise 2.1, pp. 26-29.

Step 2.   Objective: DEMONSTRATE AN UNDERSTANDING OF CHANGES IN POPULATION
(7610)   DENSITIES BY: a) DEFINING "POPULATION DENSITY"; b) IDENTIFYING THE
          MAJOR POPULATION DETERMINERS WHICH INCREASE AND THOSE WHICH DECREASE
          POPULATION DENSITY; AND c) USING THE DENSITY FORMULA TO CALCULATE THE
          NUMERICAL CHANGE IN A POPULATION WHEN THE EFFECTS OF A SPECIFIED
          POPULATION DETERMINER ARE GIVEN.

          Example: If the population density of rabbits in a field was reduced
                    from 50 rabbits/km^2 in 1960 to 25 rabbits/km^2 in 1965, which
                    one of the four population determiners was probably not a
                    factor in the change?

FIGURE 3-3

The instructional guide summarizes the relationships existing in the text to which the student has been directed. Moreover, the student is given a number of questions to answer as practice in studying the relationships between the various states of matter.

30-255-2   INTRODUCTION TO MATTER   (1,00)

Instructional Guide

Part I

Step 4

   (d) The relationships between the states of matter may be summarized in the diagram below.

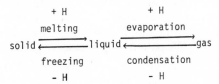

    + H means that heat is *added*.

    - H means that heat is *taken away*.

Referring to the diagram above, answer the following questions.

  1. What is the process called when a gas changes to a liquid? Is heat added or taken away?

    _____

  2. In the freezing process a _____ changes to a _____. Is heat added or taken away? _____

  3. In going from a liquid to a gas heat is _____. What is the process called? _____

  4. Some solids (such as dry ice) go directly to a gas in a process called sublimation. Would heat be added or taken away? _____

FIGURE 3-4

THE TEACHER'S SUPPLEMENT

A teacher's supplement is developed as a companion document to each TLU. It is basically a method of communicating the general framework of the planned curriculum to the teacher.

The PLAN teacher's supplements are organized on a program basis; that is, they are packaged together by level and subject area. The teacher's supplement is a comprehensive listing of modules in the program as well as the objectives in those modules. Within the modules, the TLU's are described by (1) reading level, (2) the appropriate groups to be involved, and (3) the activities pursued within the TLU. As a result, when counseling the student or preparing resource collections, it is possible for a teacher to tell at a glance whether there is a TLU within a module which calls for small group work, calls for partners working together, or calls for teacher involvement. Similarly, the teacher can tell at a glance whether or not such activities as discussions, dramatizations, drawing or painting, field trips, game playing, viewing-singing, or others are provided within the various TLU's. In this situation, the teacher would be able to advise the student regarding the learning options open to him and, if desirable, recommend the TLU which most nearly fits the student's pattern of successes in prior TLU's.

A further assistance to the teacher is provided with a master materials list and a TLU Materials Reference Chart. The TLU Materials Reference Chart provides a mechanism for graphically illustrating to the teacher the use of the various materials in the program. For example, the teacher can tell whether a material is (1) used consistently in one TLU, (2) used as a supplemental source, or (3) used as a core material in a wide range of teaching-learning units. Figure 3-5 shows portions of a Learning Materials List, a TLU Materials Reference Chart, and the student's TLU which uses one of the materials. The film strip *Flowers: Their Parts and Functions* is coded 30/7/052 on the Learning Materials List. From the TLU Materials Reference Chart, it can be seen that the film strip is used in TLU's 2 and 3 for module 30-382. The portion of the student TLU shows how the student receives reference to the film strip. This information is particularly important to the teacher in organizing classroom material.

Finally, the teacher's supplement includes special instructions to the teacher that are important considerations if the unit is to be accomplished with maximum effectiveness.

PROGRAM FLAGS

The teacher's supplement should be tied in very closely with the student's documents if it is to be functional. The best illustration of this appears at the primary level in connection with what is termed the PLAN flagging program. Figure 3-6, step *a* (in the margin), shows the IBM card used as the flagging symbol. When flags are indicated on the TLU, the student knows

A Portion of a Learning Materials List

30/7/50	Life Science, Singer Science Series, Teacher's Edition (Second Edition), Helen Dolman MacCracken, et al. (The L. W. Singer Company, 1968)
30/7/051	Dependent Plants (A427-18), from Correlated Science Series, filmstrip. [Society for Visual Education, Inc. (SVE)]
30/7/052	Flowers: Their Parts and Functions (A408-1), from The Role of Flowers and Fruits Series, filmstrip. [Society for Visual Education, Inc. (SVE)]
30/7/053	Let's Explore a Pond (A423-4), from Exploring the World of Nature Series, filmstrip. [Society for Visual Education, Inc. (SVE)]

A Portion of a TLU Materials Reference Chart

Module	30/7/045	30/7/046	30/7/047	30/7/048	30/7/049	30/7/050	30/7/051	30/7/052	30/7/053	30/7/054	30/7/055	30/7/056
30-378					2,3	2					.	
30-379			2	2		2,3						
30-380					2,3							
30-381	2	2,3										
30-382			2,3			3		2,3				2,3
30-383							2,3		2,3		2,3	
30-384			2,3	2								

A Portion of a Student's TLU

USE	DO
Flowers: Their Parts and Functions (A408-1), from The Role of Flowers and Fruits Series, filmstrip. [Society for Visual Education, Inc. (SVE)]	(c) View frames 20-51, using the Teacher's Guide and Reading Script.
Living Things	(d) Read p. 59, "Check Your Facts," 1-9. Can you answer the questions or do the activities for each of these? Think of the answers for 1, 3, 4, 5, 6, 7, 8 and 9. Do question 2 in your notebook.

FIGURE 3-5

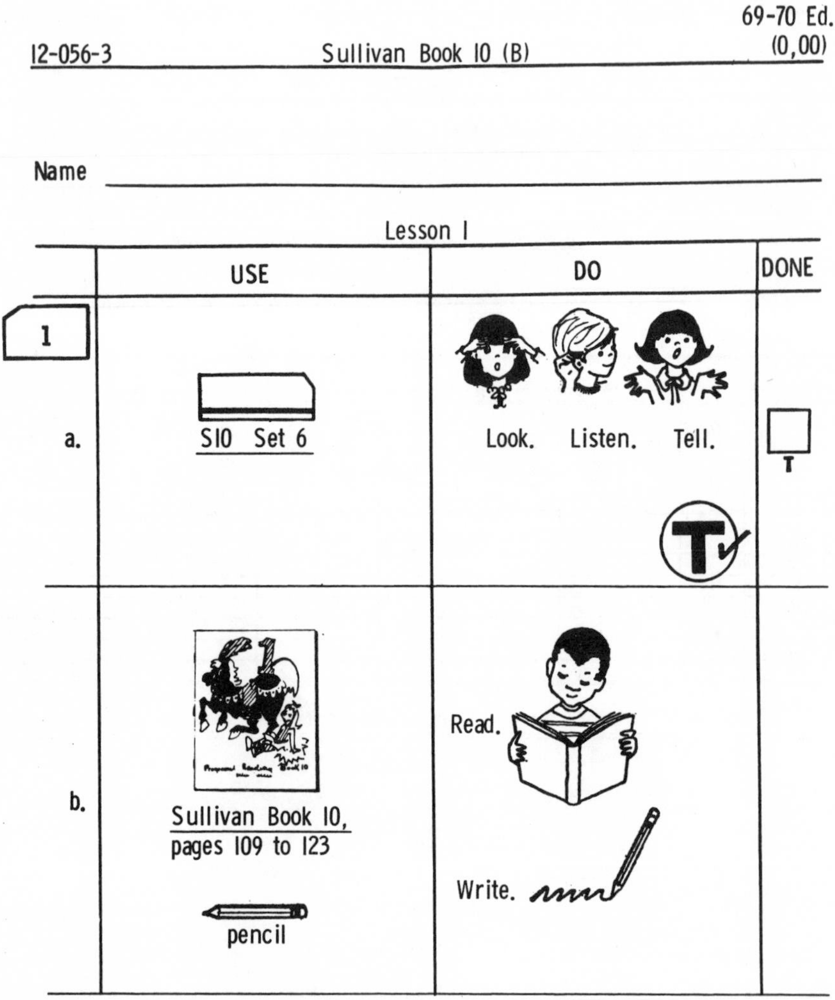

12-056-3 Sullivan Book 10 (B) 69-70 Ed. (0,00)

Name ______________________

Lesson 1

	USE	DO	DONE
1 a.	S10 Set 6	Look. Listen. Tell. T	T
b.	Sullivan Book 10, pages 109 to 123; pencil	Read. Write.	

FIGURE 3-6

12-056-3   Sullivan Book 10 (B)   (0.00)

Lesson I (continued)

	USE	DO	DONE
c.	GAME Ideal Consonant Pictures	My partner is _____. Play.	
d.	S10 Set 7	Look. Listen. Tell.	
e.	Sullivan Book 10, pages 124 to 132 pencil	Read. Write.	

FIGURE 3-6 *Continued*

that he has to submit a pre-punched card to the computer. The computer then generates a message to the teacher indicating the relevant portion of the teacher's supplement that she should review to provide necessary student support. Thus, when the student is on step *a*, he submits the first IBM card for this TLU to the computer. He then proceeds through activities *a, b,* and *c.* In this instance the teacher is notified that she should refer to step *d* of the Teacher's Supplement (see Figure 3-7). Step *d* indicates that the teacher should prepare Language Master cards labeled S-10, Set 7, and indicates the words that should be on these cards. Therefore, when the student arrives at step *d,* and requires these cards, they should be available.

A similar procedure is used to notify the teacher of other actions she should take, such as providing certain information for the students or organizing group work. In the latter instance, the teacher is told not only that the work is called for but also which students are eligible for grouping. Through the use of the flagging technique, then, it is possible for the teacher to have the *current* information she needs in order to manage a wide variety of instructional activities.

MEASURING PERFORMANCE

After the student has completed a teaching-learning unit, he is evaluated on his ability to demonstrate mastery of the objectives. Evaluation items are written with a view to eliciting relevant performance from the student. Where feasible, the student takes a multiple-choice type examination which can be directly scored by the computer. On the other hand, it is not always feasible or relevant to provide a multiple-choice evaluation. In such cases, the student is directed to perform a particular activity for the teacher, who is given the criterion of acceptability by which the student should be judged. The teacher can then transmit her evaluation of the student's performance to the computer for record-keeping purposes. A specific example of how this operates in PLAN is provided by Figure 3-8. In the associated TLU, the student has been provided with an objective which says that he should be able to locate certain items on a map of his community. At the time he is ready for evaluation, the student provides the map of his community with certain items marked on it. The directions for the teacher indicate which features the student should have marked on his map. In this way it is possible to call for a specific response to a stimulus which is locally provided.

Although the basic function of the TLU and its supporting documents may now be clear, it is appropriate to provide a final illustration showing how the student interacts with all the various components as part of a continuing process, leading to the attainment of short-range objectives and long-range educational goals. Figure 3-9 symbolically shows the main components as modules/TLU's, module tests (not shown are the placement tests), computer data base, learning materials and equipment, and resource personnel. It further shows a "typical" sequence in which these components would be used. Although this diagram is greatly oversimplified, it is clear

Teacher's Supplement
Level 2 Language Arts (Sullivan Reading)

Special Instructions to the Teacher

Module 12-056, Lesson 1 (continued)

    d. Prepare language master cards labeled <u>S10 Set 7</u>:

        1. bathrobe - handlebar
        2. stone - shone - bone
        3. rode - home - hole - chose
        4. drove
        5. thorn
        6. prick
        7. caterpillar
        8. hungry
        9. split
      10. shed
      11. chipmunk
      12. mile
      13. Jim Wise
      14. alike
      15. tunnel
      16. perfect
      17. change
      18. twinkle

    e. The student does pp. 124 to 132 in <u>Programmed Reading Book 10</u>.

    f. Partners turn to p. 177 of the Teacher's Guide and dictate the sentences at the top of the page to each other at the chalkboard.

    g. The student does Webstermasters for Book 10, pages 21, 22, and 26, and checks his work.

    h. The student makes "blend blocks" on Worksheets 1 and 2. The student draws a picture of an object that begins with each blend below it before assembling the blocks. The teacher can use the examples in the TS to show students what their blocks should look like.

    i. The student folds a piece of drawing paper into four parts and draws one part of the life cycle of a butterfly in each section. He then writes a sentence under each picture.

    j. The student does pp. 133 to 143 in <u>Programmed Reading Book 10</u>.

    k. The student takes Test 4, p. 144.

    l. The student does Webstermasters for Book 10, pages 23, 24, 25, and 27.

FIGURE 3-7

A Portion of a Student's TLU

Step 3.   OBJECTIVE:
4421   Given a map of your community, show the source of your local water
          supply, and describe the type of purification process used. Also
          trace the route and system of sewage and garbage disposal.

USE	DO
local map	(a) From the agency responsible, find out where your water comes from and locate the source on the map.
	(b) From the agency responsible for your clean water, find out the location of the purification plant. Mark it on the map.
	(c) Find out where the sewage goes after it leaves your house. On the map, locate the main sewage disposal routes and the location of the sewage treatment plant.

TEACHER DIRECTIONS   (From Teacher's Supplement)

For Item 4, examine the community map which was marked by the student during
completion of TLU Step 3.   Check to make sure that the student has indicated
the location of the local water supply, the water purification plant, the
main sewage disposal routes, the sewage treatment plant and the main dumping
areas.   When the student has indicated the correct location of all of these
to your satisfaction, mark answer space A in Row 4 of his PLAN First Test
Card.

FIGURE 3-8

that frequent choices are made by the student and he develops responsibility
for self-directed learning as a result of those choices.

SUMMARY

From a previous discussion of a PLAN module, it can be seen that each
PLAN student is provided with objectives to guide his study, is given
learning activities to assist him in achieving the objectives, and finally is
provided with assessment procedures to evaluate his progress. In this way it
is possible for the student to have a program which more nearly
accommodates his individual needs with respect to: (1) which objectives he
studies; (2) the methods he uses to master the objectives; and (3) the pace
with which he progresses through the curriculum. As PLAN continues to be

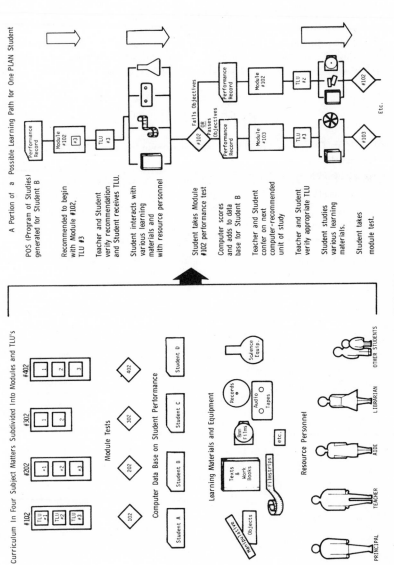

FIGURE 3-9

PLAN COMPONENTS AND THEIR POSSIBLE USE BY ONE STUDENT

developed and revised, it is expected that additional refinements will further facilitate the student's becoming an independent learner.

NOTE

[1] Research on "learning styles" is underway at the American Institutes for Research as it is at other locations. Indications of the existence of identifiable styles among PLAN students is still at an inferential stage but will be studied empirically in the next few years.

REFERENCES

FLANAGAN, JOHN C.   "Functional Education for the Seventies," *Phi Delta Kappan,* September, 1967.

GAGNÉ, ROBERT M.   *The Conditions of Learning.* New York: Holt, Rinehart & Winston, Inc., 1965.

Chapter 4. THE REVISION OF *PLAN* TEACHING-LEARNING UNITS

USE OF STUDENT PERFORMANCE DATA FOR IMPROVEMENT OF INDIVIDUALIZED INSTRUCTIONAL MATERIALS

Harold F. Rahmlow

INTRODUCTION

PLAN is a computer-supported system of individualized education dedicated to the improvement of educational results. Because PLAN is concerned with educational results, there is a strong emphasis on student performance data as the primary source of corrective feedback. There is continued effort toward improvement of the system, and the improvement is based on information gathered from the field.

This paper describes some of the kinds of data used in the improvement of the PLAN program and illustrates the improvement procedure with examples in the areas of science and reading.

SOURCE: Presented as part of a symposium: *Project PLAN: A Computer-Supported Individualized Education Program* for Division 15, American Psychological Association, Washington, D.C., September 1, 1969, by permission of the author.

BACKGROUND

PLAN (a Program for Learning in Accordance with Needs) is a joint effort of the American Institutes for Research, Westinghouse Learning Corporation, and thirteen participating school districts to improve education in grades 1-12. The combination of public schools, a research organization, and a major industrial concern provides tremendous resources which can be brought to bear upon the problem of education. Previous papers, (fnn. 1,2,6) provide detailed background information on the project.

The basic building block in PLAN is the module, which includes objectives associated with recommended learning activities, and criterion tests. A guidance system uses student data and draws upon a bank of modules available to recommend an individualized program of studies for each student. This program of studies is individualized in both the number and the type of objectives the student studies. The program is further individualized by providing alternate teaching-learning strategies, called Teaching-Learning Units (TLU's), for many modules.

A central computer is used in PLAN to collect information from remote terminals, one of which is located in each of the participating schools, and to process this information for future use of teachers and the research staff.

A correlated teacher development project involves work on the problems of the functions of teachers in an individualized education system.

TYPES OF DATA

The data base for the improvement of instructional results can be divided into two categories: hard data (objective) and soft data (subjective). In the hard data category we utilize four different test records: (1) item statistics of module tests indicating the number of students selecting each option; (2) frequency distribution of student scores on module tests on an objective-by-objective basis; (3) frequency distribution of student scores on module tests on an objective-by-objective-by-TLU basis; and (4) cross-validation data on parallel items administered at various time intervals.

It was mentioned that learning activities and evaluation items are written to specific performance objectives. Because of this principle, in analyzing items it is possible to pinpoint the validity with respect to the objectives as well as the reliability of items. A portion of an item analysis sheet is shown in Figure 4-1. The data are typical in that they indicate the frequency of student response for the various items and the correct response as well as providing in the right-hand column certain item-difficulty information. Although the specific objective to which each item is related is not shown in Figure 4-1, an alternate document provides the key to the item analyzer.

CHOICE OF OPTIONS FOR TEST ITEMS						**ITEM DIFFICULTY LEVELS**			
ITEM NO.	A	B	C	D	E	(-PASS	(-SR	(-TC	(-NP
01	021	020	099*	040	000	054	071	055	021
02	027	007	003	144*	000	079	100	078	058
03	002	010	170*	000	000	093	100	097	073
04	011	033	030	107*	000	059	079	065	006
05	023	130*	009	020	000	071	075	071	058
06	003	027	145*	007	000	080	100	078	061
07	005	004	005	168*	000	092	100	098	064
08	051	112*	017	002	000	062	088	057	039
09	120*	052	010	000	000	066	088	065	039
10	006	156*	009	011	000	086	100	090	055
11	004	173*	003	002	000	095	100	099	076
12	150*	015	013	000	000	082	100	087	045

```
TOTAL NUMBER OF TEST RECORDS0   0182
NUMBER OF COMPLETE CASES0       0015
NUMBER OF S REVIEW CASES00      0024
NUMBER OF T CERTIFY CASES0      0110
NUMBER OF NOT PASSED CASES0     0033
```

FIGURE 4-1
MODULE 30-254

If revisions of the learning activities are to lead to more effective learning, it is important to be able to relate the learner's activities to his achievement of a specific objective. This is accomplished primarily by comparing the activities indicated by the student as completed and the results of the criterion test items. If it is found, for example, that none of the activities leads to satisfactory performance, or that completion of a particular activity appears to attenuate performance, this information triggers a careful look at the module and the test.

Figure 4-2 shows an example of the objective-by-objective data. The printout shows the frequencies, percentages, and cumulative percentages of student responses on each of the evaluation items related to the given

Objective Code	No. of Items Correct	Frequency	Percent	Cumulative Percent
3013	00	1	0.7	0.7
	01	2	1.5	2.2
	02	1	0.7	2.9
	03	4	2.9	5.8
	04	129	94.2	100.0
TOTALS		137	100.0	
MEAN				3.88
STANDARD DEVIATION				0.54

FIGURE 4-2

objective. Means and standard deviations are also included. The manner in which these data are used in module revision will be illustrated shortly.

On any given set of objectives, it is very likely that more than one teaching-learning unit will be offered from which the student can choose the method he will use to accomplish the objectives. Because there are alternate approaches to the same terminal behaviors, it is desirable to be able to differentiate between the effectiveness of the various methods. To this end, information on the relative performance of the various teaching-learning units is provided. Figure 4-3 illustrates data available on alternate teaching-learning units which seek to facilitate the acquisition of the same student performance. Although it is not shown in Figure 4-3, it is also possible to examine data for different sub-populations to determine the differential effect, if any, of different TLU's upon the various sub-populations. A point biserial correlation is computed for each item as related to the overall items for the objective and can provide useful information. The correlation is useful because it gives an indication of the relationship between success on a given item and success on all items for the objective. It is a measure of the internal consistency of items for an objective. If a correct answer for one item correlates negatively with overall objective performance, this indicates a potential problem with the item. For example, if for item 1 alternative B is the correct answer, the item can be considered a good one since it correlates well (.641) with overall performance for all items on the objective. But if alternative A is the correct answer, the item would be considered a poor one since it correlates poorly (–.142) with overall performance for all items on the objective. However, as indicated by Popham (fn.3), such traditional indicators of item effectiveness can be very misleading in mastery-type learning situations. For this reason, it is desirable to examine the raw data as well as the correlation coefficient itself.

ITEM		A	B	C	D	E	BLANK
	ALTERNATIVE ANSWERS						
1	FREQUENCY	4	85	6	13	5	2
	PROPORTION	0.035	0.739	0.052	0.113	0.043	0.017
	MEAN	3.500	5.082	2.833	2.692	3.800	3.000
	PT. BIS. R	–0.142	0.641	–0.287	–0.472	–0.114	–0.147
2	FREQUENCY	3	7	4	87	12	2
	PROPORTION	0.026	0.061	0.035	0.757	0.104	0.017
	MEAN	2.333	2.714	3.000	5.034	3.583	2.000
	PT. BIS. R	–0.258	–0.333	–0.209	0.611	–0.235	–0.242
3	FREQUENCY	1	2	101	8	3	0
	PROPORTION	0.009	0.017	0.878	0.070	0.026	0.000
	MEAN	2.000	2.500	4.762	3.500	2.333	0.000
	PT. BIS. R	–0.170	–0.194	0.411	–0.204	–0.258	0.000
4	FREQUENCY	102	6	3	0	4	0
	PROPORTION	0.887	0.052	0.026	0.000	0.035	0.000
	MEAN	4.794	2.667	3.000	0.000	2.250	0.000
	PT. BIS. R	0.492	–0.314	–0.181	0.000	–0.311	0.000
5	FREQUENCY	24	12	0	79	0	0
	PROPORTION	0.209	0.104	0.000	0.687	0.000	0.000
	MEAN	3.333	3.417	0.000	5.089	0.000	0.000
	PT. BIS. R	–0.444	–0.275	0.000	0.571	0.000	0.000
6	FREQUENCY	6	69	19	21	0	0
	PROPORTION	0.052	0.600	0.165	0.183	0.000	0.000
	MEAN	3.167	5.261	3.632	3.429	0.000	0.000
	PT. BIS. R	–0.231	0.622	–0.290	–0.377	0.000	0.000

FIGURE 4-3

MODULE 31-645, TEST NO. 1, TLU 2, OBJECTIVE 7617,

N = 115, MEAN = 4.548, S. D. = 1.410

It is recognized that different competencies are evaluated on a short-term test as compared to a long-term test. In PLAN the module test whose item analysis we have been examining above is considered short term. That is, the module test is designed to measure student performance gained over an approximate two-week period. However, PLAN Achievement Tests and Developed Ability Tests are two other tests designed to assess student performance over a longer period of time. By comparing student results on the short- and long-range tests, it is possible to ascertain not only the immediate results of student activity, but also the long-range retention and synthesis of concepts. Figure 4-4 compares items from a survey test (a PLAN Achievement Test) with items from module tests.

In addition to the hard data discussed above, observational and teacher-observed behavior is also recorded. Figure 4-5 shows a portion of the questions asked of the teacher about the TLU's. This information, when used in conjunction with the item-analysis data mentioned above, provides valuable clues on the possible improvement of the program. Figure 4-6 illustrates a portion of the information relative to evaluation instruments that was collected from teachers.

Because PLAN is being developed for students, it is very valuable to collect student-response information on their perception of the program. Figure 4-7 illustrates the categories of information collected from students. Again, as with the questionnaire-type data collected from teachers, this information can be used along with the hard data as a vehicle for the improvement of the instructional program. Finally, project personnel working on the improvement of the instructional program make periodic visits to Project PLAN schools to maintain a realistic context within which to interpret data collected.

To summarize the types of data used in the improvement of the PLAN instructional program, we have seen that four basic types of objective data related to specific objectives are (1) item statistics of module tests indicating the number of students selecting each option, (2) frequency distribution of student scores on module tests on an objective-by-objective basis, (3) frequency distribution of student scores on module tests on an objective-by-objective-by-TLU basis, and (4) cross-validation data on parallel items administered at various time intervals. To supplement this data, subjective teacher judgments (TLU information, evaluation information) and student judgments are recorded. Let us now consider how these data are used in the actual improvement of instructional modules.

REFINEMENT OF A SCIENCE MODULE

To illustrate some of the procedures involved in the improvement of PLAN modules, the improvement of the module, "Introduction to Matter," will be discussed. The module can be classified in the general area of physical science. It was developed for students in the fourth- through sixth-grade

A Comparison of the Items That Appeared in Both the Module Tests and the Survey Tests

84-543

Civics Survey Test – 9th Grade

Survey Test Item No.	Module Test	Module Test Item No.	Percent Passing Module Item	Percent Passing Corresponding Survey Item	Percent Difference	One or More of the Alternates Were Changed	Position of Alternates Changed	Developmental Item	Appears on PLAN Achievement Test	Remarks
11.	44-543	23	61	67	+6	X				Item stem also changed somewhat.
11.	44-623	23	67	67	0	X				
11.	44-583	23	52	67	+15	X				
12.	44-543	25	68	78	+10				X	No change
12.	44-623	25	62	78	+16				X	No change
13.	44-544	1	97	96	-1					No change
14.	44-544	4	77	72	-5				X	No change
15.	44-544	8	77	76	+1					No change
16.	44-544	9	67	64	-3					No change
17.	44-545	7	77	71	-6				X	No change
18.	44-545	20	84	83	-1	X				Small format change

Note.—The brackets indicate that the item appears in more than one module test.

FIGURE 4-4

TLU Overall Evaluation

A.   The objectives are not sequenced correctly.

B.   TLU requires extensive teacher help.

C.   TLU needs a greater variety of learning activities.

D.   Reading level of TLU itself is too difficult for my (better, average, poor) students. (Select appropriate one for comment.)

E.   Please revise as indicated on the attached copy of the TLU.

F.   TLU should be deleted from the program.   (Why?)

G.   There is not enough difference in TLU's.   (How should they be modified?)

Student Activities

A.   Acceptable.

B.   Activities not related to the objective, or they are irrelevant to overall development.

C.   Objective needs additional activities as indicated on the form or on attached TLU in order to prepare students adequately for the achievement of the objective.

D.   The activities are not in the correct sequence.   Please revise as on the form or on the attached TLU.

E.   Activities require extensive teacher help.

F.   Too much reading required.

FIGURE 4-5

PORTION OF TEACHER'S TLU EVALUATION FORM

range. The module contained nine objectives, although only four will be discussed here. At the time the module was revised, 137 students had completed it.

A. Needs to be written in simpler language for the student. (Indicate vocabulary or structure causing difficulty.)

B. Does not appear to be related to any of the objectives of the module.

C. Format of item was confusing — needed teacher explanation.

D. Answers are ambiguous — no real distinction at the child's level of understanding.

E. Insufficient information is given in the item to know what is intended.

F. No correct answer to this item.

G. Requires too much time for the student to answer this question. (Indicate how much.)

H. Please revise as indicated on the form or on the attached copy of the test.

I. More than one correct answer for this item. (Please list.)

J. Too much teacher-time to correct. (Indicate how much.)

K. Illustrations are incorrect or ambiguous. (Indicate problem.)

L. Item seems too difficult for the objective. (Why?)

M. TLU does not prepare the student adequately.

FIGURE 4-6

PORTION OF TEACHER'S TEST EVALUATION FORM

Figure 4-2 showed the distribution of student responses on a four-item evaluation of one of the objectives, "Tell which substances are gases, liquids, and solids when given a list of ten substances." It can be seen that of the 137 students attempting the items 129 had all items correct. Moreover, the evaluation items related to this objective are clearly acceptable. For these items the student was given a list of substances and was asked to designate whether they were solid, liquid, or gas. Since the test items do match the objectives and since students were performing at an acceptable level on the objective, revision of this objective and its related learning activities and test items was not called for.

1.   What statements below best describe the reason you chose this TLU?

        A.   It was the easiest.
        B.   It uses materials I like.
        C.   It has the most interesting activities.
        D.   My teacher recommended it.
        E.   Other students recommended it.
        F.   It was the only one available.

2.   Which one statement best describes the time you spent on this TLU?

        A.   More than 15 hours
        B.   11 — 15 hours
        C.   6 — 10 hours
        D.   1 — 5 hours
        E.   Challenged test without studying the TLU

3.   What statements below describe the help you received on the TLU?

        A.   I received no help. (Circle Question Number 4, Item G, also.)
        B.   I received help from another student.
        C.   I received help from my teacher.
        D.   I received help from my parent(s).
        E.   I received help from others.

5.   Did you use more than one TLU for this module?

        A.   Yes.
        B.   No.
        C.   If you answered, "Yes," list on the "Student TLU Form" the
              additional TLU's you used.

FIGURE 4-7

PORTION OF STUDENT'S TLU EVALUATION FORM

Consider another objective for this same module. With this one there was a considerable amount of difficulty. The objective was "Write an acceptable scientific definition of the following words: *matter, molecules, atoms, electrons, protons,* and *nucleus.*" Figure 4-8 shows the distribution of student responses on the six items covering this objective. Since the distribution of responses on this objective reveals that an unsatisfactory number of students has achieved the objective, examination of the test items for this objective as well as of the learning activities was called for—and revealed the problem.

First, though the objective clearly calls for a recall of information, all six test items call for recognition. Although it is normally assumed that if the student can recall information, he should also be able to recognize the same information, recall and recognition are not the same. Therefore, the test items call for a different type of behavior than the objective. A much more serious problem is revealed by the learning activities given the students. Students were directed to read material in one or more of four textbooks. In reviewing these pages assigned to the student, it was discovered that in one book (5) there is the sentence, "All matter is made up of tiny particles called

Objective Code	No. of Items Correct	Frequency	Percent	Cumulative Percent
3011	00	0	0.0	0.0
	01	12	8.8	8.8
	02	10	7.3	16.1
	03	26	19.0	35.1
	04	23	16.8	51.9
	05	24	17.5	69.4
	06	42	30.7	100.1
TOTALS		137	100.1	
MEAN				4.19
STANDARD DEVIATION				1.62

FIGURE 4-8

molecules," and in another book (4), there is the statement, "All matter is made up of tiny particles called atoms." Thus, in two separate books, the student is given two apparently conflicting statements and then expected to respond correctly on the criterion test.

A different problem was encountered in the same module with two objectives which were ultimately combined into one. The two original objectives were: "State the difference between evaporation and condensation, explaining how heat is involved in these processes" and "Infer a relationship between melting and freezing after viewing a diagram." The distributions of student responses on the two objectives are shown in Figure 4-9. Neither of these shows a particularly good distribution of student responses. Examination of the objectives themselves indicates that though both are trying to get at different aspects of the overall problem, both are vague and poorly stated. It is difficult to know, for example, what a student will be doing when he is inferring. In this case, the objectives were in need of repair, and so one was written in a manner which tries to retain the desirable features of both of the original objectives. The new objective is "Given two states of matter, tell whether heat must be added or taken away to go from the first to the second state, and give the name of the process."

In addition to improvements made in the substance of the module, changes have also been made in the format of presentation. The original form of the module first listed all objectives and then all the steps for the achievement of those objectives. (Figure 4-10.) However, the specific relationship between the objectives and the steps was not clearly delineated.

Objective Code	No. of Items Correct	Frequency	Percent	Cumulative Percent	Objective Code	Number of Items Correct	Frequency	Percent	Cumulative Percent
3015	00	22	16.1	16.1	3016	00	39	28.5	28.5
	01	42	30.7	46.8		01	98	71.5	100.0
	02	73	53.3	100.1					
TOTALS		137	100.1		TOTALS		137	100.0	
MEAN				1.37	MEAN				0.72
STANDARD DEVIATION				0.74	STANDARD DEVIATION				0.45

FIGURE 4-9

MODULE NUMBER 30-255 | DRAFT EDITION 10/67

Figure 4-10

OBJECTIVES

INTRODUCTION TO MATTER

THE STUDENT WILL BE ABLE TO:

3011 Write an acceptable scientific definition of the following words: matter, molecules, atoms, electrons, protons, and nucleus.

3012 List the three states of matter with three examples of each.

3013 Tell which substances are gases, liquids, and solids when given a list of ten substances.

3014 State, after experimenting, that matter can change state, and cite two examples.

3015 State the difference between evaporation and condensation explaining how heat is involved in these processes.

ITEM	USE	DO	SELF-CHECK	DONE
1.	What is Matter? by Posin. Instructional Guide.	Review material from What is Matter, pp. 1-23. Read the I.G. Answer the following in your notebooks: 1. Tell what matter is. 2. List the three states of matter. 3. Define matter (See IG.)		
2.	Science 4, Laidlaw. Science notebook.	Read pp. 197-206. Do the following activities in your notebook. 1. Make a chart showing the three states of matter and give three examples of each. 2. Explain how you can tell if a fluid is a liquid or a gas. Check your answer with the material on pp. 199-201. 3. Study the picture on p. 200. State briefly in a paragraph what happened to the iodine crystals. 4. Define and give two everyday examples of evaporation and condensation. Tell how they are related. 5. Draw a diagram showing how melting and freezing are related.	Are clothes drying on a line an example of evaporation? Explain. Check pp. 205-206.	
---	---	---	---	---

FIGURE 4-10

This caused two problems. First, a student was not always aware of why he was going through certain steps. Although both objectives and learning activities were presented to him, the separation of the two and the lack of identification of the relationship of the two did not make the objectives as functional as desired. A second problem occurred when a student finished a module but had not mastered all objectives, since when objectives and learning activities are not closely related, it is extremely difficult for a student to know where to return to study. Therefore, a student might restudy the entire module, much of which he has already mastered, or he might engage in activities totally unrelated to his need. To remedy this situation, the module was rearranged so that the objectives and their related learning activities are specifically identified. (Figure 4-11.) This improved clarity has proved to be of great benefit to students and teachers, and in developmental work, it is much easier to monitor the work of a writer when the relationship between the objective and the learning activities must be made explicit.

REFINEMENT OF A READING MODULE

The work done on the reading material under consideration illustrates the effect of sequencing learning activities. Figure 4-12 illustrates the original teaching-learning unit. This teaching-learning unit relies heavily on the Sullivan reading materials but supplements these materials with a variety of activities. It can be seen from Figure 4-12 that the student is playing games, reading materials, writing, listening, looking at film strips. Students worked through the module at a reasonable pace and mastered the reading objective at the close of the work. However, teachers were able to identify a small group of students who were not succeeding with these materials. To ascertain the problems of the students who were having learning difficulties, special project personnel were assigned to monitor closely their activities.

After observing students, it was hypothesized that the sequencing or possibly the chunking of learning activities was inappropriate for these students as they seemed to have had a great deal of difficulty concentrating on the 16-page block of reading required in Activity (f). Could it be that breaking this block of reading into smaller parts and interspersing this reading with the other related activities would solve the problem for these students? Did students need a more structured way of keeping track of what they had read? Figure 4-12 shows that we had provided a "Done" column where the student can check off the activities he has completed. This aid, however, did not seem to be sufficient for these students that were having learning difficulties.

Figure 4-13 illustrates a portion of the modified version of the teaching-learning unit. The essential differences between the modified version and the original version are: (1) reading passages have been broken down into smaller units; (2) smaller units of reading have been interspersed with the other activities; and (3) a more structured format for recording the pages

Step 4. OBJECTIVE
         Given two states of matter, tell whether heat must be *added* or *taken*
         away to go from the first to the second state and give the name of
         the process.

         Example: To go from SOLID to LIQUID must heat be added or taken away?
                  What is the process called?

USE	DO
	(a) Ice, water, and steam are all made of water molecules. How are the substances different? Add them to the chart you made in Step 3(b).
What is Matter	(b) Review pp. 16-18.
	(c) Melt an ice cube. How did you do it? Evaporate the water you obtained from the melted ice cube. How did you do it? The results of your experiment could be summarized as follows:

$$ \text{ice} \xrightarrow[\text{melting}]{+H} \text{water} \xrightarrow[\text{evaporation}]{+H} \text{steam} $$

USE	DO
Instructional Guide	(d) Study and do Part I of the IG.
	(e) Check your answers in Part II of the IG.
science notebook	(f) In your notebook give as many every-day examples as you can of evaporation, condensation, melting, and freezing.

FIGURE 4-11

read is provided in the "Done" column. It should be emphasized that there were no content or activity changes from the first teaching-learning unit to the second. Everything that is included in the first teaching-learning unit is also included in the second, and no new learning activities have been added. The only modifications that have been made are in the sequencing and format of presentation. But now the students who had previously been having learning difficulties are able to proceed in a satisfactory manner using the refined materials. It should be pointed out that this work was carried out on a small sample of students, and, at this point in time, the results should not be considered generalizable to a wider target population. It is hoped that further work on the sequencing of instructional materials will provide us with more generalizable results.

Lesson 2   (continued)

	USE	DO	DONE
e.	pegboard [Sh] [Th] pegboard cards	play 4	
f.	Book 1 pencil Sullivan Book 1 pages 109 to 124	read write 6	
g.	4-D 4-D Listen and Do 4 - D crayons pencil	listen Draw a line. draw 1	
h.	Filmstrip D Tape D	look listen 1	

FIGURE 4-12
SULLIVAN BOOK 1 (2)

Lesson 2 (continued)

	USE	DO	DONE
	(T)	TM, pp. 231-236, <u>mint</u>, <u>fish</u>, <u>ship</u>	
f.	Book 1 <u>Sullivan Book 1</u> pencil	Read pages 115 to 118.	☐ 115 ☐ 116 ☐ 117
g.	pegboard pegboard cards	4 Play.	
h.	Book 1 <u>Sullivan Book 1</u> pencil	Read pages 118 to 120. Read page 120. My partner is _____	☐ 118 ☐ 119 ☐ 120

FIGURE 4-13
SULLIVAN BOOK 1 (2)

SUMMARY

The paper has presented the general rationale and types of data utilized in the improvement of individualized instructional materials within Project PLAN. Illustrations of both hard and soft data were presented. To illustrate further the techniques utilized, an illustration of the revision of a science module was presented. This revision depended very heavily on the hard data. On the other hand, an illustration was given of the refinement of a reading module during which the dependence was more on soft data. We believe that this analysis of the instructional program of Project PLAN will continue to improve educational results.

REFERENCES

1. FLANAGAN, JOHN C.   "Individualized Education," an invited address presented to Division 15, American Psychological Association, San Francisco, September 1968.

2. FLANAGAN, JOHN C.   "Program for Learning in Accordance with Needs," *Psychology in the Schools,* Vol. VI, No. 2 (April, 1969), pp. 133-136.

3. POPHAM, W. JAMES and HUSEK, T. R.   "Implications of Criterion-Referenced Measurement," *Journal of Educational Measurement,* Vol. 6, No. 1 (Spring, 1969), pp. 1-9.

4. POSIN, DANIEL Q.   *What Is Matter?* Westchester, Ill.: Benefic Press, 1962.

5. SCHNEIDER, HERMAN and SCHNEIDER, NINA.   *Science in Our World.* Boston: D. C. Heath & Company, 1965.

6. WEISGERBER, ROBERT A., and RAHMLOW, HAROLD F.   "Individually Managed Learning," *Audiovisual Instruction,* Vol. 13, No. 8 (October, 1968), pp. 835-839.

Chapter 5. **THE NATURE OF
AN OPERATIONAL
PLAN SCHOOL**

THE *PLAN* OPERATING ENVIRONMENT

Norman D. Carter

Entering a PLAN classroom is an experience not easily understood if one is accustomed to viewing standard classrooms over a period of years. Perhaps even before entering the doorway, one can hear sounds coming from a PLAN room that could be called disturbing sounds at another time and place. These are the sounds of activity, of students engaged in pursuing educational objectives that include discussing a problem or answer with others, of movement in the room, and of operation of equipment. These are the sounds of children talking with a neighbor about their learning activity, of children walking from an area of the room where they usually sit to an area where materials are displayed, and of a projector being used.

As one passes into the room, a few heads turn to see who has arrived. Someone may poke a neighbor and point out that a visitor is here again to

SOURCE: This chapter was written for this publication based on Norman Carter's experience as a PLAN principal while on leave at the American Institutes for Research.

watch. These heads will soon turn back to normal activity, closing out the watcher and the diversion that a new person brings to a class.

READING ACTIVITY

We notice that perhaps a fourth of the class is reading. One child is reading a newspaper, several are reading texts of various types, and magazines are in use by a few students. It is apparent that not all children are working on the same reading material. Book series are in use from difficulty levels above and below what would normally be expected in a standard classroom. The encyclopedia is in use by one child. Pamphlets have been collected by two students who are working as partners on one step of a TLU (Teaching-Learning Unit). They are busy reading and comparing information gathered from local sources relating to their work.

VIEWING

A student is using a filmstrip viewer at a designated station along one side of the classroom. He is watching this filmstrip alone, turning the filmstrip from frame to frame and viewing each picture frame of the story of colonization in America. Another child is operating an 8 mm single-concept film projector, showing a short film to herself, and looking for the particular process that has been called to her attention in the directing TLU—in this case, the process of a butterfly emerging from a chrysalis. The child using the single-concept film is showing the film repeatedly, viewing again a process that cannot be easily duplicated in a classroom and that requires the showing of movement in order to be understood. (Figure 5-1.) Elsewhere, the viewing of still pictures, diagrams, and charts in texts and booklets is occurring while students are pursuing step-by-step assignments through TLU's.

LISTENING

Three children with earphones are listening to a tape recording of an interview; in this case, they also have printed scripts of the tape before them. Their assignment is to identify statements made by the interviewee that are relevant to the topic of juvenile dress. Another student is using a second tape recorder, listening to directions on how to perform a mathematics operation. Still another child is listening to a record while using earphones, carefully noting particular sections of ballads called to her attention by the TLU. (Figure 5-2.)

In addition to listening to recorded materials, children are listening to explanations from classmates as well as from the teacher. At times when their teacher is busy with one child or with a discussion group, many children simply ask a classmate to help explain an idea they don't understand.

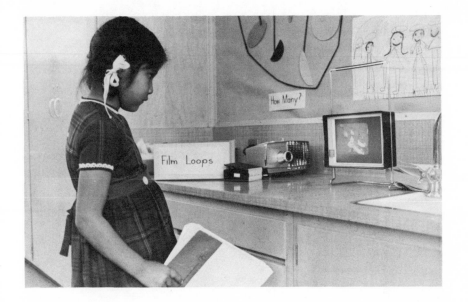

FIGURE 5-1

EXPERIMENTING

At a counter near the sink, two youngsters are involved in a science experiment where they must handle an alcohol lamp and a steam-driven apparatus. They must record their observations, make hypotheses, and draw conclusions based on what they have seen. Another boy may be by himself, examining salt crystals as they dissolve under a microscope. (Figure 5-3.) Two boys have just gotten up from their seats, have gone to a work area at the chalkboard, and are experimenting with possible combinations in a probability exercise. They are attracting no attention to themselves by their activity at the chalkboard, simply working there because it is convenient and well suited to the problem posed in their TLU. Other children are on the playground, where they are using thermometers and colored paper to determine the effects of color in relation to heat.

REPORTING

The students who have just concluded the experiment in heat are now sitting down at their desks and are reviewing notes that they recorded while outside. They must translate their estimate of temperature differences into a report called for as a learning activity in their TLU.

FIGURE 5-2

For another student, an oral report has been assigned on a process involving decision-making about the "limits" of population that are practical for his community. He is making his report to several classmates and the teacher.

Evidence of a third kind of reporting can be seen on the teacher's desk. An academically talented child in this room has submitted a "formal" paper, complete with title page, introduction, chapters, summary, and bibliography.

OBSERVING

Another child is busy looking out the window, seemingly wasting a good deal of time. If you watch him a minute more, you may see that he is watching a cloud formation, noting its type, and adding to notes or observations taken over a period of days. These observations are being graphed and written into a report to complete a science activity.

After writing an original play in language arts, a child is ready to act as a character in a scene in which two class members observe her performance and evaluate it against preset criteria prescribed for this activity. These observations will be important to the actress as judgment of her performance. The observers will have gained practice in evaluating against certain criteria.

FIGURE 5-3

DISCUSSING

Now the teacher is calling four children, who are working on the same TLU, over to a discussion area. All are known to her to have completed a portion of their work and are now asked to meet and talk over the differences between specific and general terms they have studied in this unit. The teacher is acting as a discussant in this activity, taking part in the conversation as a tutor only when her professional judgment tells her a child has missed a central idea or when the discussion drifts too far away from the behavioral objective and main topic.

TESTING

Having finished their TLU's in social studies and in mathematics, several youngsters are now moving to an area of the room set aside for test taking. They have requested their module tests through their teacher, who has questioned them briefly in order to reinforce certain major ideas and to see if they had finished the learning activities listed in their TLU's. (Figure 5-4.) Each student was handed an appropriate test along with an IBM card. For one child, the testing may go quickly; 20 minutes will be all that is needed to answer the 20 multiple-choice and true-false questions on his test. For the other child, taking a different test, two hours may be used concentrating on similar multiple-choice questions as well as a written part of the test that requires teacher certification. A third child feels he can pass the module test without working on the learning activities. He has read the module objectives and examples, feels that from his past outside reading and experience he knows the area of study, and wishes to "challenge" this unit of work. Upon passing this test, he will proceed to his next module, perhaps even challenging and passing that test.

FIGURE 5-4

TEST PROCESSING AND REPORTING

The students' test cards are processed through a remote computer terminal. Students, teachers, or aides can process them either as testing is finished or in batches at the end of the day. (Figure 5-5.) The test answers are transmitted to a computer elsewhere in the United States, scored, and returned to the school on an overnight basis.

A printout of yesterday's testing was on hand when children arrived at school this morning. With anticipation, they studied the printout for their results, looking first at what level they had passed (complete; student review; or teacher certify) and next at any objectives that were missed. After passing a module test, these students referred to their POS (Program of Studies), went to the file where all modules are kept, and with the help of the teacher selected the TLU that seemed most appropriate.

GOAL SETTING

One child, who has spent his last hour on readings directed by his TLU, feels he needs a break from that activity and is planning his own goals for the next week of work. He is making some changes in his program with the help and counseling of his teacher. As a matter of fact, his expectations for the past quarter could have been more realistically set; he neglected to plan enough time for those three extra experiments in science that were optional. Furthermore, he completely forgot about two holidays that shortened the time available. Hopefully, this quarter he won't forget to take a good look at the calendar and consider a careful estimate of time needed to complete the modules coming up.

CENTRAL MATERIALS STORAGE

The classroom observer notices that materials such as texts, kits, magazines, workbooks, answer keys, pamphlets, teacher editions and guides

FIGURE 5-5

are located in open display near as many students as possible. They are arranged systematically for ease of access according to title, author, or subject matter area.

The students are able to use all books and answer keys freely, returning each book or material item to its original place as soon as a step is completed. Marking of shelving areas for particular items has been done by a group of student library helpers selected by the teacher to maintain the materials collection. With this open-display system, students can quickly go to the shelves, find the material item called for, take it to their work area for study, and, after it has been used to the extent called for in a TLU, return it to its proper place.

Filmstrips, single-concept films, records, globes, maps, and tapes, etc., also are displayed openly and are located near the audio-visual equipment area. Children move freely to pick out audio-visual items, go to the equipment and study the item as many times as they feel necessary. After returning the audio-visual item to its designated storage spot, they continue with whatever task is called for next in their programs. Usually these children operate the devices comfortably and easily with a minimum of help from an adult. If assistance is needed, another child is only too happy to display his skill in starting a piece of equipment.

An older student, with his TLU in hand, has come into the central materials area from his room at the opposite end of this building. He has equal access to the same materials as the students in the class you have been observing, and in this instance he is looking at an item that is not typically used by his classmates. These materials were placed in the central materials area so that shared use by several classrooms of children would keep costs much lower than would be expended if each item were stocked in each room.

Since the audio-visual equipment has a high usage rate, it is imperative that regular maintenance be provided. A quick turnover time is essential on repair of recorders, viewers, and devices that could prevent a child from progressing through essential steps. Back-up equipment for use in case of long-term repair, as well as use of "loaner" replacements, has been provided for by the school principal.

SCHOOL DESIGN

The school where these activities are described was constructed according to a concept of open design, encouraging free flow of pupils between "rooms." It is equipped with detachable walls mounted on tracks, which provide the teacher with the option of using a walled area when necessary even though this is infrequent. Floor areas are fully carpeted thereby providing a helpful cushion for sound in an active classroom, where students are required to talk with their neighbor and equipment is operated freely.

The central multi-use room, adjacent to all the open "rooms," is designated as a materials center for audio-visual equipment as well as for learning materials storage. Students are under supervision at all times by an adult who may observe them from another "room" area. (Figure 5-6.)

Another design, a modular concept in school building construction, is also particularly well suited to accommodate a PLAN program. Classrooms in this circular arrangement are located around a center core. The central area or "hub" can be used as a material resource center much the same as has been described in the open-concept building.

Classrooms constructed on a linear or row concept have been adapted to the PLAN system. Often they are altered to provide a doorway between adjacent classrooms, allowing students to pass freely from one class to another with a minimum of disturbance. (Figure 5-7.) A room which is central within the wing or located in the middle of the row of rooms is used as a materials resource center. Because of this physical arrangement and the need for supervision, this adaptation is usually staffed with an aide or librarian.

ARRANGEMENTS WITHIN THE ROOM

The usual PLAN classroom has a variety of work stations and seating arrangements; some desks are in pairs, and still others are in groups of four

FIGURE 5-6

FIGURE 5-7

or five. They face no front of the class because there is no traditional lecture area from which the teacher speaks. Often two groupings are used as discussion centers and are placed at opposite corners of the classroom. Both areas may have small chalkboards, where a visual explanation can be sketched out, as well as a table around which students gather for discussion groups.

The bulletin board is used for the purposes of displaying students' creative work, for announcements, and for instructions related to classroom management.

The teacher's desk is placed wherever it seems most appropriate for a particular teacher. In the room we are visiting, it is located adjacent to the central materials storage area, allowing supervision of both the class and the multi-use room.

SUPPORT SERVICES

The teachers are given support in three ways. First is the principal, who is readily available for material needs, conferencing, counseling, and for matters that concern the operation of the school as well as the total instructional program. The second source of support is the personnel development consultant, who is responsible for training and counseling of teachers throughout the school year. She handles many schools in her assignment but visits this classroom about one day per week and more often when called upon. The third supporting ingredient is the A.I.R. Development, Evaluation and Research staff who monitor the whole program and provide contact for the schools to facilitate revision during developmental phases of PLAN (Figure 5-8.)

FIGURE 5-8

As we leave this class, students continue their varied activities, working as individuals accomplishing objectives prescribed according to their individual needs. Several children noticed us enter this classroom an hour ago, but as we leave, no child really notices our exit.

SUMMARY

An operational educational system has been described where students work in an individualized manner achieving behavioral objectives by means of teaching-learning units (TLU's). Students have been making decisions concerning their immediate learning tasks as well as planning their longer range goals. Help in decision-making has been provided through a program of studies (POS), the teacher-tutor-counselor, and the support of a computer data base.

Students have been working at a number of diverse activities leading toward mastery of stated objectives. Those students have worked with a teacher, with other children, and with varied material resources.

A learning center with materials storage has been used freely by students in pursuing tasks assigned through their TLU's.

The school design has contributed to the student's learning experience by allowing open access to material items and work space. It also has provided a motivational environment for study.

One must be aware that PLAN is a developmental system. As such, it needs continued revision and adaptation to differing state and local requirements. It is designed to accommodate such changes.

Project PLAN is a system whereby a child can gain a broad base of experience necessary for adjusting to and living in tomorrow's world. Besides offering what appears to be a fundamentally sound educational system, a PLAN classroom is an exciting place for a child to be.

Chapter 6. THE DEVELOPMENT OF *PLAN* TEACHERS

A PROGRAM OF TEACHER DEVELOPMENT FOR A SYSTEM OF INDIVIDUALIZED EDUCATION

Margaret T. Steen

In the fall of 1967 a program of individualized education was introduced in 13 school districts throughout the United States. The program, Project PLAN, was developed by the American Institutes for Research, the Westinghouse Learning Corporation, and teachers from the cooperating school districts. Project PLAN differs from the usual instructional program in its classroom organization, materials, method of instruction, patterns of curriculum, and its definition of the roles of the teacher and the student. Since the project required such comprehensive changes in the school's program, one of the most important components of the project became the program for teacher development. A Title III ESEA grant provided the means for designing, writing, implementing, and evaluating a program of teacher development for individualized education using PLAN as the prototype system.

Need for Teacher Change. In the first year in which PLAN was implemented in the public schools, the teachers began teaching with a

---

SOURCE: This is original material written especially for this volume.

minimum of training in specific skills relative to the PLAN system of individualized education. During that year, the activities in which teachers participated in the PLAN classrooms were recorded and analyzed by consultants from the teacher development staff.

The data from the classrooms revealed that during the first year of the project, teachers spent the largest amount of time during the school day in organizational and managerial activities. The description of teacher activities defined as desirable by PLAN included tutoring, counseling, and instructing students in the techniques of managing their own behavior. The actual time teachers spent in these desirable activities was minimal. This meant a new emphasis for all teachers and in most cases the acquisition of new skills. The problems for the teacher development program were identified as:

1. The need to insure that certain skills related to individualized instruction were acquired by *all* trainees

2. The limitation of time for training teachers in the skills and for practicing the subsequent transfer to the classroom setting.

The tasks for the teacher development staff could then be outlined as finding means of:

1. Helping teachers *modify* skills in their present repertoires of behavior

2. Helping teachers *acquire* new skills

3. *Reinforcing* the procedure of acquiring new skills and modifying current skills

4. Helping teachers *maintain* the new behaviors once they were acquired

5. *Extinguishing* behaviors which are viable in a regular classroom setting but not in a PLAN classroom setting.

CHOOSING A THEORETICAL BASE FOR TEACHER CHANGE

Once the problems were identified, the next step was to find the best method to use to train the teachers. With the problem of helping teachers acquire, maintain, improve or decrease certain specific behaviors, it was clear that a comprehensive conceptualization of reinforcement theory would be needed. This comprehensiveness was suggested by the work of Bandura and Walters[1] and Ullman and Krasner.[2] Some behavior could be maintained through a simple use of social reinforcement; some behavior could be improved through successive approximations; other behavior could be acquired through imitation. A program based on some form of reinforcement theory was concluded to be the most appropriate approach for the following reasons: (1) the techniques suggested several approaches to insure that certain skills were acquired by all trainees, (2) the specificity of the techniques compensated for the short period of time for achievement and the subsequent transfer to the classroom setting. Strict operant or classical conditioning were both rejected as being too limited to produce the broad scope of complex behaviors required in a public school setting. For example, this type of conditioning would require a larger number of instructors and more controlled setting than could be expected in the social system of a public school.

THE TRAINING PROGRAM

The training program which the staff developed had two phases: (1) the definition of the specific behaviors for the teacher to acquire, (2) presentation of the program to provide for acquisition, improvement and maintenance of the behaviors. The program includes pre-service conferences and in-service consultant services.

1. The Definition and Statement of Specific Behaviors

Each teacher-trainee is given an individualized program with objectives to be achieved at the conference and performance criteria for use in his classroom. The set of objectives for training is presented as a Program of Studies and the data on achievement of the objectives is stored in the computer. (See Table 6-1.) Thus, if a teacher-trainee is required to learn a specific skill in the teacher-training program, an objective is written which would indicate how the teacher-trainee would study and be tested on the skill during the training session. An example of such an instructional objective would be:

> After reading a case study of a student, you will be able to list (A) the steps you might follow and (B) possible questions you might ask for each step when evaluating a Program of Studies.

This objective would be studied and tested at the conference.

To increase the chances for transfer to the PLAN classroom setting, each objective is translated for the teacher-trainee into a performance criterion. The intent is to indicate to the teacher-trainee the conditions under which the behavior would be performed. A performance criterion for the objective stated above would be:

TABLE 6-1
PLAN

PROGRAM OF STUDIES AND PROGRESS REPORT FOR: <u>ANDERSON JAMES</u>

<u>SCHOOL</u>: BISHOP MEMORIAL HIGH   <u>CONSULTANT</u>: MRS. SUSAN CARTER   <u>LEVEL</u>: SECONDARY

Objective	Date Finished
The teacher is able to catalogue learning material to meet the criteria presented in the Materials Organization Guide.	August 27
The teacher is able to arrange subject matter centers which include catalogued materials, furniture, and learning equipment to meet the criteria presented in the Materials Organization Instructional Guide.	August 27
The teacher is able to identify teacher-monitored materials as defined in the Materials Organization Guide and give reasons for their identification.	August 27
The teacher is able to instruct students in understanding the rationale, as defined in the Materials Organization Instructional Guide, behind their locations of work, location of learning materials, and equipment.	August 27

Planning the Program of Studies and the Individualized Schedule
 	
   a. After reading a case study of a student, you will be able to (a) list the steps you will follow and (b) list possible questions you might ask for each step when setting up a Program of Studies, according to the procedures described in "Planning the Program of Studies."
 	
   b. Based on the "Description of Student-Managed Behavior," you will be able to place sample student behaviors on the continua and assess student managed behavior using a checklist.
 	
   c. Using the sample form "Behavior Measures Relative to Student-Managed Behavior," you will be able to recognize those behaviors which need modification and suggest possible questions for discussion at the teacher-student counseling session.	

Following the criteria in the instructional guide, demonstrate with two of your own students the planning of a Program of Studies for each student.

The performance criteria are a basis for evaluation by the PLAN consultant during visits to the classroom and are also used during in-service planning meetings. A summary of the resulting evaluation is made available to both the teacher-trainee and consultant. (See Table 6-2.)

2. *Acquisition, Improvement and Maintenance of Behavior*

The training program consists of two pre-service conferences followed by ongoing in-service consultant services.

The pre-service conferences are designed to cover several categories of information about PLAN classes; (1) materials organization, (2) room arrangement, (3) computer services, (4) individualizing the student's

TABLE 6-2

Teacher's Name _____ *Mrs. Young* _____

School _____ *Valley* _____

Consultant _____ *Betty Smith* _____

MATERIALS ORGANIZATION AND ROOM ARRANGEMENT

OBJECTIVE	COMPUTER RESULTS/DATE
1. The teacher is able to catalogue learning material to meet the criteria presented in the Materials Organization Guide.	*#88063 Complete 9-5-69*
PERFORMANCE CRITERION	**OBSERVATION DATES**
1. The student is able to locate and return TLU related material with ease.	First *9-30-69*
	Second *10-7-69*
a. Primary: all materials are catalogued so as to meet the criteria presented in the Materials Organization Guide.	Third
	Criterion Met *10-7-69* (date)
b. Intermediate/Secondary: (see above)	Comments: *Teacher/consultant agree on student ability to locate and return TLU related material.*
(Five students are randomly selected. Using a TLU and a checklist a consultant notes these five students easily locate and return material and equipment.)	

programs, and (5) tutoring and counseling skills. The instructional material is presented in the form of modules consisting of a set of related objectives and the activities necessary to complete those objectives. The modules can be completed independently, with a partner, or with a small group. They include written material, filmstrips, slides, and problem-solving games. An example of a training TLU is illustrated in Table 6-3. Teachers complete a test of the objectives after finishing the activities in the module or at any point they feel they have achieved the objectives.

The in-service program is focused on the set of performance criteria. The PLAN consultant visits each teacher's classroom to identify those behaviors which the teacher-trainee is demonstrating. These behaviors are then reinforced by the PLAN consultant.

Any behaviors stated in the performance criteria but not demonstrated in the PLAN classroom become the basis for an in-service program with that individual teacher. To help the teacher-trainee acquire these behaviors, any of several techniques could be followed. (1) The conference material could be reviewed or supplemented with other materials. (2) Approximations of the appropriate behaviors could be reinforced. (3) Some type of modeling procedure could be used to help the teacher acquire the appropriate behavior. None of these techniques is mutually exclusive. The decision is made by the PLAN consultant as to which or to what extent any one technique is used.

For example, a teacher-trainee who has not been doing any special-interest tutoring but finally begins to do some, even though using poor techniques, would be reinforced for the tutoring but not for the techniques. This could also be an appropriate time to introduce some supplementary written materials on tutoring skills and techniques. To further help the teacher-trainee acquire the appropriate techniques, the PLAN consultant could model the procedure himself (observational modeling), provide a description of another teacher's approach (symbolic modeling), or take the teacher-trainee to observe another model (observational modeling).

INDIVIDUALIZATION AND INVOLVEMENT

Necessarily, the description of the actual procedures to change behavior has been simplified. There are obviously many variables in the affective domain to consider when helping individuals change their behavior. Two of these variables which have been most important to the teacher development staff are the individualization of the techniques used by the PLAN consultant and the involvement of the teacher-trainee in decisions about his own behavior.

The first factor, the individualization of techniques, is accomplished through the unique relationship which develops between each teacher and

TABLE 6-3

OBJECTIVE #1: AFTER READING A CASE STUDY OF A STUDENT, YOU WILL BE ABLE TO
               LIST A.) THE STEPS YOU WILL FOLLOW AND B.) POSSIBLE QUESTIONS
               YOU MIGHT ASK FOR EACH STEP WHEN EVALUATING A PROGRAM OF STUDIES
               (POS), ACCORDING TO THE PROCEDURES DESCRIBED IN "PLANNING THE
               PROGRAM OF STUDIES."

PERFORMANCE IN THE CLASSROOM: Demonstrate with two of your own students the
                               planning of a POS, according to the procedures
                               described in "Planning the Program of Studies."

USE	DO
1. Instructional Guide, "Planning the Program of Studies."	1. Read the Introduction and Procedures, pages 1 through 5.
2. Field Consultant	2. Discuss the following topics related to the instructional guide: a. What is the POS? b. What procedures would you follow in planning the POS?
3. Tape of case study (either intermediate or secondary). Tape recorder Written version of case studies in Instructional Guide, Part 3, page 15 or part 4, page 16.	3. Listen to the tape of the case study appropriate for your level. You may want to follow the written version at the same time. Study the corresponding suggested POS for the student.
4. Suggested POS for the students in each of the case studies, Instructional Guide, part 5 or 6.	4. List the procedures you would use with the student in evaluating the POS.
5. Audio tape, "Eavesdropping on the Planning of a POS", Intermediate or Secondary. Tape recorder Instructional Guide, "Planning the Program of Studies." Partner if desired.	5. Listen to the tape appropriate for your level. Using the checklist on page 5 of the instructional guide, check the procedures as they occur on the tape.

the PLAN consultant. The training program was designed to *require* teacher-consultant interaction and, moreover, for these interactions to provide opportunities for verbal and non-verbal reinforcement appropriate to *particular* teachers. The number of interactions and type of reinforcement during the interactions are responsibilities of the PLAN consultant. The teacher-trainee is ultimately responsible for his own behavior change and the PLAN consultant is merely the facilitating agent. The PLAN consultant works to help the teacher-trainee maintain appropriate behaviors only as long as necessary. Because each behavior is essential to the classroom operation it facilitates rather than hinders the teacher's learning of the skill. In other words, the behaviors have "pay-off" for the teacher and are thus maintained.

An example of a behavior which becomes self-reinforcing is the use of the computer for storage and retrieval of information. One purpose of the computer in the PLAN system is to eliminate the clerical task of keeping track of 30 students, all with different sets of objectives. If a teacher tried to keep complete records for all students there would be little or no time for instructional activities. Once the teacher-trainee understands how to report information to the computer and how to retrieve it and recognizes the advantages in time saved, with more accurate records, the teacher voluntarily continues to use the computer for this purpose.

The biggest job is in assisting the teacher to learn the initial behavior. Once the behavior is learned, the maintenance role of the consultant can be diminished in direct proportion to the pay-off value for the teacher.

The goals of the training program are not ends in themselves. A creative teacher will complete the training program as outlined here and with the help of the PLAN consultant find many individual ways to complement and extend the skills acquired during training. The limit to teacher effectiveness and individualization is not controlled by the program but by the extent to which a teacher is able to understand the differences among students and to individualize instruction with each student. The more effective the teacher is in accomplishing this, the more unique each teacher's role will become.

NOTES

[1] Albert Bandura and Richard H. Walters, *Social Learning and Personality Development* (New York: Holt, Rinehart & Winston, Inc., 1967).

[2] L. P. Ullman and L. Krasner, *Psychological Model for Abnormal Behavior* (New York: Holt, Rinehart & Winston, Inc., 1969).

Part B

**Individualized Programs at
the National Level:
The IPI System**

Introduction

In 1963 a joint effort to develop a *system* of Individually Prescribed Instruction (IPI) was begun by the Learning Research and Development Center, at the University of Pittsburgh, and the Baldwin-Whitehall Public Schools, of suburban Pittsburgh. A K-6 grade level school, Oakleaf, was chosen as the experimental site. Building upon a firm base of research established in prior years, and with support from the U.S. Office of Education, the IPI project had multiplied from the original Oakleaf School into 99 demonstration schools by the 1968-69 school year. Presently the field testing and dissemination of IPI are a responsibility of Research for Better Schools, Philadelphia.

Concentrating first in the areas of reading and mathematics, the IPI system has stressed testing for identification of learner needs, for monitoring their progress, and for program revision and improvement. Initially, the time requirements associated with scoring and the logistics problems associated with maintaining vast quantities of sheets of instructional material, as well as other factors, necessitated the supplementation of school staffing with teacher aides. Recently experimentation was undertaken to employ computers as a way of assisting the teacher in the management process.

In Chapter 7, William Cooley and Robert Glaser describe the IPI Management and Information System which is the forward look, the model, for IPI's future development. Of particular importance in this new model is the increased attention to (1) specification of goals, (2) measurement and diagnosis of the pupil's initial behavior, (3) assignment of instructional objectives, (4) continuous monitoring and assessment, and (5) procedures for adaptation and optimization.

Chapter 8 represents a description of the IPI system as it is currently being disseminated to the schools. This chapter is meant to answer some of the questions typically posed by those who are not familiar with IPI's operational aspects.

In Chapter 9 Richard Cox and C. M. Lindvall analyze in depth the various ways that evaluation of learner behavior takes place in the IPI program for planning and monitoring student progress and providing for program improvement.

Next, John Bolvin, in Chapter 10, explains how the IPI program provides for program revision through systematic analysis of data from the field.

In Chapter 11, Donald Deep describes the Oakleaf School's operation during one of the early years in which the IPI system was used. He emphasizes the effects of the program upon the teachers' changed roles.

This is followed by Chapter 12, in which Robert Scanlon and Claire Moshy review the status of teacher retraining in schools that are now adopting the IPI system.

Chapter 7.   THE *IPI*/MANAGEMENT INFORMATION SYSTEM

THE COMPUTER AND INDIVIDUALIZED INSTRUCTION

William W. Cooley
Robert Glaser

One of the most important potential uses of computers in schools is their use to individualize the educational process. However, as the history of attempts at individualization indicates, little can be accomplished unless the educational process is operationally defined and translated into specific school practices. The basic requirement for this is the presentation of an instructional model which underlies and generates (i) the instructional procedures, materials, and school environment and (ii) the data and research information needed for performing the desired educational functions effectively.

Therefore, before any fruitful discussion on how the computer might facilitate such education can begin, it is necessary to specify just how

SOURCE: Reprinted from W. W. Cooley and R. Glaser, "The Computer and Individualized Instruction," *Science,* Vol. 166 (October 31, 1969), pp. 574-82, by permission of the authors and publishers. Copyright 1969 by the American Association for the Advancement of Science.

individualization is to be accomplished. The instructional model can serve as the beginning of a system which can then be improved on the basis of information obtained from the model's application. If there is no model, or if it is ambiguous, it is difficult to structure operations and essentially impossible to make continuous improvements in the total educational system. It is in this light, and with this as a base for discussing the individualized school and the computer, that we present a model of educational practice which can underlie individualized instruction.

Individualized education is essentially the adaptation of instructional practices to individual requirements. Three major factors are involved, each of which defines a set of variables in the system: (i) educational goals, (ii) individual capabilities, and (iii) instructional means. *Goals* are defined to suit the individual, as when individuals choose different courses of instruction for different desired vocations. The term *individual capabilities* refers to the capabilities that the individual brings to a particular instructional situation; these are influenced by prior background and schooling. *Instructional means,* which include what is taught and how it is taught, are dictated by both the nature of the individual's capabilities and the nature of his educational goals. These three factors may change in the course of one's education or one's life, but in any particular span of time, during a specific teaching act, it is assumed that a particular educational goal or level of competence is to be attained; that the individual has particular capabilities; and that there is available a set of instructional means and conditions relevant to assessed capabilities and to criteria of competence.

Thinking about the educational process in this way suggests the following general instructional model, which is presented as a sequence of operations.[1]

1.   The goals of learning are specified in terms of observable student behavior and the conditions under which this behavior is to be manifested.

2.   When the learner begins a particular course of instruction, his initial capabilities—those relevant to the forthcoming instruction—are assessed.

3.   Educational alternatives suited to the student's initial capabilities are presented to him. The student selects or is assigned one of these alternatives.

4.   The student's performance is monitored and continuously assessed as he learns.

5.   Instruction proceeds as a function of the relationship between measures of student performance, available instructional alternatives, and criteria of competence.

6.   As instruction proceeds, data are generated for monitoring and improving the instructional system.

The implementation of these operations requires both research and application. Various degrees of automation can be used in implementing the model. It is possible to begin without any automation at all. With a redesigned school organization and appropriate tests and materials, teachers and teacher aides can carry out individualized instruction in a particular school. The system known as Individually Prescribed Instruction (IPI), introduced at the Oakleaf School,[2] was such a nonautomated version during its early years. The effectiveness of individualized education is not necessarily related to the degree of automation involved. However, it seems possible that automation can be a significant aid in the conduct of an individualized system and in the collection of research data on which improvements can be based.

Automation can be introduced in individualized education as a *means of assisting the teacher* in managing the process. The computer can service classroom terminals which assist the teacher in assessing the student's capabilities and prescribing a course of instruction. When automation is used in this way it is referred to as "computer-managed instruction" (CMI).[3] In CMI, the primary function of the computer is to assist the teacher and student in planning instructional sequences, where the actual instruction may be self-instruction packages (automated or not) or more conventional instruction. On the other hand, when the computer is used by the student as a *means of instruction,* the term commonly used is "computer-assisted instruction" (CAI). Both CMI and CAI carry out educational functions. CMI can be used without CAI, but if CAI is used, the information necessary for CMI is usually present. CMI will probably precede CAI in the evolutionary individualization of a school.

The general instructional model presented can be implemented in any one of three modes: nonautomated instruction, CMI, or CAI. It is highly probable that increasing levels of automation can improve individualized education, but only if more is learned about adapting education to individual requirements. A CMI system can obtain such information in addition to being used for operational implementation. The nonautomated version (IPI, during the early years of its use at the Oakleaf School) represents a first application of the general instructional model. After a period of pilot work, CMI is being introduced at the school to speed up collection and analysis of the data required for the design of an improved system.

INSTRUCTIONAL DECISION-MAKING

All teaching involves decisions about how instruction should proceed. Individualized instruction requires instructional decisions relevant to each student. The differential decision-making function in individualized instruction is a central issue. These decisions require a great deal of information about the individual student, such as the following. (i) What criteria of competence should be applied? These criteria have traditionally been stored in the form of test grades, teacher judgments of quality, and so on. (ii) What is the student's background? This information has been stored in the student's written record, in the form of intelligence-test and aptitude-test scores. (iii) How does a student proceed in his learning? This information is usually based on the teacher's impression of the student as slow or fast, attentive or inattentive, and is rarely documented. (iv) What instructional means are available for teaching certain lessons? These have been catalogued in the teacher's head or on a resources list. In the model of individualized instruction envisioned here, a sizable amount of information is needed for each student on a daily basis. It is obvious that the teacher will need assistance of some kind in storing, and acting upon, such data.

A computer management system has as its objectives the collecting and processing of information on each student and the supplying of this information to the teacher in summarized form such that it is directly applicable to human decision-making. It is possible that, at each decision point, data can be summarized for the teacher at his request, or supplied to him on a regular basis. It also seems possible that such information, in a form different from that in which it is supplied to the teacher, can be supplied to the student and used by him in choosing or discussing with the teacher his next instructional sequences. With this approach, the teacher's time can be reserved for the most subtle and difficult educational decisions. The computer can be programmed to suggest decisions to the teacher, based upon analysis of the learning process and of past experience with similar students. The teacher can then decide whether to accept, revise, or reject the recommendation.

We should emphasize the fact that the primary function of the computer in a CMI system is to make possible more complicated decision processes than would be possible without the computer, and to do this on a continuous basis. Automation cannot be justified if the computer is used simply to keep records. Clerks tend to be cheaper record keepers than computers. In an individualized system, the teacher continuously needs information and assistance in making instructional decisions. By providing decision tables in the computer, help can be given the teacher on a continuous basis. The computer itself is not making the instructional decisions. The computer is the means whereby the psychologist and the teacher can work together on a day-to-day basis to provide a continuously improving system of decision-making.

IMPLEMENTATION OF THE MODEL

Let us examine the procedures that would be followed in an individualized school proceeding according to the model mentioned above. The system is oriented around the instructional decisions required for adapting the educational environment to the student. The procedures involved supply information about the student to both the teacher and the student; also, information is supplied concerning the effectiveness of the procedures and materials that are used in the school.

1. Specification of goals, subgoals, and decision nodes. Educational goal-setting is a complex problem that cannot be ignored; goals are inevitably involved, whether explicitly or implicitly, whenever instruction takes place. The educational technologist does not set the goals for American education. Instead, his task is to identify goals that are valued in his society and then to develop the procedures for achieving those goals. When he has finished his task he can say to educators, parents, and students, "In order to attain goal A, consider doing X, Y, and Z." The eventual result is a variety of goals from which the learner is free to select and for which instructional means are defined and made available.

Schools must provide not only the means for attaining various goals but also the mechanism whereby goals can be identified or selected for each student. Although selecting goals is often seen as a guidance function differentiated from subject-matter teaching, the two functions are not separable. The guidance technology required to institute a system of goal setting for the individual must be defined and implemented if the school is to offer the means of attaining alternative goals and alternative paths toward these goals. No one will argue that all students should have the same educational goals or that goals must remain constant for a given student, although it is probably true that elementary school, directed as it is toward the teaching of fundamental skills and knowledge, permits less freedom for goal-setting than later schooling does. Up to a point, in the individualized elementary school, the choice is more among instructional means than among ultimate goals.[4]

The goals specified for a given student imply a series of subgoals. The arrangement of these subgoals is a function of the structure of the subject-matter goals that have been selected, the approach of the course designer to the subject matter, and the instructional path that the student elects or that his performance suggests. Different students may follow different paths through these subgoals, so for any particular individual the subgoals may be omitted, added to, recombined, or rearranged. These changes take place as a function of instructional alternatives. These are discussed below; we should make the point at this time, however, that the subgoals provide nodes at which instructional decisions are made by the teacher with the aid of the psychologist, by way of the computer. Experience and research data serve to "validate" subgoal hierarchies, permissible paths, and so on. Specifying subgoals essentially involves describing student behavior and ways of measuring it. The data obtained serve to establish the degree of effectiveness with which this is done.

2. Measurement and diagnosis of the student's initial state or behavior on entering an instructional situation. Initial diagnosis requires two kinds of information: long-term history and short-term history. Long-term history refers to information on characteristics such as intelligence and aptitudes. Short-term history refers to the student's performance during recent

instruction in relevant subject matter. In a CMI system, a teacher would have access to a file of test information (both long-term and short-term) from a computer terminal and would be able to ask specific questions about the characteristics of each student. Then the computer could be used to give subject-matter placement tests pertaining to the course of instruction, and the results would be put in the student's record. The teacher could examine the data and make decisions about student placement. Or suggested placement decisions could be displayed for the teacher, who could accept, reject, or amend the suggestions on the basis of a perusal of the record.

The necessary research for developing this aspect of an individualized system would be study of the reliability of the placement tests and their relationship to instructional decisions in terms of helping the student achieve maximum learning efficiency and motivation. As such information was obtained, placement decisions could become increasingly useful.

3.   The assignment of instructional alternatives. On the basis of the information obtained from the diagnosis discussed in step 2, a student is assigned, guided to, or allowed to select means of instruction. In CMI, the range of instructional alternatives could be displayed on the classroom terminals for either the student or the teacher to choose from. Various allocations of teaching resources could be suggested to the teacher, through displays indicating which students might be available to tutor other students and which students might be grouped together for a discussion or a teacher presentation.

A basic question is what instructional alternatives are made available and how they are decided upon. Alternative instructional experiences might involve different content relevant to different subgoals, or they might utilize different instructional procedures. The student's placement test scores can indicate his present level of accomplishment and his mastery of prerequisites. Measures of general intelligence may suggest whether or not he requires more closely or less closely sequenced instruction and whether or not he can effectively manage his own progress. However, these relationships are far from clear. Aptitude measures of the kind typically used today may be somewhat predictive of long-term academic and vocational success and, as a result, may assist the student in the selection of vocational goals. Such aptitude measures, however, appear to be less relevant in determining immediate instructional requirements. For example, there is little information available about whether spatial or mechanical aptitude is related to particular ways in which the student learns. In contrast, measures of the student's behavior obtained in the course of instruction, as performance is continuously assessed, should provide better information about the kinds of instructional alternatives that should be made available to him.

4.   Continuous monitoring and assessment. As the student proceeds along the course of instruction, his performance is monitored and

continuously assessed in terms of the established decision points. Measures similar to those used to assess initial placement are obtained, but, in addition, new measures are obtained which are specifically related to the student's learning characteristics. For example, how much practice does he require? What kind of instructional alternatives does he enjoy? Is he slow and steady, or impulsive? How well does he retain what he has learned? Information of this kind, updated as the student progresses, should provide the primary information for the decision-making required to guide student learning. This information would incorporate and supersede initial long-term aptitude measures and placement information.

Implicit in the proposed model of individualized instruction is the assumption that most or all of the students can attain, to a defined criterion of competence, the goals and subgoals along the path of learning. The basic task in adapting instruction to individual differences is to determine the methods and materials that will enable most students to attain these goals. It is no longer assumed, as it is in conventional instruction, that student achievement will follow a normal distribution of grades—some students failing, some excelling, and some falling in between. What eventually distinguishes students is their degree of understanding of a subject matter, and this is a function of how much they learn and of the extent to which they are taught to use their knowledge to learn new things, to generalize to new situations and thus solve problems, and to be creative.

The foregoing assumptions require techniques for measuring student achievement that are different from those generally used. In the context of the instructional model, a student's performance can be measured with reference to the behavior described in each subgoal. The measure of achievement indicates the degree to which the student has attained or surpassed the described level of competence. The measure gives information about the nature of the student's performance and gives the relative standing of the student in a group of his peers. Most standardized and generally used measures of achievement assume a distribution of attainment and provide only information about a student's performance in relation to others: for example, grade placement or percentile scores. These measures do not provide information about student performance in terms of criterion levels of achievement. In the model for individualized instruction, achievement measures do provide such information and make it possible to assess the outcomes of learning at each selected decision point.

5.   Adaptation and optimization. As the student learns, information is obtained about the characteristics of his learning, instructional assignments are made, and his performance at the subgoal decisions points is assessed. This procedure is carried out continuously throughout the course of instruction. Of obvious importance is the nature of the criterion measures of performance at the subgoals. Since the measures of the student's learning history are expressed, and the instructional alternatives are evaluated, in

terms of his subgoal performance, the question of which measures of mastery are selected becomes critical. Depending upon the measures used, some gains will be fully recognized and others overlooked; some kinds of student performance may be inadvertently overlooked unless they are stated as goals and explicitly assessed. It is for this reason that the model requires criterion-referenced measures of the desired outcomes of education. The continuous pattern of assessment and instructional prescription is a multistage decision-making process which is directed toward establishing the most effective sequence of instruction, as judged by the student and the teacher, for attaining selected educational goals.

In practice, an underlying concept of the way in which learning proceeds influences the interaction between outcome measures, instructional variables, and individual learning characteristics. Different measures and different instructional alternatives can provide a very large number of possible learning paths; however, many of these paths are ruled out if constraints are supplied concerning the way in which learning occurs. In a nonautomated individualized system the teacher's concept of the learning process influences the decisions he makes, and the information with which he is supplied also provides constraints. In CMI, the displays to the teacher and any more detailed suggestions presuppose concepts about the nature of learning, and since both teacher and computer are involved, the concept built into the system and the teacher's concepts interact.

6.   Evolutionary operation. A primary property of the instructional system described here is the fact that it accumulates information which is used to improve its own functioning. Improvement takes place in two ways. (i) The system uses procedures and materials in keeping with the current state of knowledge, and, through data obtained during the operation of the system, these procedures and materials are made more efficient. (ii) New knowledge about the learning process and about the conduct of individualized instruction can be obtained. Since each individual's learning is carefully monitored, the system makes it possible to explore a variety of research questions. In fact, when the system is first used there should be excess monitoring for this purpose; as it becomes operational, less information is needed.

A plan for research and development in individualized instruction at the Learning Research and Development Center (LRDC) at the University of Pittsburgh includes the transition from a nonautomated individualized procedure to a CMI system which eventually will include CAI as one available means of instruction. Nonautomated IPI forces redesign of the organization of the school. It also calls to the teacher's attention the need for detailed information about the individual student. This has facilitated the introduction of teacher-inquiry terminals to be used for CMI. After the teachers have become familiar with the potential of computers, various computer-based components in various areas can be introduced. The general instructional model described above should permit incorporation of each of these components as appropriate knowledge and technology become available.

IPI AS AN IMPLEMENTATION OF THE MODEL

In Individually Prescribed Instruction, the entire curriculum in each subject area is broken down into instruction units for subgoals of achievement. For example, the mathematics curriculum has identified 430 specific instructional objectives. These objectives are grouped into 88 units. Each unit is an instructional entity which the student works through at any one time. On the average there are 5 objectives per unit, the range being 1 to 14. A set of units covering different subject areas in mathematics comprises a level; levels may be thought of as roughly comparable to a school grade level. On entering the school the student takes a placement test; on the basis of his performance he is placed in a particular unit. If his placement test profile is scattered, he begins work on the lowest numbered unit. Associated with the unit are a preliminary test (a "pretest") and a post-training test (a "posttest"), and associated with each objective (or skill, as it is called in the subsequent printouts) are one or more "curriculum-embedded tests" (CET). Following assignment to a unit, the student takes the unit pretest, designed to give an evaluation of his skills within the unit. For example, he may have mastered skills 1, 2, 4, and 5, but not 3, 6, 7, and 8; at this point the teacher prescribes work related to the skills he has not mastered. As a student works through a lesson, he takes, at the teacher's discretion, the "curriculum-embedded test," which shows whether or not he has mastered the skill and also to what extent he has attained some competence on the next skill. When he has attained all the objectives he takes the unit posttest. If his grade is 85 percent or more, he begins work on the next unit; if it is not, he is reassigned an appropriate objective in the unit he has been working on. The teacher is allowed a certain discretion in deciding whether to keep the student in a given unit or to move him ahead.

COMPUTER ASSISTANCE FOR *IPI*

Designing and implementing a computer system to facilitate the operation and evaluation of IPI was simplified by the fact that the IPI system had already been in operation at the Oakleaf School for three years. The clerical operations which had evolved over that three-year period helped to clarify the nature of the data generated and the types of questions that teachers, evaluators, and researchers tended to ask on the basis of these data. In addition, experienced staff members prepared memoranda summarizing the types of questions they wanted to ask of the IPI data base. All of this helped define the content and the organization of the data files. An analysis of the types of data generated by the operation of IPI and the types of inquiries that teachers, evaluators, and researchers wanted to make on the basis of the data determined the design of a first approximation to a computer-management system for IPI.

The system design also took into account available computer hardware. This includes the University of Pittsburgh IBM 360 Model 50 computer, an IBM 1050 terminal with card-reader attachment, and three IBM 2741 typewriter terminals. The central processing unit has an extended core which allows up to 131,000 characters per on-line terminal. A 250-million-byte disk and six tape drives are also part of the computer configuration. The card-reading terminal is located at the Oakleaf School and connected by leased line to the computer on the University of Pittsburgh campus. The typewriter terminals are located at the Research and Development Center. This CMI system is called the IPI Management and Information System (IPI/MIS).

The major aspects of the IPI/MIS system as it is operating today are summarized in Figure 7-1. The basic data are recorded on optical scan forms by teachers, students, or clerks located throughout the school. These forms

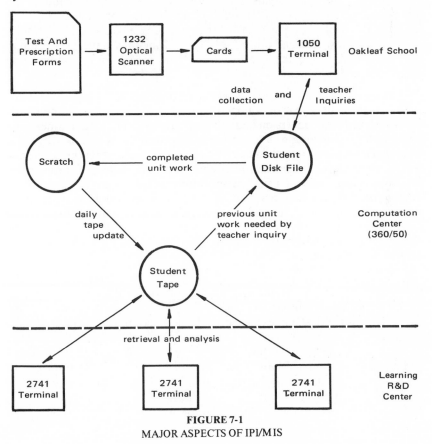

FIGURE 7-1
MAJOR ASPECTS OF IPI/MIS

are brought together and processed at the IBM 1232 optical scanner. The resulting punched cards are then read by the terminal at the school, and the data are edited and added to the current student file stored on disk at the computer. If errors are detected in the editing, the diagnostics are sent back to the school terminal for correction. The student file stored on disk contains test and prescription data pertaining to the unit in which the student is currently working, and selected background data. When a student completes a unit, the data obtained during his work on that unit are written out on a scratch file stored on disk. At the end of the day, a program updates the student tape from the scratch file. The student tape contains all the instructional history available for each student. The tape file is organized by student and consists of a variable number of fixed-length records for each student, the number depending upon the number of instructional units he has completed. Also included are background data collected at the beginning of each school year, such as standardized test results, home background data, the student's sex, his homeroom, and so on.

There are four major functions which the MIS can provide in an individualized school; it can (i) collect data; (ii) monitor student progress; (iii) provide information as a basis for prescribing a course of instruction; and (iv) diagnose student difficulties. These functions have two primary objectives: to increase the effectiveness of the model for individualizing instruction and to increase the productivity of the teacher operating the IPI system.

During the fourth year of IPI operation at the Oakleaf School, the school personnel included one principal, 12 teachers, and 12 teacher aides. The aides' primary function was to score tests and record test results. They also tabulated data pertaining to inquiries by the principal, the teachers, and the LRDC research and curriculum design staff. The teachers' three main functions have been writing prescriptions for courses of instruction, diagnosing student difficulties, and tutoring individuals and small groups of students. The clerical and teacher load can be reduced by having teachers and students enter data directly at classroom terminals. The teacher load can be further reduced by having the computer assume some of the prescription and diagnostic functions.

A description of three reports typical of those now available from the terminal at the school should help illustrate how the system is facilitating school operations. Printout 1 (Figure 7-2), which is a unit summary for a particular student (last names have been deleted), is a report of the kind most often used. A printout of this kind is most frequently requested following failure on a posttest, so that the student's work in that unit can be reviewed and appropriate prescriptions can be made. In Figure 7-2, the numerals in the group at the top summarize the student's pretest and posttest scores for each skill in the unit. Shown at the bottom of this group are the dates (the day of the school year) upon which these tests were taken. Prescriptions and "curriculum-embedded test" scores appear in the lower part of Figure 7-2, again listed by date and skill. For this unit, for example, it is possible to trace what this student did in mathematics from the 59th day of school to the 80th day of school, and how well he did.

The computer report illustrated in printout 2 (Figure 7-3) summarizes all the work being done by the students in a particular homeroom. This summary of where each student is in the curriculum and how long he has been there is used in the teachers' group-planning sessions, together with printout 3 (Figure 7-4), to help decide which students have gotten bogged down and which ones might be used to help in tutoring. Also, printout 3 provides information on which students might be brought together for group work in a unit.

One shortcoming of the present system is that the school has only one terminal, and it is in the data room and not in the classroom. The teacher who is prescribing courses of instruction on a continuous basis does not have time to send "down the hall" for the required report, so those needed reports must be anticipated by the teacher or the system, or both. Also, it usually takes a day or two for the scan forms to go through the various processing steps before reaching the computer's disk storage.

Apparently the next step in the development of IPI/MIS is to install a terminal network at the school so that both teachers and students can have convenient access to computer terminals. A single terminal in the school cannot provide the data-collecting, the monitoring, and the teacher-inquiry and diagnosis functions needed. Classroom terminals would make it possible to enter data directly into the system quickly and easily.

Terminals in each classroom would also facilitate diagnosis of student difficulties. Occasionally a student will get bogged down in a particular unit, and none of the available tests for that unit reveals the nature of his difficulty. That is, the tests for a given unit measure the unit's objectives and not the prerequisite skills. Although the student may have previously "mastered" prerequisite skills, he may have moved on to another unit prematurely, due to errors of measurement, or he may not have retained the knowledge and skills needed as prerequisites for the unit in which he is currently having difficulty. At present, the teacher attempts to diagnose the difficulty through questioning the student in a kind of clinical branch testing. It is possible that this can be done much more effectively through a computer-assisted branch-testing approach. Given the unit in which the student is currently having difficulty and given the knowledge and skills prerequisite for that unit, items can be presented for on-line student response which should facilitate identification of the missing knowledge or skills. Prescriptions for appropriate lesson units can then be written.

Experience gained during the first year of developing and implementing IPI/MIS suggested several changes in both the instructional system (IPI) and

```
          0977   R . . . , DAWN              DATE - 085

CURRENT MATH IS LEVEL D SYSTEM OF MEASUREMENTS

              PRETEST              POST-TEST SCORES
 SKILL        SCORES        1ST    2ND        3RD        4TH

    1           71          86
    2           43          86
    3           25          75
    4           99          99
    5           50          50

 DATE          054          071


PRESCRIPTIONS AND CETS

 DATE     SKILL                          PAGE - SCORE

  059      01          03-90    04-90    06-90    08-90    09-90
                       13-90    14-90
                       CET 16   PART 1-29   PART 2-67

  061      01          17-90    18-90    19-90    20-90    21-90
                       CET 22   PART 1-57   PART 2-99

  063      01          10-90    11-90    12-90    15-90
                       CET 16   PART 1-71   PART 2-99

  065      01-M        14-90
                       CET 22   PART 1-86   PART 2-99

  066      02          CET 21   PART 1-71   PART 2-99

  068      02-M        01-90    05-90    08-90    13-90    17-90
                       19-90    20-90
                       CET 21   PART 1-86   PART 2-99

  068      03          CET 15   PART 1-50   PART 2-99

  070      03-M        05-90    06-90    09-90    12-90    14-90
                       CET 15   PART 1-99   PART 2-99

  070      04-M        CET      PART 1-    PART 2-

  070      05-M        CET 09   PART 1-99   PART 2-

  078      05          94- 0    17-90    19-90    20-90    22-90
                       CET 23   PART 1-75   PART 2-99

  080      05-M        CET 13   PART 1-99   PART 2-

          SUGGESTED NEXT UNIT IS D GEOMETRY
```

FIGURE 7-2

PRINTOUT 1: UNIT SUMMARY FOR A SINGLE STUDENT

ID	NAME	SKILL	UNIT	DAYS
	GRADE 6 MRS. F		DATE - 036 MATH	
0306	A . . , JOHN	04	F COMBINATION OF PROCESSES	8
0317	A . . , LOUANNE	05	E FRACTIONS	31
0339	B . . , LINDA	01	F DIVISION	4
0341	B . . , ROBERTA	05	F MULTIPLICATION	31
0352	B . . , MARK	04	E MULTIPLICATION	30
C374	D . . , RICHARD	05	E NUMERATION	5
2052	C . . , MARLENE	02	D SYSTEM OF MEASUREMENTS	8
2096	H . . , GILBERT	01	E ADDITION	3
2041	H . . , ROBERT		E MULTIPLICATION	1
0705	K . . , PAUL	04	E FRACTIONS	31
0693	Z . . , JANICE	06	E FRACTIONS	31
0682	W . . , KIMBERLY		F NUMERATION	5
0671	V . . , EDGAR	07	E COMBINATION OF PROCESSES	31
0669	T . . , MICHELE	04	E DIVISION	29
0636	S . . , MARY ANN	02	E MONEY	5
0614	P . . , DENISE	08	F DIVISION	31
0603	P . . , TIMOTHY	02	D SYSTEM OF MEASUREMENTS	
0591	P . . , ROBERT	11	E MULTIPLICATION	31
0567	M . . , PEGGY	03	F MULTIPLICATION	28
0545	M . . , MICHAEL	05	D SYSTEM OF MEASUREMENTS	24
0512	M . . , KELLY	08	F DIVISION	32
0501	L . . , LINDA	07	E NUMERATION	33
0498	L . . , RONALD	04	E MULTIPLICATION	9
0487	L . . , MICHELE	02	E NUMERATION	5
0443	K . . , KEVIN	06	E SYSTEM OF MEASUREMENTS	31
0432	K . . , KAREN	04	G MULTIPLICATION	7
0421	K . . , MICHELE	03	G NUMERATION	31
0419	J . . , WILLIAM	01	E MONEY	3

FIGURE 7-3

PRINTOUT 2: CLASS LIST SHOWING HOW LONG EACH STUDENT
HAS BEEN WORKING IN HIS CURRENT UNIT

the computer support system. However, it is clear that more fundamental advances will come through a systematic program of evaluation and research. The availability of the MIS should facilitate such a program.

IPI RESEARCH AND EVALUATION

The IPI educational system, consisting of units geared to assessable objectives, is very amenable to the type of evaluation called for in step 6 of the instructional model. The instructional units are used in an environment in which relevant information on the participating students and teachers is readily available. Information regarding the relative effectiveness of

```
GRADE 6  MRS. F                    DATE - 035 MATH
                                        SKILL
   D SYSTEM OF MEASUREMENTS
      2052     C . . , MARLENE          02
      0545     M : . : MICHAEL          05
      0603     P . . , TIMOTHY          02

   E NUMERATION
      0374     D . . , RICHARD          05
      0487     L . . , MICHELE          02
      0501     L . . , LINDA            07

   E ADDITION
      2096     H . . , GILBERT          01

   E MULTIPLICATION
      0352     B . . , MARK             04
      2041     H . . , ROBERT
      0498     L . . , RONALD           04
      0591     P . . , ROBERT           11

   E DIVISION
      0669     T . . , MICHELE          04

   E COMBINATION OF PROCESSES
      0671     V . . , EDGAR            07

   E FRACTIONS
      0317     A . . , LOUANNE          05
      0705     K . . , PAUL             04
   .  0693     Z . . , JANICE           06

   E MONEY
      0419     J . . , WILLIAM          01
      0636     S . . , MARY ANN         02

   E SYSTEM OF MEASUREMENTS
      0443     K . . , KEVIN            05

   F NUMERATION
      0682     W . . , KIMBERLY

   F MULTIPLICATION
      0341     B . . , ROBERTA          05
      0567     M . . , PEGGY            03

   F DIVISION
      0339     B . . , LINDA            01
      0512     M . . , KELLY            03
      0614     P . . , DENISE           03

   F COMBINATION OF PROCESSES
      0306     A . . , JOHN             04

   G NUMERATION
      0421     K . . , MICHELE          03

   G MULTIPLICATION
      0432     K . . , KAREN            04
```

FIGURE 7-4

PRINTOUT 3: CLASS LIST, SORTING STUDENTS BY UNIT

different units designed to meet the same objectives can be systematically collected so that decisions can be made regarding which units are more appropriate for what kinds of students at what points in their educational development. Weak units among those offered can be identified and replaced. Objectives for which no adequate units are now available will be discernible, and appropriate units can be developed. This, in turn, will lead to a more potent system of education for each student, one whose results more and more closely approximate desired goals.

In addition to facilitating evaluation studies of the "is it working?" type, the retrieval and analysis system and the IPI data bank provide a vast resource for basic learning and measurement studies. The scientist has quick and convenient access to the data, so if he gets "hot" on a particular question he can interact with the data and evaluate his hypotheses at the moment, rather than wait for weeks after getting an idea before seeing the first printout. Evaluation and research requirements have been given a high priority in development of the IPI/MIS. The system is now operational to the extent that psychologists and curriculum evaluators can sit at the computer terminal and retrieve data for selected students or units according to search parameters which the researcher types in as verbal requests. He can edit the requested data if necessary, and proceed with an appropriate data analysis of the retrieved, edited data. The student history file, containing all the data collected on all the students for one academic year, can be searched in 3 to 5 minutes, depending upon the demands being placed on the computer by other terminals at that time. An example of such a search is provided in printout 4 (Figure 7-5).

In printout 4 the investigator was interested in examining selected data for all the students who had taken the pretest in E-level subtraction in mathematics (unit e4). Line four (4.) of the search parameters is the primary selection criterion; this is indicated by the period at the end of the line. This command directs the search routine to select only those students who had taken the pretest for unit e4. The exclamation point at the end of a line indicates data to be retrieved for the selected students if it is available; for example, line five (5.) is a request for the prescription information on students who worked on the first skill in unit e4. This search resulted in a work file (called "e4 stuff" by the terminal user) for 32 students. The file contained the unit performance data for those students plus some background data requested for them—their Otis IQ scores and their Stanford arithmetic computation percentiles, if these were available in the file.

Current research applications of the MIS are primarily concerned with three major aspects of IPI and their interrelationships: (i) the diagnostic tests; (ii) the "prescription behavior" of teachers; and (iii) the content and sequence of the curriculum materials. In IPI's first three years a tremendous effort was needed to develop the necessary tests and curriculum materials. Also, teacher retraining was a large task. These developmental activities were primarily and necessarily departmentalized: a group of test specialists developed the test battery, while authorities on subject matter in the various curriculum areas developed the materials and their sequence. Other staff members worked with the teachers in developing their new mode of teaching. The real challenge now is to investigate the functioning of all these components and their interactions. The computer information system makes this large task more feasible.

```
Search Example:*

    >$$logon e65wwc.
    >$$att d stutape as xx.
    >$$load d search.

    TYPE THE FILE NAME OF THE STUDENT TAPE.

    >xx

    THE STUDENT TAPE IS DATED 042068.
    LIST YOUR SEARCH PARAMETERS.

    1. >id.
    2. >otis iq!
    3. >st acptile!
    4. >math pret,e4,=1.
    5. >math presc,e4,skill 1(1),cet!
    6. >math presc,e4,skill 2(1),cet!
    7. >math presc,e4,skill 3(1),cet!
    8. >math post,e4,=1!
    9. >end.

    PARAMETER LIST COMPLETE
    DO YOU WANT YOUR OUTPUT ON TAPE OR DISK?
     >disk

    SPECIFY DATASET NAME.
     >e4stuff.
    COMPILATION BEGINS.

(diagnostics printed here if there were errors in the search parameters)

    COMPILATION COMPLETE
    OUTPUT FORMAT:

    ONE BACKGROUND RECORD OF 09 BYTES PER STUDENT.
    ONE OVERALL RECORD OF 91 BYTES PER STUDENT.
    SEARCHING BEGINS

    YOUR OUTPUT FILE CONSISTS OF 32 STUDENTS.
    THE SEARCH IS COMPLETED

    M:  END OF JOB
```

---
*
 Lines typed following the > were typed by the terminal user. The
other lines were typed under computer program control.

FIGURE 7-5

PRINTOUT 4: ILLUSTRATION OF THE TAPE RETRIEVAL PROGRAM

For example, Bolvin[5] has observed that there is considerable variance in "prescriber behavior." Some teachers tend to assign a bare minimum of study and practice and then assign a posttest to see whether the student requires more study and practice for that particular unit; they thus go back and forth between prescription and posttest until mastery is apparently achieved. Other teachers tend to "follow the book" strictly in terms of the pretest scores; they prescribe no work if these scores are 85 percent or higher; if the scores are lower than 85 percent, the extent of the assignment is determined by the degree to which the pretest score deviates from that percentage. Still a third type of individual tends to "over-prescribe"—that is, to assign students much more work than would seem to be indicated by the pretest scores. A systematic analysis of the data involving prescriber, prescription, and subsequent student performance will help clarify the relative effectiveness of these different prescription behaviors and will suggest whether or not they should be varied for different students and different units. For example, it may be important that the student be given extensive practice in certain skills (computation, for example) so that in subsequent, more complex units requiring those skills he is not hampered through lack of retention. Printout 5 (Figure 7-6) shows data relevant to this area of concern. Note how the number of tasks prescribed varies for the same pretest scores, depending in part upon who did the prescribing.

Another line of current concern is the structure of curriculum sequences. For only ten objectives there are over 3 million possible sequences. Fortunately, most of these sequences are ruled out by content structure and by concepts of the learning process. Instructional sequences can, however, also be empirically studied. Techniques similar to multiple scalogram analysis[6] of available placement and pretest results can assist in determining whether or not the skills are being taught in the order of their difficulty and in an order that facilitates the next learning stage. It is also possible to see whether or not the extent to which failure to present skills in the order of their difficulty affects (i) the time it takes students to master that particular sequence of skills and (ii) their eventual ability to use what has been learned.

A more fundamental task which MIS can facilitate is the development of alternative forms of instruction that can be adapted to the needs of particular students. Of course, at present a student can be assigned material in which he shows a lack of mastery and need not be assigned lessons in skills that he has mastered. But, in addition, lessons may involve different kinds of vocabularies; they may involve more closely or less closely sequenced instruction; or they may involve instruction which gives the student more, or less, responsibility for managing his own progress. Essentially, the problem is to determine different instructional alternatives that are related to different patterns of learning. The goal of the IPI/MIS is to help with empirical work which would determine the measures most efficient for assigning individuals appropriate alternatives and determine what alternatives should be made available.

TOWARD *CAI*

The development and adoption of the type of individualized model proposed here seems to be a necessary prerequisite for bringing CAI out of the "back room" and into the classroom. It seems unlikely that CAI will ever provide all of the instruction for all of the students all of the time. Yet it is virtually impossible to incorporate CAI into traditional schools where the

```
>$$att d d8stuff(e65wwc) as F8.
>$$load d main.
LOADING STARTS AT LOC 070200

PRETEST, PRESCRIPTIONS, AND POSTESTS FOR MATH D8 SKILL 2.
```

ID	PRETEST	PRESCRIPTIONS (UNIT TASK NUMBERS)	PRESCRIBER	POSTEST
294	70	1 2 3 5 6 7 15 16	6	90
102	70	2 3 8 9 10 13 14 15 17	6	99
124	60	4 6 7 10 11 13	6	60
168	80	9 12 3 16 17 15	6	80
181	70	4 6 7 8 9 10 12 14 16	0	99
226	70	1 2 3 4 5 6 7 8 10 11 13 14 15	9	80
317	80	1 5 6 7 16 17	5	99
341	80	4 6 9 11	5	90
352	70	1 2 3 4 5 7 9 10 12 14 17	10	90
363	70	6 7 8 9 10 11 12 14 17	10	99
385	60	5 6 7 8 12 13 14 15	5	99
408	70	2 3 4 6 7 13 15	10	99
432	80	5 6 7	10	90
476	50	1 2 3 4 6 7 9 11 12 14 17	10	70
501	60	1 2 4 6 7 8 9 13 15	5	90
567	60	1 2 6 7 11 13 15 16 17	5	70
578	50	4 5 6 7 11 13 15 16 17	5	90
614	80	1 5 7 11 12	10	90
636	30	1 3 6 10 13 14 17	5	99
647	70	1 16 17	5	99
669	60	1 2 3 4 7 9 11 13 15 17	10	80
671	70	5 6 7 11 12 13 14 15 16	5	90
682	80	5 7 8 9 22 23 13 15	5	99
693	60	1 2 3 4 5 6 7 9 10 13 15 16 17	5	80
1058	50	1 2 3 4 5 6 7 8 10 11 12 13 14	4	70
1036	80	3 7 8 9 13	4	99
1025	70	1 2 10 16 17	4	80
1014	60	1 2 3 4 5 6 7 8 9 10 11 12 13	9	80
999	60	1 2 3 4 5 6 7 8 9 10 11 12 13	4	70
738	50	1 2 3 5 6 7	4	50
1105	80	7 11 13 9	3	99
1116	50	1 2 3 4 5 6 8 10 13 15 17	3	80
1173	80	1 2 3 4 5 3 8 9 11 13 15 16 17	11	90
1231	60	1 2 3 5 6 8 10 11 12 14 17	3	99
1242	70	3 4 5 6 7 8 9 15 16 17	3	90
1297	50	1 2 3 4 6 7 8 10 11 13 15 16 17	3	90
1333	0	1 2 3 4 6 7 13 14 16 17	3	99
1377	70	1 3 5 6 7 8 9 10 11 12 13 14 15	3	90

```
M:END OF JOB
```

FIGURE 7-6

PRINTOUT 5: DATA PERTAINING TO PRETESTS, PRESCRIPTIONS, AND
POSTTESTS FOR SKILL 2 OF MATHEMATICS-UNIT D DIVISION

classroom is the basis for instructional decisions and scheduling. On the
other hand, it is easy to incorporate CAI lessons into IPI/MIS as those lessons
become available for solving specific instructional problems. The computer is
there, the terminal capability is there, and the flexibility of an individualized
school organization is there. Most important, a model for individualization
is there. It seems reasonable to believe that the same instructional model that
guided the development of IPI and is guiding IPI's "automation" can guide
the development and implementation of CAI in an individualized school.

Some mix of these aspects seems to be the end toward which we are currently striving.[7]

NOTES

[1] R. Glaser in M. C. Wittrock and D. Wiley (eds.), *Evaluation of Instruction* (New York: Holt, Rinehart & Winston, Inc., 1970).

[2] R. Glaser in *Proceedings of the 1967 Invitational Conference on Testing Problems* (Princeton, N.J.: Educational Testing Service, 1968), pp. 3-36; C. M. Lindvall and J. O. Bolvin in P. Lange (ed.), *Programed Instruction* (Chicago: National Society for the Study of Education, 1967), pt. 2, pp. 217-54. Oakleaf is an elementary school in the Baldwin-Whitehall School District near Pittsburgh.

[3] Although we are not completely happy with all of the connotations of the term *computer-managed instruction,* it does seem to be the term most frequently used by people currently working in this area of concern. It should be emphasized that the computer is used as a tool in the management of the information needed by teachers in planning individualized education.

[4] See, for example, W. W. Cooley, "Computer Systems for Guidance," paper presented before the American Educational Research Association Annual Meeting, February, 1968, Chicago, for a more detailed consideration of guidance in the individualized school.

[5] J. O. Bolvin, "Evaluating Teacher Functions," Working Paper No. 17, 1967, Learning Research and Development Center, University of Pittsburgh.

[6] J. C. Lingoes, *Educational and Psychological Measurement,* Vol. 23 (1963), p. 501.

[7] The specification of models for individualizing education, the development of IPI, the implementation of CMI, and the eventual incorporation of CAI in individualized schools are major activities at the Learning Research and Development Center, University of Pittsburgh. We thank our many colleagues and students who have contributed to these efforts. The preparation of this article and the research and development described were performed pursuant to a contract with the U.S. Office of Education, Department of Health, Education, and Welfare. Additional support has been provided by the General Learning Corporation, New York.

INDIVIDUALLY PRESCRIBED INSTRUCTION

Research for Better Schools

HISTORY OF INDIVIDUALIZATION

A survey of the history of instruction indicates that formal learning began very much as an individual affair—that is, pupils came to school to receive instruction individually from the teacher. Education was generally for a select few; therefore, fewer pupils attended school. This made possible the provision of individualized instruction for those students. For example, in the one-room school, pupils proceeded on an individual basis rather than as intact groups. As educational advantages were offered to a larger proportion of the population, it became necessary to deal with pupils in grade-level groups, and individualized instruction diminished. Since then, however, as awareness of individual differences among pupils increased, many efforts were made to individualize instruction even within the context of schools offering mass education.

Source: *Individually Prescribed Instruction,* Phila.: Research for Better Schools, Inc., p. 16.

Individually Prescribed Instruction consists of planning and conducting with each student a program of studies that is tailored to his learning needs and to his characteristics as a learner. Team teaching, nongraded classrooms, programmed instruction, grouping, etc., all have attempted to administratively accommodate within the classroom these differences among individuals. Individually Prescribed Instruction takes a new direction in this continuing search for ways to adapt instruction to the individual. In it, there have been taken into account such parameters of individual differences as rate of learning, amount of practice and, to some extent, preference for mode of instruction.

The Learning Research and Development Center at the University of Pittsburgh has currently adopted instructional materials in elementary mathematics, reading, science, handwriting and spelling that are designed for the individual student.

1.   The rate of speed at which each child progresses depends upon his own capacities. He places himself on the continuum by taking both placement tests and pre-tests.

2.   The curriculum material is arranged in a sequential order called continuum. The assignments are given by a prescription to fit his individual needs. (A prescription is an individual lesson plan for each student each day.)

3.   The student's mastery of the curriculum is judged by curriculum-embedded tests and post-tests. He is required to perform at a level of 85%.

4.   The child works independently in most cases, thus building up his sense of responsibility and also his confidence in his own knowledge. He begins to realize that learning is a process that is dependent on his own participation and initiative.

BACKGROUND INFORMATION

The Learning Research and Development Center

The Learning Research and Development Center at the University of Pittsburgh is the creator of Individually Prescribed Instruction and specializes in the research and basic design of new educational technology.

Individually Prescribed Instruction was developed by Drs. Glaser, Bolvin and Lindvall with the cooperation of the University of Pittsburgh and the Baldwin-Whitehall Public Schools of suburban Pittsburgh, Dr. W. R. Paynter, Superintendent of Schools.

During the school year of 1963-64, the Learning Research and Development Center and the Baldwin-Whitehall Public Schools of suburban

Pittsburgh initiated an experimental project to investigate the feasibility of a system of individualized instruction in an entire K-6 school. This came about as a result of a series of prior exploratory studies, begun in 1961-62, designed to test preliminary notions on a smaller scale in single classrooms. The work started with the use of programmed instruction in an intact classroom, "intact classroom" being defined as a classroom unit in which the teaching practices were oriented around the conventional grade-by-grade progression of learning.

As work proceeded, it soon became apparent that the significant individualization feature of programmed instruction could not be manifested unless the intact classroom changed its organization to permit a more flexible progression.

As a result, a second set of studies was instituted, using programmed instruction and other materials in a more flexible context. Out of this experience grew the Individually Prescribed Instruction project currently in progress, in which various combinations of instructional materials— including programmed materials, special workbook and test procedures— and teacher practices are being used for the purpose of adapting them to individual student requirements.

DISTINGUISHING FUNDAMENTALS

1. Individually Prescribed Instruction must be based on a carefully sequenced and detailed listing of behaviorally stated instructional objectives. Such listings must be used in planning most other aspects of the program and should have the following characteristics:

a) Each objective should tell exactly what a pupil should be able to do to exhibit his mastery of the given content and skill. This should typically be something that the average student can master in such a relatively short time as one class period. Objectives should involve such action verbs as solve, state, explain, list, describe, etc. rather than general terms such as understand, appreciate, know, and comprehend.

b) Objectives should be grouped in meaningful streams of content. For example, in arithmetic the objectives will typically be grouped into such areas as numeration, place value, addition, subtraction, etc. Such grouping aids in the meaningful development of instructional materials and in the diagnosis of pupil achievement. At the same time, this grouping does not preclude the possibility of having objectives that cut across areas.

c) Within each stream or area the objectives should, to the extent possible, be sequenced in such an order that each one will build on those that precede it and, in turn, be a prerequisite to those that follow. The goal here is to let the objectives constitute a "scale" of abilities.

ipi STUDENT PROFILE

Name _____ Grade _____ Room ___

ipi MATHEMATICS PLACEMENT PROFILE

STUDENT
NUMBER _____

STUDENT
NAME _____

GRADE _____ ROOM _____

SCHOOL STAMP   PLACED AT LEVEL

MATHEMATICS AREA	DATE OF TEST		PLACEMENT LEVELS B–H						
			B	C	D	E	F	G	H
NUMERATION (01)		MAX. PTS.							
		SCORE							
		%							
PLACE VALUE (02)		MAX. PTS.							
		SCORE							
		%							
ADDITION (03)		MAX. PTS.							
		SCORE							
		%							
SUBTRACTION (0									
ADDITION/ SUBTRACTION (34									
MULTIPLICATION (05)									
DIVISION (06)									
MULTIPLICATION/ DIVISION (56)									
COMBINATION OF PROCESSES (07)									
FRACTIONS (08)									
MONEY (09)									
TIME (10)									
SYSTEMS OF MEASUREMENT (11)									
GEOMETRY (12)									

Based upon prototype originated by
Research and Development Center. As
by
Research for Better Schools, Inc.

ipi MATHEMATICS PRESCRIPTION SHEET

STUDENT
NUMBER _____

STUDENT
NAME _____

SCHOOL STAMP   UNIT _____

GRADE _____ ROOM _____

DATE PRES.	PRES. INIT.	SKILL NO.	PAGE NO.	INST. TECH CODES	INSTRUCTIONAL NOTES	TOTAL POINTS

INSTRUCTIONAL TECHNIQUES

CODE	SETTING
01	Teacher, Tutor
02	Peer Tutor
03	Small Group
04	Large Group
05	Seminar
07	Independent Study
11	Tutor of Others
	MATERIALS
06	Curr. Texts
08	Film Strip
09	Records/Tapes
10	Research
12	Manipulative Devices

d) Within the sequence of objectives in each area the objectives should be grouped into meaningful sub-sequences or units. Such units can be designated as representing different levels in progress and provide break-points so that when a student finishes a unit in one area, he may either go on to the next unit in that area or may switch to a unit in another area. (For example, upon completing Level B Addition the pupil may either go on to Level C Addition or move to Level B Subtraction.)

2.   Individually Prescribed Instruction lesson materials must be geared exactly to the instructional objectives and must be such as will permit pupils to proceed quite independently and with a minimum of direct teacher instruction.

3.   A basic aspect of the Individually Prescribed Instruction procedure is a rather detailed provision for diagnosis of pupil skills and abilities and continuous monitoring of pupil progress.

4.   The unique feature of Individually Prescribed Instruction is its requirement that each pupil's work be guided by written prescriptions prepared to meet his individual needs and interests.

5.   As is true with most types of classroom instruction, the work of the teacher is a key aspect of Individually Prescribed Instruction. Among the essential aspects of the change in teacher performance are:

a)   Little time is spent in lecturing to a group.

b)   Much time is spent in evaluating the individual pupil's record, in diagnosing his needs, and preparing individual learning prescriptions for each child.

c)   Most time is spent in helping individual pupils.

d)   Frequent and regular staff conferences are held to discuss individual pupils, to evaluate and adapt materials and procedures, and to make future plans for each child on an integrated part of the system.

6.   The success of any type of educational curriculum will rest ultimately on the quality of the experiences that the pupils have. Individually Prescribed Instruction is pupil-oriented instruction and differs from other procedures in terms of activities in which pupils are engaged.

FOUR TYPES OF DIAGNOSTIC INSTRUMENTS ARE USED IN THE INDIVIDUALLY PRESCRIBED INSTRUCTION

Type I—Placement Instruments

Placement instruments developed by Dr. Richard Cox, LRDC are used to assess mastery of units of work along the learning continuum. The placement instrument permits a general diagnostic evaluation of levels of work mastered for each unit of the learning continuum. The placement instrument has the following characteristics:

1.   It measures mastery for each unit of work.

2.   It measures the mastery level within each unit of work.

3.   It provides a gross profile for any student along the learning continuum.

4.   It is an indicator of strengths and weaknesses of a student.

5.   It focuses on the area or areas that need further exploration for proper diagnosis.

Type II—Pre-Test Instruments

Since several specific objectives are assigned to each unit and level of work, an instrument is needed to discover which specific objective within the unit and level a student knows or does not know. The pre-test instrument is designed to measure the specific objectives within a specific unit and level of the learning continuum. The following functions of the pre-test should be noted:

1.   A pre-test is needed for each unit and level of the continuum.

2.   Determination of the proper pre-test to administer is based on the placement profile of each student.

3.   The pre-test measures each specific objective within the one level and unit.

4.   Pre-tests are assigned prior to any teaching within the unit.

5.   Information as to strengths and weaknesses of each objective within the level and unit of work helps to determine the learning tasks.

6.   The pre-test score can be considered the entering behavior of the student for each objective within a level and unit of work.

Type III—Post-Test Instruments

The post-test is an alternate form of the pre-test and is assigned at the end of each unit of work to determine the pupil's mastery of the unit. The post-test score also indicates growth in total behavior for each student of that level and unit.

Type IV—Curriculum-Embedded Test

The curriculum-embedded test is a short test of a student's progress toward a particular objective within a level and unit of work. It has two parts, the first part measures his progress toward a particular objective, and the second part serves as a short pre-test of his ability to achieve the next objective within the unit and level of work.

SUMMARY

Individually Prescribed Instruction is an instructional system based on a set of behavioral objectives correlated with diagnostic instruments and curriculum materials and teaching techniques. The objectives are:

1.   To enable each pupil to work at his own rate through units of study in a learning sequence.

2.   To develop in each pupil a demonstrable degree of mastery.

3.   To develop self-initiation and self-direction of learning.

4.   To foster the development of problem-solving thought processes.

5.   To encourage self-evaluation and motivation for learning.

There are six elements which distinguish Individually Prescribed Instruction from conventional elementary school procedures:

1.   Detailed specifications of educational objectives;

2.   Organization of methods and materials to attain these objectives;

3.   Careful determination of each pupil's present competence in a given subject;

4.   Individual daily evaluation and guidance of each pupil;

5.   Provision for frequent monitoring of student performance, in order to inform both the pupil and the teacher of progress toward an objective;

6.   Continual evaluation and strengthening of the curriculum and instructional procedures.

RESEARCH FOR BETTER SCHOOLS, INC.

Research for Better Schools has the major responsibility for the field development, field testing, and dissemination of Individually Prescribed Instruction. Included in this responsibility is the study of problems encountered in a variety of institutional settings. It also includes the investigation of the strategies that are necessary for widespread

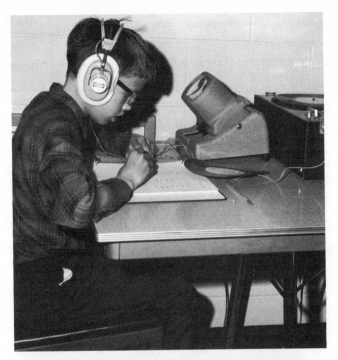

Photos: Courtesy of Research for Better Schools, Incorporated, Philadelphia, Pennsylvania.

dissemination of IPI. This activity is of major proportion, since the task of implementing this type of instruction in a variety of ongoing school programs is quite different from that of implementing IPI in the Oakleaf School.

Research for Better Schools has established six demonstration schools in different socioeconomic settings so that educators can see the IPI program in action.

RBS has established a general strategy for the involvement of schools with IPI. The specific criteria that were established to insure commitment and understanding are as follows:

Administrative Commitment

This means a self-study of IPI on the part of the local administrator. Firsthand knowledge about the essential elements of IPI and an understanding of some of the financial implications involved are the main objectives. When this study is completed, the administration must be able to say that it can support IPI not only in philosophy and operation, but financially as well.

Teacher Commitment

Teachers of any given school have the same right as the administration to investigate a new instructional system that is to be used in their school. Therefore, the faculty, or at least faculty representation must be given the opportunity to visit an IPI demonstration school and talk to other teachers in this instructional system. The teachers also must be involved in the basic decision as to whether their school should become an IPI situation.

Participation in Research

Both the teachers and the administrators must know quite clearly the research questions that are being asked, the kinds of data that are being collected, and the need for this information if IPI is to succeed.

Retraining of Administrators and Teachers

Both the administrator and the teachers of any particular school must know the need for a new role in using IPI. This understanding must include knowledge about the training and the time needed for such training.

Uniqueness of Situation

RBS, in using this criterion, is trying to take into consideration the past history of any given school in terms of its interest and efforts to promote individualization.

The second phase of the strategy for controlled expansion of IPI involves the retraining of administrators. Specific administrative training programs are offered to help the principal successfully implement this change. The administrative training programs thus have the following objectives in order to cope with the above deficiencies in the conventional principal's role.

To learn the operation and procedures of IPI.

To develop strategies for training teachers for IPI.

To work with the IPI materials.

To learn the administrative tasks involved in implementing IPI.

To develop communication skills useful in IPI.

To formulate an implementation plan for the operation of IPI in each individual school.

Retraining of teachers has received considerable attention from RBS. The teacher education efforts have been concentrated on the development of a teacher-training program that would enable the school to work on its own training program. This program enables the teacher to conceptualize a model of IPI as a basis for instructional decision making. It equips the teachers to plan and conduct IPI in the classroom. The present retraining program being used by RBS has been constructed upon a model of IPI as a basis for instructional decision making, and contains five specific packages. Each consists of behavioral objectives, pre- and post-tests on the objectives, self-instructional materials and equipment, and recommended learning settings. Each package provides six types of activities: concept building related to IPI, analysis and application of the concepts to IPI, practice in using IPI skills and materials as routine exercises, role-taking of teacher aide and student while working through the math continuum, discussion designed to provide an opportunity for clarification, and expression of reactions to IPI. The last activity was the development of skills for planning sessions in order to cover suggested topics, questions or case studies. The packages that have been prepared for the training of teachers have several general principles under which they operate. They include individualizing the training program for teachers so that we can practice what we preach; and, developing it in such a way that the administrator can, with some help, lead his faculty through the program.

A fourth aspect of the implementation strategy has been to develop a systematic way of collecting data about the progress that the youngsters are making in the IPI system, and assessing the degree of implementation which each school brought to the IPI program. During the course of each school year, specific information is collected from each of the participating schools to determine student growth and the degree of implementation. A team of monitors from the RBS staff is available to follow up each school and help resolve some of the problems.

Research for Better Schools, unlike the Learning Research and Development Center which operates in an experimental and research environment, functions in the world of the day-to-day problems of helping children learn. Its role is to test and perfect new innovations in the field and bring better education to the attention, and within reach, of the public schools of America. This of course means that considerable efforts must be made in testing, evaluating, and modifying educational innovations.

For Individually Prescribed Instruction, five major kinds of data are collected to answer the question—"How does this innovation work in the pilot schools?" These are information about:

1. The materials

2. The pupils

3. The teaching staff

4. The community setting

5. The Individually Prescribed Instruction concept as an educational system.

How well the materials do the job of helping pupils learn, how adaptable they are to the varying requirements of each pupil, how the individual pupil responds to this different approach, how the teacher's role changes, what happens to the pattern of staffing the school, what the effects are on the community and its expectations of the "system," and the variations in cost are all carefully monitored and compared with other schools not using Individually Prescribed Instruction.

In this manner, Research for Better Schools is able to feed back to the Learning Research and Development Center information needed to improve the system (or, in some cases, Research for Better Schools makes the improvements itself) and to determine generally how effective this change in the school pattern really is under as differing circumstances as possible. Does Johnny really learn more? Quicker? Faster? Are there side effects that are undesirable? Do we need to retrain teachers? Is it possible to lower the cost of Individually Prescribed Instruction? The job of the laboratory only starts there, however. When these questions have been satisfactorily answered, the laboratory then changes its field-testing role to a dissemination role and sets up demonstration centers in a number of typical schools in a variety of typical communities. Other schools in other communities are invited to examine the program in action in a real setting much like their own school.

Courtesy of Research for Better Schools, Incorporated, Philadelphia, Pennsylvania.

It is obvious that it takes time to answer the questions raised about how good a new program is. When these questions have been satisfactorily answered, the laboratory is then ready to respond in a different role. It is now the role of the laboratory to figure out strategies for diffusing the product to the public schools as rapidly as possible.

CURRICULUM

The mathematics curriculum includes 13 specific areas—numeration, place value, addition, subtraction, multiplication, division, combination of processes, money, time, system of measurement, geometry, fractions, and special topics. A total of 434 specific objectives have been established as part of the mathematics continuum.

The reading curriculum has been developed by sequencing the specific reading skills that need to be mastered by each youngster. The skills are worked into units and levels of work much the same as in the mathematics continuum. The beginning reading program is built around the first 14 programmed texts by Sullivan Associates. This material is supplemented by Center-prepared records and special work sheets. A second phase of the reading program is built around paperback published materials. The third phase of reading is the independent reading program, in which children select their reading material from the school's library. During the independent phase of the reading program, students are also working on prescribed skills material.

New curricula under development include: elementary science, social studies, spelling and handwriting. LRDC and RBS working with students and faculty at "Oakleaf" and the five demonstration schools will design this curricula using the technology applied in mathematics and reading.

NUMBERS OF BEHAVIORAL OBJECTIVES FOR THE MATHEMATICS CONTINUUM 1968-69

	A	B	C	D	E	F	G	TOTALS
Numeration	12	10	8	5	8	3	8	54
Place Value		3	5	9	7	5	2	31
Addition	3	10	5	8	6	2	3	37
Subtraction			4	5	3	1	3	16
Multiplication				8	11	10	6	35
Division				7	7	8	5	27
Comb. of Processes			6	5	7	4	5	27
Fractions	3	2	4	5	6	14	5	39
Money		4	4	6	3	2		19
Time		3	2	10	9	5	3	32
System of Meas.		4	3	5	7	3	2	24
Geometry		2	2	3	9	10	7	33
Special Topics			1	3	3	5	4	16
TOTALS	18	38	44	79	86	72	53	390

EXAMPLES OF BEHAVORIAL OBJECTIVES
FOR THE MATHEMATICS CONTINUUM

	level E	level F
ADDITION	1. Column addition, no carrying, 3 or more digit numbers, more than 2 addends. 2. Uses commutative principle of addition. 3. Uses associative principle for addition to add 2 or more place numerals. 4. Adds with carrying for 4 or more place numerals with 2 addends. 5. Adds 2 mixed numbers to thousands (whole no.'s) and hundredths (decimals). 6. Solves multiple-step word problems.	1. Adds — carrying 4 or more place numbers, more than 2 addends. 2. Adds, 2 or more numbers with whole number parts and decimals to the millionths.
MULTIPLICATION	1. Uses repeated addition to solve multiplication problems. 1 place times 1, 2, 3 place number. Combinations 9 X 9. 2. Timed test products through 9 X 9. 3. Uses commutative principle for multiplication. Solves problems, 1 place times 2 place factor. 4. Uses associative principle for multiplication. Multiplies more than 2 numbers with single digit factors. 5. Uses distributive principle to simplify multiplication problems. 6. Multiplies 1 digit factor times 2 digit factor. Uses mult. algorithm. 7. Multiplies 1 digit factor times a 3 or more digit factor. Uses mult. algorithm. 8. Finds squares of numbers 1-10. Writes exponential form — identifies base and exponent. 9. Uses algorithm for multiplication by 10's to 100,000. 10. Multiplies 2 digits by 2 digits using algorithm. 11. Solves multiple-step word problems.	1. Checks products by inverting factor order. 2. Uses associative principle to simplify multiplication of 1 & 2 digit numbers. 3. Uses distributive principle to simplify multiplication of 1 & 2 digit numbers. 4. Uses multiplication algorithm for a 2 digit number times a 2 or more digit number. 5. Multiplies a 3 digit number times a 3 or more digit number. To 1,000,000. 6. Finds products of 11's, 12's tables. 7. Multiplies decimal number times a whole number. 8. Multiplies decimal number to 10ths by a decimal number to 10ths. 9. Multiplies a 1 place decimal number times a one or more place decimal number. 10. Solves two-step word problems.
DIVISION	1. Finds missing factors or quotients for division problems thru 81 ÷ 9. Timed. 2. Uses distributive principle, simple numbers, simplify division problems. 3. Uses "ladder" division with 1 digit divisor, 2 or more digit dividend. No remainder. 4. Divides with remainders, 1 digit factor and product. 5. Divides with remainders, 1 digit factor, 2 or more digit products. 6. Checks division problems by inverse operation of multiplication for 2 or more digit products. 7. Solves 1-2 step word problems.	1. Uses repeated subtraction to solve division problems. 2. Divides a 2 or more digit dividend by a 2 or 3 digit divisor. 3. Rounds numbers to estimate quotients. Dividends to 2000. 4. Uses division algorithm with 2 or 3 place factors, writes R, remainder. 5. Uses fractional notation as a way of solving division problems written as fractions. 6. Writes remainder as fraction. Divisors to 12. 7. Divides decimal by whole number. 8. Two-step word problems.

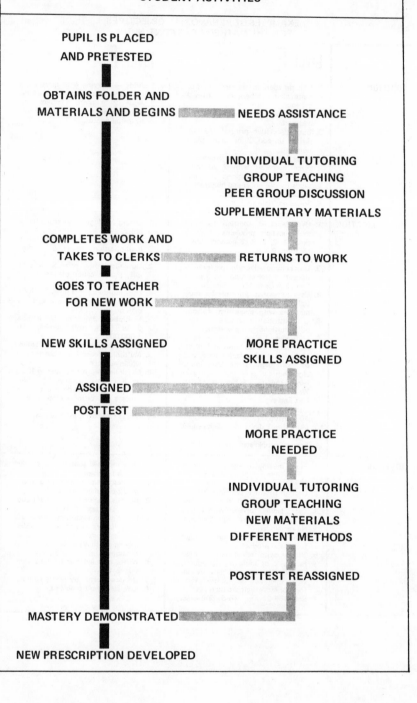

STUDENT ACTIVITIES

PUPIL IS PLACED
AND PRETESTED

OBTAINS FOLDER AND
MATERIALS AND BEGINS — NEEDS ASSISTANCE

INDIVIDUAL TUTORING
GROUP TEACHING
PEER GROUP DISCUSSION
SUPPLEMENTARY MATERIALS

COMPLETES WORK AND
TAKES TO CLERKS — RETURNS TO WORK

GOES TO TEACHER
FOR NEW WORK

NEW SKILLS ASSIGNED — MORE PRACTICE
SKILLS ASSIGNED

ASSIGNED

POSTTEST

MORE PRACTICE
NEEDED

INDIVIDUAL TUTORING
GROUP TEACHING
NEW MATERIALS
DIFFERENT METHODS

POSTTEST REASSIGNED

MASTERY DEMONSTRATED

NEW PRESCRIPTION DEVELOPED

Q. Where can those interested see Individually Prescribed Instruction demonstrated?

A. The following schools are available for demonstration. Feel free to contact them to make arrangements for visitation:

> McAnnulty Elementary School
> Baldwin-Whitehall School District
> 5151 McAnnulty Road
> Pittsburgh, Pa. 15236
> (412) 655-4517
>
> Downey Elementary School
> 1212 Monroe Street
> Harrisburg, Pa.
> (717) 234-6131
>
> Richland Elementary School
> 500 Fairview Avenue
> Quakertown, Pa. 18951
> (215) 536-2300
>
> West Elementary School
> Forest Avenue
> Dover, Delaware
> (302) 734-4718
>
> Washington Elementary School
> Emory Avenue
> Trenton, N.J.
> (609) 396-7646
>
> Daniel J. Flood Elementary School
> North Washington Street
> Wilkes-Barre, Pa.
> (open Sept. 1969)

Q. Does Individually Prescribed Instruction need a specially built school?

A. No—school buildings vary in design.

Q. Are students selected for this project?

A. No—assignment procedures remain the same.

Q. What is the relationship between the Learning Research and Development Center (LRDC) of the University of Pittsburgh and Research for Better Schools (RBS)?

A. The Learning Research and Development Center is responsible for development and improvement of the model.

Research for Better Schools is responsible for field development, testing and dissemination of Individually Prescribed Instruction.

Q. What are some implications for teacher-education courses in colleges and universities?

A. There appears to be a need for courses in small-group dynamics, tutorial instruction, individual progress diagnosis, prescription writing, child psychology, child behavior and learning patterns, and testing and measurement.

Q. From whence do the Learning Research and Development Center and Research for Better Schools receive their funds?

A. The Learning Research and Development Center is funded by the U.S. Office of Education and the University of Pittsburgh with additional grant and contract support from:

A. W. Mellon Education and Charitable Trust
The Buhl Foundation
Carnegie Corporation of New York
The Ford Foundation
Office of Naval Research

Research for Better Schools is funded by Title IV—ESEA of 1965.

Q. Who is in charge of the Individually Prescribed Instruction projects?

A. For the Learning Research and Development Center the project is directed by J. O. Bolvin and its steering committee is chaired by Dr. C. M. Lindvall. For Research for Better Schools, Dr. Robert Scanlon is the Director of the Project.

Q. Do the pupils in Individually Prescribed Instruction receive the New, or Modern, math?

A. Strictly speaking, No. However, the math curriculum does include many concepts which can be considered modern math.

Q. What kind of training do you have for the teachers?

A. All teachers are asked to work in the summer IPI workshop. The best training seems to be on the job, where a new teacher is associated with an experienced person for a short period of time. Special materials have been ordered by RBS to permit the individualization of teacher training.

Q. What kind of grouping do you do in IPI?

A. There is no homogeneous grouping. The pupils in the self-contained classroom are heterogeneous. On occasion, when the need arises, pupils from the same or different classrooms are grouped for instructional purposes. These pupils have similar problems relating to a common skill or unit.

Q. At the present time, can IPI be initiated in a conventional elementary school at a cost compatible with that school's operational budget?

A. No. But with continuous refinements in the system and more research designed to lower the cost, it is hoped that IPI can be placed in a conventional elementary school at a reasonable cost in the very near future. Most important is the complete cooperation needed from all persons involved in this initiation.

Q. What kind of progress report goes home to the parent?

A. This varies from school to school. No one way has been found to be best.

Q. Who scores the pupil's work?

A. A child's work page is either scored by himself or by an aide. The teacher's time is spent on evaluating the work after it is scored. All tests (Placements, Curriculum-Embedded, Pre-, and Post-) are scored by the aides.

Q. How long has the project been in existence?

A. It began in 1963.

Q. Do you have group instruction in Individually Prescribed Instruction?

A. Yes. The teacher is concerned with prescribing materials and settings for students. Students may work independently or in various size groups.

Q. What is Individually Prescribed Instruction?

A. Individually Prescribed Instruction is a system of managing instruction so that each child's work can be evaluated daily and, if necessary, the teacher can make an assignment for each child which is tailored especially for him.

Q. How does IPI allow the teacher to prescribe for many children?

A. Individually Prescribed Instruction rests upon information and materials. In order to evaluate and make assignments for each student the teacher needs a great deal of up-to-date information about the work and academic history of each student. When she makes an individualized assignment, the assigned materials must be readily available without fail.

Q. What subjects are involved in the Individually Prescribed Instruction procedures?

A. K-6 Mathematics and Reading. (Limited experimentation in science at the Oakleaf School.)

Q. Why are these subjects chosen?

A. Because these are the basic tools of intellectual development which must be used in any future job or future learning. Lack of mastery in these areas causes a child to fall farther and farther behind his classmates. A third area, science, is currently under development.

Q. How is the curriculum arranged if every student is working independently on his own assignment?

A. The curriculum is spelled out in a few hundred objectives for each subject. These objectives are stated in terms of what the student must do at every step in order to convince the teacher (and himself) that he has mastered the curriculum objective and that he is ready to go on.

At other times the size of a group varies from 3 to 15 pupils, depending on the learning task. The decision that certain pupils with similar problems in math and reading should be grouped for instruction usually comes out of a planning session. The length of the grouping period may vary from 10 to 40 minutes.

Q. What are the Individually Prescribed Instruction teachers' functions?

A. Administer placement and pre-tests, diagnose needs of learner, prescription writing (review background information and test scores), analyze student progress, provide guidance, prescribe post-test, and determine mastery.

Q. Do pupils from different grades ever receive instruction together?

A. Yes. If two children in fifth grade are having a problem similar to three children in sixth grade, the pupils may be brought together in a small group for instruction. After the instruction they return to their usual work area and continue their Individually Prescribed Instruction work.

Q. How is the library related to the Individually Prescribed Instruction reading?

A. The library is always open for the pupils and there is no limit to the number of books a child may take out. Sometimes complete IPI classes are held in the library. At other times children are seen going in and out of the library for different purposes. An honor system is used in the checking in and out of books.

Q. Is there any homework in IPI subjects?

A. Generally, no. However, several of our schools have used the prescription material as homework assignments in specific cases.

Q. Doesn't the daily writing of prescriptions become boring?

A. No. Teachers accept the challenge of prescribing informational materials in a more professional manner.

Q. What help does the teacher receive in the record-keeping, scoring and material management which IPI requires?

A. The IPI system, as now operated, requires the use of nonprofessional staff (teacher's aides). While scoring and checking information is vital to the success of the program, in some cases students can correct their own material.

Q. Doesn't the freedom and individual attention of IPI create discipline problems?

A. No. All our experience indicates that discipline problems decrease at our IPI institutions.

Q. Does IPI mean that the student is always working alone?

A. No. Teachers as diagnosticians and prescribers of instruction place each youngster in the setting in which he functions best. This may mean group instruction.

Q. How do parents react to Individually Prescribed Instruction?

A. Current indications are extremely high.

Q. What happens to a student from another school who comes into an IPI school?

A. Diagnostic instruments permit quick assessment of his strengths and weaknesses. Therefore, proper instructional setting and tests can be quickly assigned.

Q. What happens to an IPI student who goes to another school?

A. The IPI school is able to provide more specific information about the student to his new school. What that school does with the information varies.

Chapter 9. EVALUATION IN *IPI*

EVALUATION IN A STRUCTURED CURRICULUM MODEL FOR INDIVIDUALIZED INSTRUCTION

Richard C. Cox
C. M. Lindvall

It is obvious that educational evaluation in individualized instruction takes many forms and serves a great number of functions. It is also the case that the term "evaluation" has a variety of meanings in the educational context. Because of the many uses of the term it may be clarifying to specify how it will be used in the present chapter. For the most part it will be used in the following two ways.

Evaluation as a procedure for gathering pupil data to use in planning and monitoring individual programs. — Planned programs for individualizing instruction require extensive data concerning pupil aptitude, achievement, interest, learning styles, and other qualities having implications for the diagnosis and planning of educational programs. An evaluation program of

SOURCE: This paper has drawn considerably upon the chapter entitled "The Role of Evaluation in Programs for Individualized Instruction," in *Educational Evaluation: New Roles, New Means,* sixty-eighth yearbook of the National Society for the Study of Education, 1969, by permission of the authors and publishers.

this type must include not only the plans and procedures for gathering data but also rather detailed suggestions for the use of each type of data collected.

Evaluation as a procedure for gathering and analyzing data in such a way that it leads to improvements in materials and in the instructional system. — Individualized instruction, with its needs for extensive information concerning pupil progress, provides an excellent opportunity for studying and improving instructional resources on the basis of such data. Furthermore, the effective functioning of an individualized system probably requires this type of continuing improvement even to a greater degree than does conventional group instruction.

A STRUCTURED-CURRICULUM MODEL FOR INDIVIDUALIZED INSTRUCTION

Most teachers are aware of the range of individual differences represented by the students in their classes and probably make some type of effort to individualize instruction. This individualization may take such forms as are represented by the elementary teacher who tries to go from pupil to pupil to provide individual help during a period in which the class is working on a common assignment or by the college professor who uses the lecture method in his class sessions but gives each student some choice in selecting the topic for a term paper. Although such relatively unstructured procedures as these can, when used by a skilled teacher, achieve a considerable degree of individualization, the term "individualized instruction" is usually reserved to denote procedures which provide for having each pupil working on an individualized assignment in the classroom and proceeding through his work at a pace suited to his own needs and abilities. It is procedures of this latter type that are considered in this chapter.

Basically, the structured-curriculum model for individualized instruction involves the following elements:

1.   Sequences of instructional objectives to define the curriculum

2.   Instructional materials to teach each objective

3.   An evaluation procedure for placing each pupil at the appropriate point in the curriculum

4.   A plan for developing individualized programs of study

5.   A procedure for evaluating and monitoring individual progress.

ORGANIZING OBJECTIVES

Sequencing and organizing objectives are key steps in the design of a program for individualized instruction. Some type of order is essential for determining how far advanced each pupil is within the curriculum, for planning his next learning experiences, and for monitoring his progress. Much of the organization will be determined by the hierarchical or prerequisite nature of the objectives.

Of course, the ordering or organizing of objectives does not dictate the order in which every pupil will master the abilities involved. They may merely provide the basic organization from which various paths may lead.

The considerations involved in sequencing may be illustrated by reference to Figure 9-1. It presents a small portion of the objectives for the reading curriculum for Grades K-6 of the Individually Prescribed Instruction Project being developed at the University of Pittsburgh.[1] In this curriculum a type of "spiral" progression is employed so that the student will move through many of the same topics (vocabulary development, literal comprehension, etc.) at successively higher levels (A, B, C, D, E, and so on). The organization is such that a level C topic should be studied prior to the same topic at level D. There is an attempted hierarchical ordering across levels. Also there is some attempted ordering within levels so that, for example, the vocabulary development unit is prerequisite to the literal comprehension unit which, in turn, is prerequisite to the interpretative comprehension unit.

The basic diagnostic instruments in programs of individualization must be the tests and other techniques that provide information concerning where the pupil is in the curriculum and what progress he is making. These instruments will be useful only to the extent that they are referenced to specific objectives and specific units and consequently to the instructional materials that teach these abilities. Tests that are useful for individualization must tell the student (and his teacher), "If I have test scores of this type, then I should start my study here," and "If I do poorly on this test, then I should endeavor to acquire this ability by studying these materials." All teachers have been told many times that results from standardized tests and from a variety of other sources provide them with information about individual pupils which they should use to help them fit instruction to the needs of each pupil. Unfortunately, the teacher is then left to his own devices in determining how he is to accomplish this highly complex and difficult task. The result is that the use of such a recipe for individualization is almost uniformly unsuccessful. Evaluation and diagnosis that is to be useful for individualizing instruction should begin with a careful specification, sequencing, and structuring of detailed instructional objectives.

INSTRUCTIONAL MATERIALS AND THE DIAGNOSTIC PROGRAM

A second major step in the development of a program for individualized instruction is the development or selection of instructional materials and activities for teaching each objective. Although such materials, strictly speaking, are not a part of the diagnostic program, their proper selection and

LEVEL C	LEVEL D
Vocabulary Development	**Vocabulary Development**
1. Identify words that have similar meanings. 2. Identify words that have opposite meanings. 3. Select words that rhyme with a written or pictured word. 4. Identify the correct meaning of a word from the context of a sentence.	1. Mark consonants and consonant blends for dictated or pictured words. 2. Draw picture to illustrate meaning of new words. 3. Match pictures with sentences or paragraphs which they illustrate. 4. Select the word which correctly completes a sentence.
Literal Comprehension	**Literal Comprehension**
1. Match words that form an associative pair. 2. Copy statements answering recall questions. 3. Answer questions requiring recall of facts from written passages. 4. List main characters from a story after reading it silently.	1. Complete a statement based on content read. 2. Select words to complete statements based on recall of material read. 3. List, in order of occurrence, the main events of a story read.
Interpretative Comprehension	**Interpretative Comprehension**
1. Order sequentially two to four sentences. 2. Select the event that happened first in a short story just read. 3. Read a sentence silently and write what might happen next. 4. Read a poem or story and indicate, in writing, the mood expressed. 5. Read a story and write a description of the idea expressed.	1. Underline part of a sentence that answers a given question. 2. Describe a story he has read as happy, sad, funny, or exciting. 3. Select the sentence describing the main thought of a story. 4. Give oral account of a story read. 5. Explain cause-effect relationships in stories read silently.

FIGURE 9-1

OBJECTIVES FOR SELECTED UNITS AT LEVELS C AND D IN THE
INDIVIDUALLY PRESCRIBED INSTRUCTION (IPI) READING CURRICULUM

use are essential to meaningful diagnosis. As suggested in the preceding section, each piece of lesson material and each specified learning activity must be keyed or referenced to some one objective. This type of identification must take such a form that when it is known that a student is to work on the mastery of objective 6, he can do this by studying materials R, S, T, U, V, or W. Only when this is the case can diagnosis lead to meaningful prescription of an individualized lesson plan.

However, the development of lesson materials probably must involve more than this. Effective individualization should be based on something more than having each pupil work at his proper point in the curriculum continuum. He should be engaged in activities suited to his interests, aptitudes, learning style, and other relevant personal qualities. Diagnosis that leads to individualization on such bases is dependent on the availability of materials and learning experiences adapted to differences in such qualities. Unfortunately, not enough is known about how to adapt to such differences. However, some things are known and many others can be explored within the context of the development and improvement of an individualized system. A key place to start this type of exploration is in the provision of a variety of types of materials for teaching each objective. Some students may learn certain concepts and principles quite readily from verbal materials alone. Other pupils may be able to achieve mastery only through the help of diagrams and pictures. Still others may require learning experiences involving the physical manipulation of objects and devices. Some students may learn most things readily by working quite independently; others may require considerable interaction with a teacher or with other students. These and many other pupil differences should be taken into account in building the lesson materials and the specified learning activities for each objective and unit. Without the availability of this variety in the learning experiences that can be employed, diagnostic procedures will be of little use. Every teacher has an almost infinite store of information concerning ways in which his students differ. A successful program for individualized instruction must provide ways for adapting learning experiences to the most meaningful of these differences.

EVALUATING PUPIL PERFORMANCE IN A STRUCTURED CURRICULUM

Diagnosis of performance is important not only for assessing what each pupil is able to achieve at any given time but for identifying the next instructional assignment for that pupil. This requirement indicates the need for content—or criterion-referenced measures as opposed to norm-referenced measures.[2] Norm-referenced measures indicate a pupil's relative position with respect to other pupils in some norm group. For example, standardized achievement tests yield norm-referenced scores in the sense that they tell how pupils in a given class or school rank in comparison with the pupils in the test-standardization group. They do not provide information as to what the pupil can perform in reference to a specified area of content.

On the other hand, a criterion- or content-referenced measure indicates how pupil proficiency corresponds to some desired criterion. In the individualized instruction model being proposed, the detailed behavioral objectives define the criterion behavior which is expected of pupils. Measurement of pupil performance must, therefore, be accomplished by using tests clearly referenced to the content objectives within each learning continuum.

Tests of pupil performance which are currently in general use are typically not appropriate for use in the individualized instruction model being proposed. What is required, then, is the development of tests which provide measures referenced to the sequences of instructional objectives. Performance measures which are to be useful as a basis for the continuous planning of instructional experiences for individual pupils in a program for individualized instruction should include *(a)* placement tests, *(b)* diagnostic tests for given units, and *(c)* curriculum-embedded tests for monitoring pupil progress.[3]

EVALUATING PUPIL PERFORMANCE FOR PLACEMENT IN THE LEARNING CONTINUUM

One of the first diagnostic requirements for an individualized system is the placement of each pupil in a learning continuum at a level which is commensurate with his performance level. It would be wasteful to have the pupil assigned to a unit of instruction which he had already learned, while, on the other hand, it would be frustrating for the pupil to be given an assignment for which he did not have the necessary prerequisites and which, therefore, he could not accomplish. What is required is a type of placement measure that is criterion-referenced and that will provide the information about the performance level of each pupil that enables the teacher to determine the appropriate place for assignment in the curriculum.

Placement tests should be administered at the beginning of the school year or when the pupil enters the individualized program. The major function of the placement measures is to provide a general profile of individual pupil performance over many units of work. What is being suggested is that placement tests should be broad in scope. If the individualized instruction program covers several subjects, the placement test battery must cover all of these subjects. If only the mathematics continuum is being individualized, the only placement tests needed are those for mathematics. It is certainly true that within any grade level there is a great deal of interindividual differences in achievement. The placement measures must therefore span some considerable sequence in the learning continuum.

Placement testing should be efficient, that is, it should yield a maximum of information in a minimum of time. Also, placement tests should be constructed by selecting items which test representative objectives along the continuum.

In most cases the length of any one placement test should be restricted to a time limit that is reasonably consistent with the length of the attention span of the group to which the test is to be given. The validity of the measures for placement should not be diminished by fatigue on the part of the test-taker.

Consideration should be given to certain item types which may accomplish diagnosis in a most efficient manner. Objectivity is highly desirable. Of course, teachers will make subjective judgments based on the results of tests and on other information available on each child such as general achievement, type of learner, and so on; however, the results of the tests in terms of proficiency in a curriculum area should be unequivocal. Certainly, multiple-choice and short-answer items should be considered. This is not to say, by any means, that the format of test items should dictate what is to be tested. Just the opposite is true. If the curriculum objective states that the child should respond by solving a problem or by constructing a certain response, the test item should demand this behavior. What is being suggested is only that, when alternative item types are possible, the test constructor should choose those items which allow for greatest objectivity and ease in scoring.

An example of a placement test battery for use in individualized instruction which illustrates some of the principles that have been cited is the Individually Prescribed Instruction (IPI) placement test series.[4] The IPI system is designed to achieve a certain type of individualized instruction in Grades K-6 in the subject areas of mathematics, reading, and science.[5] Each of the IPI curriculums is defined by a series of behavioral objectives or skills which are organized into content areas and levels. The mathematics curriculum, for example, is divided into the content areas of numeration, place value, addition, subtraction, multiplication, division, combination of processes, fractions, money, time, systems of measurement, geometry, and special topics. It is also structured into nine levels starting with very elementary mathematics at level A and systematically building in difficulty to level I, which is quite advanced junior-high-school mathematics. The objectives for a content area at a given level are defined as a *unit*. This means that each unit is designated with a descriptive title such as "Level A Addition," "Level D Multiplication," and so on. The basic task in placement testing, then, is to determine the level at which a pupil is prepared to work in each of the several areas.

Placement tests have been constructed for each level of the curriculum so that, in a sense, each placement test represents a certain well-specified achievement level which is similar to the achievement defined by a grade level in a graded school. The level E placement test in mathematics, for example, includes items which test each content area in the curriculum at that level. At the outset of individualization, the teacher must decide which is the most appropriate placement test for each pupil. This decision, in most cases, is made after obtaining information about past achievement of each pupil, examining the content of the placement test, and then matching these. This means that, in a given class, pupils will start taking placement tests at a variety of levels depending on achievement variability in that class. (After the individualized system has been in effect for a year, the placement testing provides an indication of retention or lack of retention over the summer months.) In order to cover a wide range of achievement, each pupil typically will be assigned placement tests for more than one level.

Intraindividual differences will readily appear as a result of placement testing. A pupil may demonstrate proficiency in certain content areas and lack of proficiency in other content areas. In order to obtain an achievement profile for each child, certain sections of the next higher or lower level test will be administered.

The result of placement testing is a profile of pupil performance over all content areas of the curriculum. Figure 9-2 shows a mathematics profile for a hypothetical third-grade pupil. Each check mark indicates successful performance in that unit.

The pupil's placement tests are scored in such a way that he is reported as having mastered each area at the highest level at which he exhibited mastery of the items on the test. The hypothetical third grade pupil mentioned would have "scores" of C-Numeration, C-Place Value, C-Fractions, D-Addition, D-Subtraction, D-Multiplication, D-Division, D-Combination of Processes, E-Systems of Measurement, E-Time, E-Money, and E-Geometry. Such scores are criterion-referenced measures in that they tell where the pupil is in the sequence of levels in each area. As criterion-referenced measures, they provide specific information concerning what abilities the pupil has mastered and at what levels or in what units he is ready to begin work.

Student A

	A	B	C	D	E	F	G	H
Numeration	✓	✓	✓					
Place Value	✓	✓	✓					
Addition	✓	✓	✓	✓				
Subtraction	✓	✓	✓	✓				
Multiplication	✓	✓	✓	✓				
Division	✓	✓	✓	✓				
Combination of Processes	✓	✓	✓	✓				
Fractions	✓	✓	✓					
Money.	✓	✓	✓	✓	✓			
Time	✓	✓	✓	✓	✓			
Systems of Measurement	✓	✓	✓	✓	✓			
Geometry	✓	✓	✓	✓	✓			

FIGURE 9-2
EXAMPLE OF A PERFORMANCE PROFILE INDICATED
BY MATHEMATICS PLACEMENT TESTS

DIAGNOSTIC TESTING FOR PLANNING INDIVIDUAL PROGRAMS

Placement measurement in the theoretical model for individualizing instruction provides a broad diagnosis of pupil performance that can be utilized in the identification of instructional units appropriate for each pupil. Placement-test information can indicate the possible curriculum units to which a pupil may be assigned with a high probability of his being successful. This initial diagnosis, however, will not provide detailed information needed for the assignment of exact instructional materials for the unit. What is demanded is a further diagnosis of a pupil's competencies specific to the particular instructional unit which he is about to study.

For each unit of the curriculum there needs to be a pretest of the objectives included in the unit. This measurement is an extension of placement testing for each specific unit in the curriculum. Pretesting must be, as placement testing, content-referenced so that the results of the pretest can be used to indicate the objectives in the instructional unit in which the pupil has or has not indicated proficiency. This is necessary for several reasons. Take, for example, a given instructional unit which contains ten objectives. The placement test has indicated that the pupil should be assigned this unit since he has not demonstrated proficiency on the test item or items representing the entire unit. This is not to say, however, that the pupil needs to be assigned work on each objective in the instructional unit so that the teacher has information for specific assignments in the unit. It must be possible for a child to pretest out of certain parts of a unit. In fact, as the child proceeds through the curriculum he may pretest out of an entire unit of work. This may result as a function of content learned in a lower level unit or in a related unit.

The length of a pretest will be determined by the number of objectives in the instructional unit and by the number of items used to test each objective. In general, the number of items testing the same objective like "the pupil can solve simple addition problems involving all number combinations" will require more items than would an objective like "the pupil must select which of three triangles is equilateral." Certain objectives may be stated in such a manner as to limit the ways in which successful performance can be tested. If only one item per objective is used, the test will generally be less reliable than if more items are used. On the other hand, it may be assumed that, if a pupil can perform well on five or ten items of similar content, he can perform well on twenty or fifty such items.

The results of the unit pretest are not the only information on which the teacher prescribes work in the curriculum. In the individualized model being proposed, a case-study approach needs to be taken for each child. In order to prescribe instructional materials suited to each learner, the teacher should know not only the pretest results but also the general performance level of each child as defined by such measures as the placement tests, standardized achievement tests (when relevant), and by general intelligence measures. Reading level would certainly be a consideration in assigning instructional materials in any content area. Pupil interests and learning styles should also be considered. Pretests indicate to the teacher only the objectives in which the pupil is deficient, not which instructional materials are appropriate for this given pupil. The continuous planning of individual programs must be based on a combination of variables and must be updated as a pupil proceeds through the curriculum.

EVALUATION IN THE MONITORING OF INDIVIDUAL PROGRESS

As a pupil proceeds by working on specific objectives in the units of the curriculum, there is a need for evaluation of the required criterion performance. Two types of measures are demanded for this evaluation. The first of these is what may be called "curriculum-embedded tests," which are an integral part of the instructional sequence. A curriculum-embedded test (CET) is a measure of performance on one particular objective in the sequence. It is used to assess performance on the skill stated in the objective so that the teacher has information with which to make a decision to advance the pupil to the next objective or to assign additional instructional exercises for the same objective. A CET will be prescribed for each pupil at specified intervals in the sequence of instructional materials for the objective.

The CET, like placement and preunit tests, must be content-referenced to the particular objective it is intended to test. Since only one objective is being tested, these tests will, in general, be quite short and should be considered as just another task in the instructional sequence, i.e., a part of the curriculum. The item types need not be limited in any way, except that they follow logically from the objective being tested. Behaviors required by the test items should be quite similar to the learning tasks defined for that objective. Since this is the measurement for the most basic curriculum element, the objective, the tests should specifically evaluate the criterion behavior specified in the objective.

A second type of evaluation used to monitor individual progress in an individualized model is the postunit test. The pupil proceeds by attaining proficiency on the CET's for the objectives in his instructional sequence. When satisfactory performance has been attained on all the objectives in an instructional unit, there is a need for reassessment of performance on the unit as a whole. This is another decision point for the teacher. Diagnosis of performance is required so that information is available to help the teacher decide whether or not the pupil should proceed to the next unit of work in his program. Success on the posttest indicates that the pupil has the prerequisites for subsequent units; failure indicates that remedial work is necessary on one or more objectives.

In most cases the postunit test will be an alternative form of the preunit test. If there is an interest in whether or not a pupil can apply the knowledge learned in the instructional unit to another situation, an item testing this ability may be included in the posttest. Remediation of failure on this type of items would be difficult, however, unless these objectives and instructional materials are part of the curriculum.

The function of each test may be seen by examining the flow chart for the IPI system as presented in Figure 9-3.

THE ROLE OF EVALUATION IN THE IMPROVEMENT OF INDIVIDUALIZED PROGRAMS

Continuing improvement is crucial to the success of individualized programs. In such programs the quality of diagnosis and prescription is judged on the basis of how well the pupil performs. If the pupil does poorly, not because diagnosis and prescription are invalid but because instructional materials are inadequate, his performance may be incorrectly interpreted as suggesting the need for changes in diagnosis. That is, in a complex system of instruction, all elements are highly interdependent, and proper functioning requires that all parts be characterized by a high degree of effectiveness.

Fortunately, a structured system of individualized instruction is typically one which continually provides data concerning the effectiveness of each part of the system. With tests that are clearly and definitely referenced to specific objectives, it is easy to gather data concerning the general effectiveness of the materials and activities designed to teach a given objective. Likewise, if the system calls for scoring each lesson sheet, this assessment can be used to judge the quality of each such item. Data such as this may suggest modification or replacement of given materials. Similarly other data may be used to indicate needed changes in other aspects of the program. Since individual prescriptions are usually developed in written form, they provide a record which can be related to subsequent pupil performance in such a way as to suggest the points at which changes might be made in prescription-writing procedures. An earlier section of the chapter suggested the need for a continuing investigation of new bases for individualizing instruction. Evaluation data are essential to the appraisal of any such new procedures.

In summary then, an individualized system can achieve its true potential only if all of its elements are evaluated on a continuing basis and if information acquired is used as feedback for improvement. Hence, such a system should involve a planned program for gathering and analyzing data to accomplish this purpose.

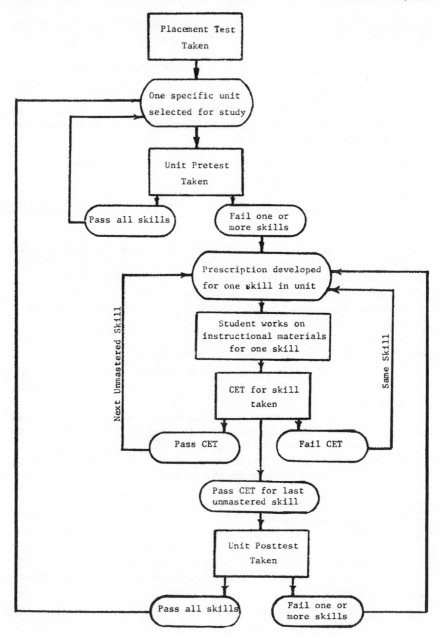

FIGURE 9-3
FLOW CHART OF STEPS IN THE CYCLE FOR EVALUATING AND
MONITORING OF PUPIL PROGRESS IN THE IPI PROCEDURE

NOTES

[1]C. M. Lindvall and John O. Bolvin, "Programed Instruction in the Schools: An Application of Programing Principles in Individually Prescribed Instruction," in Phil C. Lange (Ed.), *Programed Instruction* (Sixty-sixth Yearbook of the National Society for the Study of Education, Part II (Chicago: Distributed by the University of Chicago Press, 1967), pp. 217-54.

[2]Robert Glaser and Richard C. Cox, "Criterion-Referenced Testing for the Measurement of Educational Outcomes," in R. A. Weisgerber (Ed.), *Instructional Process and Media Innovation* (Chicago: Rand McNally & Co., 1968), pp. 545-50.

[3]To make the description of the evaluation procedures for an individualized instruction program as specific as possible, the writers have based these sections largely on the Individually Prescribed Instruction (IPI) program with which they are associated.

[4]Richard C. Cox and M. Elizabeth Boston, "Diagnosis of Pupil Achievement in the Individually Prescribed Instruction Project" (Working Paper No. 15, Learning Research and Development Center, University of Pittsburgh, 1967).

[5]Lindvall and Bolvin, *op. cit.*

THE USE OF FIELD DATA FOR IMPROVING IPI MATERIALS AND PROCEDURES

John O. Bolvin

The Individually Prescribed Instruction Project represents an investigation into the requirements for and the problems encountered in developing a system for individualizing instruction. The definition of individualization used for IPI is that the individualization of instruction requires the adaptation of the educational environment to individual differences. The aims and goals of this project have been described previously and will not be repeated here. Also, the specification of the system to arrive at these goals has been described in several articles such as Glaser,[1] Lindvall and Bolvin,[2] and Bolvin and Glaser.[3] In all of the discussions of the elements of the IPI system, one important component that has relevance for the use of data in improving the program is that the system has built into it strategies for information feedback in order to provide means for constant evaluation and improvement of the system.

SOURCE: Reprinted from a paper presented at the Annual Convention of the American Educational Research Association, Los Angeles, Calif., February 5-8, 1969, by permission of author.

PLAN	OPERATION
A Testing Program that:	The Testing Program:

a. Provides information for proper placement in the instructional continua.

b. Aids in the diagnosis of specific pupil needs.

c. Provides for frequent assessment of mastery.

d. Tests pupil on objectives and units when he is ready.

e. Facilitates the planning of effective individualized programs.

f. Provides information that has real meaning to the student.

Prescription Writing Procedures that:

a. Are based upon valid and meaningful diagnoses.

b. Start the pupil at the proper point in the instructional continua.

c. Specify learning experiences suited to the pupil's ability and other personal qualities.

d. Are suited to the pupil's rate of learning.

e. Provide guidance to the pupil so that he can secure proper materials and proceed.

a. Is used to place pupils at correct points in the instructional continua.

b. Provides valid diagnosis of pupil needs.

c. Provides a valid assessment of mastery of objectives and of units.

d. Is administered so that the pupil is taking CET's and unit tests at proper times.

e. Provides data that are found useful by the teachers for developing valid prescriptions.

f. Provides data that are meaningful to the student.

Instructional Prescriptions

a. Are based upon proper use of test results and specified prescription writing procedures.

b. Provide learning experiences that are a challenge but permit regular progress.

c. Vary from pupil to pupil depending upon individual differences.

d. Permit pupil to proceed at his best rate.

e. Are interpreted and used correctly by the pupil.

FIGURE 10-1 *

PLAN AND OPERATION FOR SELECTED ELEMENTS OF THE IPI SYSTEM

* Individually Prescribed Instruction: Outline of Basic Elements in Development and Evaluation. Learning Research and Development Center, University of Pittsburgh, May 13, 1968.

f. Provide for adjustment as
   pupil proceeds.

                        f. Are modified as required.

Instructional Materials and
Devices that:

The Instructional Materials and
Devices:

a. Are referenced to a specific
   objective.

a. Are easily identified with the
   proper objective.

b. Enable the student to achieve
   mastery.

b. Have demonstrated instructional
   effectiveness.

c. Permit a maximum of indepen-
   dent.study and individual
   progress.

c. Are used by pupils largely in
   individual independent study.

d. Permit packaging into individualized instructional
   sequences.

d. Are used by pupils in individualized packages.

e. Require active responses on
   the part of the pupil.

e. Keep the pupil actively involved.

f. Are primarily self-instructional.

f. Require a minimum of direct
   teacher help to pupils.

g. Are regularly revised and
   improved on the basis of
   performance data.

g. Are shown to teach more effectively as they are revised.

Teacher Classroom Activities
that:

The Teacher Classroom Activities
are such that:

a. Provide the pupil with help
   when he needs it.

a. There is little delay in the
   pupil's getting help when he
   needs it.

b. Provides individual help on
   individual problems.

b. Teacher assistance to pupils
   is largely on an individual
   basis.

c. Permit the teacher to spend
   considerable time in diagno-
   suing needs of individual
   pupils and in preparing
   prescriptions.

c. The teacher will spend some
   class time in examining pupil
   work and in developing prescriptions.

d. Reinforce the pupil's learning
   and attention.

d. Positive reinforcement of desirable behavior is employed.

FIGURE 10-1 *Continued*

e. Give the student considerable freedom in determining when and how he works.

f. Facilitate progress on an individual basis.

e. Teachers give the students considerable freedom.

f. Little time is spent on lectures (etc.) to the group, and individual or small group tutoring is employed.

Classroom Management Procedures that:

a. Use teacher aides to score papers and tests and provide quick feedback on results.

b. Permit pupils to score some of his papers.

c. Provide for the pupil's procuring his own instructional materials.

d. Allow the pupil to decide when he has completed a lesson and is ready to have it scored.

Classroom Management Procedures are such that:

a. Teacher aides score papers and record results in an efficient manner.

b. Pupils score some work pages.

c. Pupils procure own lesson materials.

d. Pupils decide when to have lessons scored.

FIGURE 10-1 *Concluded*

Like other programs, IPI has a set of *goals* to be achieved. It has a *plan* to achieve these goals, and this plan has been put into *operation* to see if the stated plan does achieve the desired goals. For the past several years, the major concern of the developers of IPI has been the evaluation of the operation to determine where changes in elements of the system must be improved to make the operation consistent with the plan. For instance, five elements of the IPI plan are: (1) a testing program, (2) prescription writing procedures, (3) instructional materials and devices, (4) teacher classroom activities, and (5) classroom management procedures. Each of these elements has sub-elements that are expressed in terms of the plan and in terms of the operation. (See Figure 10-1.)

During the school year 1967-68, IPI was field tested in approximately 25 schools throughout the country. During this field testing the developers collected information which could be used to determine where improvement was needed to make the operation more consistent with the plan. However, before using data for this purpose, it had to be determined whether or not the schools were in fact adopting and applying the system as designed. Miss Weinberger has addressed herself to this point previously. Once we had determined what schools represented true replications of the IPI model and hence could be used for data analysis, the staff of the Learning Research and Development Center then selected the essential data to be analyzed.

Examples of parts of the IPI operation for which data was gathered for this purpose are as follows:

1. *Prescription Writing.* One of the essential requirements of the system is that prescriptions or plans vary from pupil to pupil depending upon individual differences. To determine whether this was happening, the prescription data was analyzed: first by objective, then by unit, and subsequently by age or grade.

Figure 10-2 is a modified version of the Prescription Form being used in the IPI system. Each teacher develops a prescription for each student in his class for each day or, at most, several days. The form itself is organized in such a way to provide the student and teacher with information relative to the student's progress, and secondly, to provide information for program evaluation. In the example of the question just asked, "Do plans vary from pupil to pupil depending upon individual differences?" the first step in arriving at an answer would be to determine if the plans varied from pupil to pupil. The Prescription Form provides some information relative to this

MATHEMATICS PRESCRIPTION SHEET

SCHOOL STAMP   STUDENT NAME ________   STUDENT NUMBER ________

GRADE ________   ROOM ________   UNIT ________

	PRES. DATE	PRES. INIT.	SKILL NO.	PAGE NO.	INST. TECH CODES	SCORE	MAX. POINTS

CURRICULUM TEST PART 1		CURRICULUM TEST PART 2		SC'S INIT	DAYS* WORKED IN SKILL	NOTES
SCORE	%	SCORE	%			

CODES	INSTRUCTIONAL TECHNIQUE
01	TEACHER TUTOR
02	PEER TUTOR
03	SMALL GROUP (2-10)
04	LARGE GROUP (11-UP)
05	SEMINAR
06	CURR. TEXTS
07	OTHER TEXTS
08	FILM STRIPS
09	RECORDS, TAPES
10	RESEARCH
11	TUTOR OF OTHERS
12	OTHERS

CURRICULUM TEST

ENTER SKILL NUMBER	ENTER POINTS PER SKILL	PRE	%	POST	%	POST	%	POST	%

FIGURE 10-2

question. In the lower right-hand corner of the form is the pretest information. This information is available for each objective within the unit before the student begins work in this unit. In the lower left-hand portion are alternative techniques and settings that can be prescribed. In the body of the prescription the teacher specifies the order of tasks, the techniques of instruction, and whose choice it was, the student's or the teacher's, that the student work on these tasks.

Sample data from the 25 schools for several objectives are given in Table 10-1.

TABLE 10-1

SUMMARY INFORMATION ON NUMBER OF LESSON PAGES AND
INSTRUCTIONAL ALTERNATIVES USED FOR SELECTED *IPI* MATH OBJECTIVES

Objective	No. of Students	Range of Pages	Mean No. of Pages	Alternatives Used	Percent of Alternatives*
D–Add–2	65	3–14	8.5	Booklets	97%
				Teacher Tutoring	3
				Seminar	15
				Other Texts	2
D–Add–3	72	1–9	6.0	Booklets	100%
D–Sub–3	125	3–21	13.3	Booklets	94%
				Teacher Tutoring	9.2
				Peer Tutoring	2.7
				Small Group	1.5
				Large Group	1.2
				Seminar	5.8
				Records, Tapes	1.1
				Other	1.2
D–Sub–5	147	1–25	11.8	Booklets	97%
				Teacher Tutoring	10.4
				Peer Tutoring	2.2
				Small Group	1.0
				Large Group	1.4
				Seminar	2.1
				Textbooks	1.0
				Other Text	3.1
				Other	2.0
E–Mult–5	175	5–28	13	Booklets	100%
				Teacher Tutoring	10
				Seminar	5
				Curriculum Texts	1.4
				Other Texts	1.4
				Film Strips	3.6

*It is possible to use more than a single alternative for any one objective.

In general, an examination of this information indicated that prescriptions did vary from child to child but there was more variation in terms of paper-pencil activities than there was with alternate settings or instructional techniques. This provided important information concerning needed modifications in the system to increase the probability of greater variations in prescriptions with respect to settings and techniques used. The Center is now attempting to provide more systematic procedures to assist the teacher in utilizing the alternatives available.

2. *Objectives.* Another question of interest to the system developers is whether all the objectives listed, for instance in the Math Curriculum, are necessary. An examination of the pretest data from the 25 schools for each of the 400 objectives in the Math program revealed that there were some objectives for which large numbers of students had proficiency at the time of the pretest. Table 10-2 is a summary of these data.

TABLE 10-2

Percent of Students Having 85% or More
Proficiency of Each Objective as
Measured by Pretest through D-Division

Unit	Skill	Number	Percent with 85% or More Proficiency
Num–C	1	1049	87%
Num–C	3	1048	85%
Num–E	4	602	89%
PV–C	3	709	88%
PV–D	3	738	96%
PV–D	4	738	97%
PV–E	3	415	83%
Add–B	2	425	93%
Add–C	5	333	85%
Add–D	1	373	99%
Sub–C	3	425	92%
Sub–D	1	614	90%
Mult–D	1	335	96%
Mult–D	2	335	94%
Div–D	1	523	85%
Div–D	2	523	87%
Div–D	4	523	85%

Information of this type leads us to two considerations: (1) to question each objective as to the necessity for including it or as to its placement, (2) to question the test that is used to measure this objective. From the 1967-68 data, we found instances of both types of errors in the program.

3. *Lesson Materials.* Another use of the information from the tryout schools was to determine some of the more serious problem areas in terms of materials available for student use. In addition to teacher comments and comments from the various monitors visiting the schools, we also analyzed the number of CET's and Posttests assigned for each objective. Table 10-3 is a sample of this type of information.

TABLE 10-3

Percent of Students Requiring Indicated
Number of Tests Before Showing
Mastery of Each Objective
in Two Sample Math Units

Unit	Objective	% Passing CET 1	% Passing CET 3 or More	% Passing 1st Post	% Passing 3 or More Post
D-Add	2	80	0		
	3	75	0		
	4	80	0		
	5	50	13		
	6	72	0		
	7	64	7		
	8	67	0		
	All			76%	15%
E-Mult	1	50	0		
	2	100	0		
	3	100	0		
	4	80	0		
	5	0	33%		
	6	80	4%		
	8	67	8%		
	9	100	0		
	10	50	21%		
	11	60	11%		
	All			68%	21%

These two units were used as examples since they represent units that were identified as particularly troublesome. In the unit D-Addition the students had very few problems in reaching the 85% proficiency on the CET's but seemed to have trouble reaching the desired proficiency on the first posttest. An examination of the materials, tests, and teacher comments indicated a need for the restructuring of the entire unit adding several missing objectives. In the case of E-Multiplication the major problems uncovered were: (1) inadequate materials for objectives 5, 8, 10, and 11; (2) missing objectives relating to the use of associative principle; and (3) inadequate sampling of desired outcomes on the posttest.

In summary, the information collected in the IPI system to assist the teacher and student in decision making relative to the child's progress is also useful information for assisting in the determination of whether the operation is consistent with the plan. During the school year 1966-67 with only 25 schools involved, it was possible to collect nearly all of the available data. However, as the number of schools increases we will become more and more involved with systematically sampling relevant data to continue the improvement of the materials and procedures necessary.

NOTES

[1] Robert Glaser, "Adapting the Elementary School Curriculum to Individual Performance," in Proceedings of the *1967 Invitational Conference on Testing Problems* (Princeton, N.J.: Educational Testing Service, 1968), pp. 3-36.

[2] C. Mauritz Lindvall and John O. Bolvin, "Programed Instruction in the Schools: An Application of Programing Principles in 'Individually Prescribed Instruction,' " in *Sixty-Sixth Yearbook of the National Society for the Study of Education* (Chicago: University of Chicago Press, 1967), pp. 217-54.

[3] John O. Bolvin and Robert Glaser, "Developmental Aspects of Individually Prescribed Instruction," *Audiovisual Instruction* (Washington, D.C.: National Education Association, October, 1968).

THE TEACHER'S CHANGING ROLE

Donald Deep

The fall of 1967 saw great unrest among teachers across the United States. The unrest itself was not surprising to many in education; however, the reason for the unrest in many instances was quite revealing.

Conscientious teachers throughout our country cried out for improved teaching conditions and the best possible atmosphere for teaching. Teachers demanded that their role become more professional and modern. The classroom teacher no longer wanted to be a clerk, simply an imparter of knowledge, a Jack-of-all-trades, but a teacher—one who guides pupils to their full attainment.

Teachers realized that their pupils were the chief victims of the conditions under protest and that ways must be found to correct the injustice to the children. Teachers sought conditions that would make it possible for each

SOURCE: Reprinted from *The Elementary School Journal,* Vol. 69, No. 2 (November, 1968), pp. 84-88, by permission of the author. Published by the University of Chicago Press with the Department of Education of the University of Chicago. Copyright 1968 by The University of Chicago.

pupil to profit fully from the education extended him. This is nothing new. Teachers everywhere have been striving toward this goal, but only recently have programs been set up that lead to it.

There are many paths to a new challenging role for teachers. The University of Pittsburgh and the Baldwin-Whitehall School District have launched a program that fits the changing role. The program, only four years old, has won praise from an important critic—the teacher.

At Oakleaf Elementary School in Baldwin Township just south of Pittsburgh, a number of subjects are taught in an individually prescribed program. The subjects are mathematics and reading from Kindergarten through Grade 6, science from Kindergarten through Grade 4, and spelling in Grades 3-6. Pupils in heterogeneous classes work on different skills simultaneously. In mathematics, one child may be working on geometry, another on addition, another on fractions. More than likely no two pupils will be working on the same topic at the same time. In this program, the teacher must know the subject matter, for in one day she may have to help one child in geometry, another in multiplication, and then another in measurement. Since the class is individualized, the variability of the pupils has increased. In fourth grade, the range of achievement is approximately four years. Clearly, teachers at Oakleaf must have more than a mastery of skills for their grade level. Teachers must be familiar with the entire curriculum. The individualized program has encouraged the integration of mathematics and reading in the primary and the intermediate grades. Confinement to a one-grade textbook has been eliminated.

Just how does the program work? Again, the mathematics program will serve as an example. The curriculum is divided into nine levels—A through I. Most levels are subdivided into units. There are units on numeration, place value, addition, subtraction, multiplication, division, combination of processes, fractions, money, time, measurement, and other special topics. Each unit is designed to develop specific skills called *behavioral objectives*, which the pupils are expected to master. The entire curriculum has more than four hundred behavioral objectives. Here is an example of a behavioral objective from Level E, Unit on Multiplication, Skill 4: "Uses the associative principle for multiplication to multiply more than two numbers with single digit factors."

Once the curriculum has been defined, the next step is to determine where a pupil at Oakleaf should begin work. A series of placement tests is given to each pupil to learn his starting level and unit. Each child is then given a pre-test on that unit to identify the skills he needs to master. A particular pupil may require lessons and drill in only three of six skills. A score of 85 percent or higher is considered mastery.

The teacher evaluates the pre-test and is responsible for writing an individual "prescription" to develop the skills the pupil needs to master. A

A second-grader does mathematics drill at a computer.

Teacher and fifth-grader talk over a prescription.

prescription assigns the child various learning activities. He may be assigned
to a teacher for individual tutoring. Or he may be assigned, with a few other
pupils, to a teacher for small-group instruction. Or he may be assigned, with
many pupils, to a teacher for large-group instruction. He may be asked to do
work pages, to listen to a disc, a tape, or a language master. He may be asked
to view a film or a filmstrip. After the pupil completes his prescription for the
skills in the unit and the teacher evaluates his lessons, the pupil is given a
post-test, an alternate form of the pre-test, to check his mastery of the unit. If
he has not mastered the unit, the teacher prescribes supplemental work. If he
has mastered the unit, he is given the pre-test for his next unit of work.
Because the teacher is continually diagnosing each pupil's weaknesses and
strengths, children are not subjected to boring drill in areas where they have
demonstrated mastery.

In the subjects covered by the program, each pupil is given responsibility
for "filling" his prescription. He obtains his own work pages, materials, aids,
discs, as prescribed. Most pupils proceed through the prescribed materials
with very little direction and instruction from the teacher. Almost all the
work is scored by teacher aides or by the pupil himself. The teacher makes
the final evaluation of the work. Teacher aides score all tests of diagnostic
skill, but the teacher evaluates the test results. Our hope at Oakleaf is that
each child will gain a sense of responsibility for the work he is doing and will
take an active interest in his progress. Pupils are encouraged to become more
self-reliant and independent while working on the individually prescribed
instruction programs.

In this program teachers rarely lecture. They are too busy observing the
child's progress, evaluating his diagnostic tests, writing prescriptions, and
instructing individuals or small groups of pupils who need help. In this
program the teacher's role is what experienced teachers have been seeking
for years—that of teaching, evaluating, and making important educational
decisions. Each prescription for an individual pupil is reviewed by the
teacher each day. Most of the prescriptions do not last more than one class
period.

An important aspect of the program is complete assurance that teachers
have time for planning. Group planning sessions are held weekly for each
subject area. At these sessions, teachers discuss specific problems or changes
in the program. During the school day teachers have time not only for group
planning, but also for individual planning. Most clerical tasks are handled by
teacher aides. The aides, who are paid an hourly wage, are housewives in the
area who have a high-school education.

Usually the teacher has all the prescriptions prepared before class. At the
beginning of the class, the pupils' folders are handed out. Each child looks at
his prescription sheet for his day's lessons. Children who need new materials
for their lessons get them at a designated place. The teacher then goes about
various tasks. She may help pupils who need assistance. She may evaluate

pupils' check tests, pre-tests, and post-tests on certain skills. She may help pupils who have a prescription, "See teacher." She may direct one pupil to teach another, oversee pupils in supplemental activities, or write new prescriptions.

This program does not make the job of the elementary-school teacher any easier, but the rewards are immediate and the role is fast approaching professional standard—exactly what it should have been years ago.

Chapter 12. TEACHER TRAINING IN *IPI*

TEACHER EDUCATION FOR INDIVIDUALIZED INSTRUCTION

Robert Scanlon
Claire Moshy

Research for Better Schools has as its major focus individualization and humanization of education. One of its specific projects is the field development and testing of Individually Prescribed Instruction, an instructional system engineered by the Research and Development Center of the University of Pittsburgh. RBS assumes the major responsibility of installing IPI in a variety of school settings. During the initial phases of these efforts, it became obvious that teacher training was one factor that had to be considered very seriously.

The first year of operation included the training and retraining of teachers in the schools of Harrisburg, Trenton, Dover and Quakertown. Most of the training in these four school systems was handled by Research for Better Schools personnel who had previous training in the IPI laboratory school

---

SOURCE: Reprinted from *Teacher Education and Individualized Instruction,* mimeographed paper, Philadelphia: Research for Better Schools, Inc., May, 1968, p. 10, by permission of the publisher.

maintained by the Research and Development Center. RBS staff members concentrated their training efforts in in-service sessions with the teachers in their respective schools. As long as there were only four schools involved, teacher training was not a major problem. However, after the first year of operation, 20 additional schools were introduced to the IPI system and training problems began to loom large. These increased training needs were handled in several ways.

Research for Better Schools in cooperation with the Learning Research and Development Center, the School of Education, University of Pittsburgh, and the Baldwin-Whitehall School District planned, designed and conducted a summer institute two years in a row. The six-week sessions were divided into two broad areas for presentation. The morning sessions were conducted at a local elementary school using the IPI procedures in its summer program. Institute members had an opportunity to observe IPI teachers in action, act as teacher aides, and eventually serve as classroom teachers. The afternoon sessions were designed to follow-up the morning sessions and to provide an opportunity for the theoretical presentation of the assumptions and principles upon which IPI is based.

During the summer of 1967, RBS also conducted six other training programs. These programs varied in length from 3 to 6 weeks. All sessions were aimed at one particular faculty and attempted to prepare the school for Individually Prescribed Instruction. During all of the summer sessions, youngsters were involved so that we could keep teachers where the action was.

During the 1966-67 school year, RBS established a demonstration school in the Baldwin-Whitehall School District which is also used as part of the training cycle. The demonstration school was used as part of the training cycle by having teachers who were being trained in different locations spend anywhere from 3 to 5 days working with experienced teachers. This meant, then, that at least one week of actual experience in individualized situations was part of the training experience offered all teachers. The demonstration school had established specific kinds of programs which varied depending upon the number of days involved and the sophistication of the teacher being trained.

These experiences from the past year and a half in retraining teachers were indication enough to conclude that, first of all, programs must be developed that practice what they preach. That is, a retraining program for teachers is needed that is individualized about individualization. The second conclusion that has been reached is that teachers when retrained for specifics of the IPI program, tend to overemphasize the mechanics of the system. It is obvious that a conceptual model of individualization must be part of the retraining.

As RBS again considered the expansion of its training facilities, three areas requiring systematic attention were identified:

Area 1. Preservice training and the need to work with schools of education to establish some type of curriculum that can introduce prospective teachers to individualized instruction in the early stages of their preparation.

Area 2. Retraining of existing staff and the need to work with school systems to conduct an in-service program on the individualization of instruction and specifically the system of Individually Prescribed Instruction.

Area 3. Continuous training of staff and the need to prepare administrators in staff development related to individualized instruction and Individually Prescribed Instruction.

Having identified these three major areas of training needs: Preservice, In-service Retraining, and Continuous Training, RBS was able to use its past experiences to describe the kind of training programs needed to answer these needs.

The staff of RBS has initiated specific projects in each of the three areas. The following discussion is a summation of these projects and events in each area.

The first area is Preservice Training. It is obvious that prior to the student teaching experience, prospective teachers need to have much more information about the importance of individualizing instruction and some experience with specific projects that purport to individualize instruction.

A seminar on preservice teacher training was held by Research for Better Schools on February 26 and 27, 1967. All of the 104 colleges and universities in Pennsylvania, New Jersey and Delaware which are involved in teacher training were invited to send two representatives. The final participants of the conference represented 52 of these institutions.

The focus of the seminar was to provide information concerning the national emphasis on individualized instruction and to discuss the implications of this for teacher training. Underlying these concerns were the questions of how those responsible for training teachers feel about individualizing instruction and what they see as the goals for education.

In order to provide a common experience in individualization, all participants were invited to visit McAnnulty Elementary School, the IPI demonstration school in Baldwin-Whitehall, Pennsylvania. The experience at McAnnulty illustrated one means of individualizing instruction and, hopefully, provided a stimulus for looking at individualized instruction in any setting.

The keynote address was given by Dr. Glen Heathers. He presented an eight-step model of individualization and an overview of relevant programs throughout the country. From his speech, it was apparent that there is a strong interest in individualization prevalent today, but simultaneously, it was realized that there is a gap between what is being said and what is being done.

Small group discussion sessions on February 27 had the general purpose of reviewing the groups' experiences at McAnnulty, examining individualized instruction as a system, and discussing what it implied for teacher training. The participants also shared information about current practices at their institutions in terms of training teachers for individualization. During this conference, representatives from the schools of education addressed themselves to the implications for teacher training and listed some 20 appropriate strategies that could be used by teacher training institutions, not necessarily being used, however. The conference also concluded that more research was needed about the effect of individualized programs to convince colleges of the need to update their programs.

Following this conference, Research for Better Schools was approached by the East Stroudsburg State Teachers College about the possibility of establishing a course for college juniors about individualization. Their specific request was twofold. (1) They wanted to introduce the Individually Prescribed Instruction program into their laboratory school and (2) they wanted to introduce a course for juniors about individualization and IPI, prior to their student teaching experience. This effort was welcomed by RBS and we cooperated in both endeavors. A one-semester course based on the theory of individualization and the specifics of the IPI math program was developed. The second group of students are now half-way through the course. At the end of this semester, the plan will be revised and expanded as it was at the end of the first semester.

Area two, Retraining of Teachers has received more attention from RBS. RBS has concentrated its efforts in teacher education on developing a teacher-training program that will (1) enable the school to conduct its own training program; (2) enable the teachers to conceptualize a model of individualized instruction as a basis for instructional decision making in IPI; and (3) enable the teachers to plan and conduct IPI in their classroom.

The training program is being constructed upon the model of Individually Prescribed Instruction and contains five specific packages each consisting of behavioral objectives, pre- and post-tests of the objectives, self-instructional materials and equipment and recommended learning settings. Each package provides four types of activities. They include: concept-building related to individualized instruction; analysis and application of the concepts to IPI; practice in using IPI skills and materials as routine exercises; working through the math continuum and assuming the role of teacher, aide, and student as needed; discussion designed to provide opportunity for clarification and expression of reactions, to develop and use skills for planning sessions to cover suggested topics, questions or case studies. The five packages of training materials are concerned with (1) The Theory of Individualization and the Pretest IPI Mathematics Program, (2) The Theory of Behavioral Objectives and the IPI Mathematics Program, (3) Diagnosis of Learning, (4) Prescription Writing and (5) Planning for Individualized Instruction including analysis of data. The selection of these areas was based on past experience of needs of teachers to retrain them for Individually Prescribed Instruction.

The training program has been given a preliminary field test during the months of October, November and December in two New Jersey schools that were preparing to install IPI in January. Revisions and refinement of the program have taken place. A second testing will take place this summer in 100 schools.

The five packages that have been prepared for the retraining of teachers have several general principles under which they operate. The first one is development of the specific packages of material to permit the individualization of the training program for teachers so we can, for once in our lives, practice what we preach. Secondly, the materials have been developed in such a way that they can be carried by the U.S. mail and that, hopefully, with some help, administrators can lead their faculties through these particular packages. Also, it was very important to introduce each of the packages with a theoretical base and move from that theory to its specific application in the IPI program. However, during the first field testing of packages, the teachers resisted this latter approach. They appeared more concerned about the here and now, the practical application of IPI and how it affects them. Therefore, the later packages have had to blend more closely the theory and the practice. Said in another way, RBS' initial efforts and initial thinking was to build all of the packages with some foundation, some basis in theory, and then move this to the specifics that are involved in the IPI math program. At this point, some of this thinking has changed, because of the needs and the demands of the teachers.

To gather data about the packages of materials being used for the retraining, specific instruments and techniques have been prepared. Information is being gathered about (1) the implementation of the program and (2) outcomes from the program. One instrument is used by the teachers to report their reactions to the training procedures and materials. The trainer uses two instruments. One to report the procedures used to conduct the sessions, and another to summarize and evaluate each session. In addition, all sessions are taped for further analysis. Since all packages contain pre-tests and post-tests, outcome data are gathered by running item analyses on these tests. Finally, all RBS staff members who are concerned with IPI work through the packages and critique the contents.

The successful development of packages of materials to retrain teachers, hopefully, will put Research for Better Schools out of the institute business and shift the responsibility for retraining local staff to local administration and college resources. However, it should be pointed out that before successful implementation of a retraining program can be carried out by local administrators, some very precise information must be prepared and developed for his retraining. This is also an area of current concern.

The third area of teacher training labeled as Continuous Training is based upon the premise that this innovation can only be successful if strategies are developed to keep the teachers abreast of what is happening and to refine their skills about individualized instruction. Research for Better Schools has established a team of monitors. Each monitor works with a specific school that is involved in IPI and systematically gathers data about the teachers and the patterns they use in diagnosis and prescription writing, and the students and their performance in the program. These data are gathered on a weekly basis, generally taken from prescriptions that are written for each youngster by each teacher. The information is being used to develop strategies for the administrator to use in his Planning Sessions with teachers to improve their sophistication and to continue training for a better individualized program. Presently, data is being gathered about each teacher concerning her style in writing prescriptions. Regularly, this information is sent back to each teacher in a "non-judgmental" way. With the help of the administrator, teachers make their own judgment about this feedback of material. Styles do change.

Other dimensions that the monitors are involved in include the self-study of work that is being done by Dr. Daniel Prescott in his child-study program in the Omaha Schools. They are attempting to adapt his ideas to design a set of diagnostic procedures suited to individualized instruction and IPI. This kind of information as it is collected and summarized is then fed back to the local administrator who in turn can take it back to his teachers.

RBS feels that Continuous Training and the specific strategies to make it work, must be part of this program. This opportunity to gather these data and make the suggestions is an excellent one, since information can be collected systematically and specific strategies can be supplied for administrative training and continuous training of staff.

RBS, as a part of its responsibility for providing regional leadership in the area of Continuous Training in IPI and in cooperation with the R.&D. Center, conducted a Conference of Teachers and Administrators using IPI on February 3-5, 1967. During this time, the participants probed deeply into the areas of role definition and training needs as well as the problems and issues involved in the interactions between various IPI roles. Besides contributing to the continuing education of the conference participants, invaluable feedback data on operation of IPI as a system was obtained. A second conference of teachers was held. Again teachers addressed themselves to specific problems and made very specific suggestions. A separate report about both conferences is available.

Briefly then, Research for Better Schools is concerned with the three phases of teacher training: Preservice, Retraining and Continuous Training. Efforts are being made to attack all three areas. A major effort, now underway with the development of packages of materials that can train teachers about individualization, is being field tested in several schools with anticipation of rewriting all the materials and broader field testing the summer of 1968 and next school year.

Part C

**Individualized Learning:
The Present in
the Elementary and
Secondary Schools**

Introduction

The concept of independent study is not new. For over 50 years there have been schools which have employed the concept as a regular part of the instructional program. There was a marked surge of interest in "upgrading" the schools during the early forties, but it was not until the early sixties that the practice really caught hold. In large measure this was due to the writing and speaking efforts of John Goodlad and Robert Anderson, both of whom were concerned directly with elementary school programs. As evidenced by their respective chapters in the 1962 yearbook of the National Society for the Study of Education, entitled *Individualizing Instruction*, they described nongraded education as a system of organization applied to curriculum and instruction to facilitate continuous student progress without reference to "assumed" grade-level standards.

In 1962, Goodlad estimated that there were close to 1,000 nongraded schools in existence in the United States. It is a certainty that this number has greatly increased since then. Unfortunately, no count would be very realistic because of the difficulty in matching the label with actual programs. There have evolved a number of educational practices which have the *effect* of nongrading but are labeled quite differently. Chief among these are the Continuous Progress Plan, the LAP (Learning Activity Package), the UNIPAC Program, the Unit Study Plan, the Learning Contract Method, and so on.

While there are differences in what these program labels stand for it is more useful to consider what they have in common, namely:

1. A reorganization of the curriculum into smaller units of study, often prepackaged according to topic and level of difficulty.

2. A greater mobility of the individual child through different kinds of settings for learning, e.g., variations in grouping and in supervision received.

3. A greater dependence on instructional media, remote resources, and learning centers all readily accessible to facilitate independent study.

4. An attempt to evaluate student readiness more personally and to suggest learning experiences which are thought to be individually relevant to each learner.

5. A shift in the role of teacher away from being the information source and toward the role of designer of "appropriate" learning tasks.

In Chapter 13, R. H. Ringis describes the I/D/E/A (Institute for the Development of Educational Activities) curriculum bank for instructional materials. These materials, teacher-developed lessons called UNIPACS, are intended to facilitate the introduction of individualized learning into group-process oriented schools. The I/D/E/A program is a national project, funded by the Kettering Foundation.

Next, in Chapter 14, Philip Kapfer describes a strategy for self-paced learning developed at Valley High School, in Las Vegas. In his paper, Kapfer emphasizes the relationship between subject matter, instructional objectives, learning materials and activities, self-tests, and "quests", i.e., student initiated problem confrontation and resolution.

Fountain Valley, California, described in Chapter 15 by E. M. Brick, its superintendent, is a school district that has not only incorporated the nongraded approach into its curriculum but has pursued an active construction program to ensure that school buildings facilitate rather than impede the independent learner. Included in the chapter are illustrations of how the learning center concept is reflected in various floor plans in the district's schools.

A school that has utilized Learning Activity Packages—(LAPS) as a basis for individualizing the curriculum is Nova, an innovative school located at Fort Lauderdale, Florida. Its program is described in Chapter 16 by Jan McNeil and James Smith.

This is followed with an example of a LAP, in Chapter 17. This LAP, developed by A. V. Rapp at Nova, concerns micro-techniques. An examination of the LAP makes clear that it consists of objectives, guided learning activities, content-centered instructional material, self-tests, and illustrations. There is also a built-in provision which allows students to "challenge" the LAP by taking the self-test immediately, if they feel they already have mastery of the objectives.

While the development of Learning Activity Packages or UNIPACS represents a valuable resource for educators in a school that adopts a nongraded or continuous progress plan, it is also true that teachers in traditional school programs can innovate in their classrooms by experimenting with "modules" of instructional material which they have developed. This exploration of new instructional methods is best implemented with caution, so that informal trial and refinement of the instructional module takes place over several semesters of classes. Without the help of control groups or other empirical methods there can be little certainty about the learning effects that such a single teacher is able to bring about in an otherwise formal school program, though there may be considerable student enthusiasm generated. In Chapter 18, James Hargis has given an example of a learning exercise which he developed to provide independent study opportunities for students in his electronics class. Efforts such as his often establish the initial leadership which encourages others in the school to follow suit.

In Chapter 19, Ernestine McDonough and Maurice Blum tell how a school has reorganized to provide more attention to the individual. The key to the approach at Meadowbrook Junior High School is the Unit Plan. Essentially, this is an organizational way of introducing independent study, based on restructuring of the class to allow a more flexible pattern of teacher-student interaction. In part, this flexibility is dependent on the availability of a learning resource center and a variety of learning materials.

Learning resources can be accessed by students who go to a center and directly obtain needed materials but a number of schools are using modern technology to facilitate access from remote study locations. In many cases dial access systems are used and both audio and video materials can be "called up" from study carrels situated throughout the school plant. In Chapter 20, H. Eugene Hollick describes an individualized school program which relies heavily on dial access retrieval of curriculum materials and which enjoys a high degree of student approval of the new approach.

In relatively few schools is the self-direction of learners carried as far as it is at Wilson School, at Mankato, Minnesota. This experimental school is operational with self-selected student-planned curricula, optional attendance in courses, self-selected holidays, elimination of all K-12 course requirements, and a great many other student freedoms. Chapter 21 is a description of the activities at Wilson School, reported by Don Glines, its Director.

One of the special problems in meeting individual needs is simply the identification and description of those needs in terms relevant to learning. Personalization of learning is not only dependent on diagnosis of initial learning needs but it presumes that the diagnostic process *continues* as the learner progresses from one level of attainment to another. In Chapter 22, Phyllis Green describes the rationale and test procedures which have been developed as a part of the Project for Intensification of the Learning Process, an undertaking of the Bucks County Public Schools, Pennsylvania. Another part of the chapter illustrates a Pupil Description Worksheet, an Individual

Student Profile, and an initial Personalized Educational Prescription (PEP) as developed by the project staff.

Another critical consideration in the school that moves toward individualization is that of the changed teacher's role. An analysis of these new teacher roles, based on high school requirements, is provided by Gary Lonnon and Richard Bodine in Chapter 23.

In Chapter 24, Cleone Geddes and Beverly Kooi describe an Instructional Management System (IMS) which depends on the computer to monitor the progress of pupils, to make decisions on the pace of instruction and the sequence of lessons, and to decide whether instruction should be individualized or conducted in the group mode. The IMS approach is intended to facilitate gradual change from the group process to the individualized process by providing specialized assistance to the teacher, especially in the area of diagnosing learners' needs on a current basis. The system is in an evolutionary state, and will require more development in the number and variety of instructional resources available for remediation as well as further teacher training in proper use of the system.

Lastly, when a new program has been brought into a school or school district there is a responsibility to make objective appraisals of the educational benefits brought about by the changes. In Chapter 25, J. D. Prince reports from the field, writing as a user of computer technology to individualize parts of the "on-line" instructional program. In a school district in McComb, Mississippi, experimental comparisons were made between the computerized and noncomputerized teaching of mathematics skills. The comparisons were made on a (1) group to group, (2) teacher to teacher, and (3) school to school basis. By way of results, the findings were sufficiently encouraging that Superintendent Prince now seeks to expand the use of computers for drill-and-practice, providing this can be accomplished on economic terms. A proposed future modification of the computer system is included in his paper.

THE "BANK" CONCEPT:
A WAY TO FACILITATE
INDIVIDUALIZED INSTRUCTION

R. Herbert Ringis

It has been well over a decade since the first major changes in education were instituted in the name of individualized instruction. Why hasn't individualized instruction caught on? What has been the major stumbling block to tailoring instruction to more closely meet the needs of individuals? Embodied in the answer to the second question is, of course, the answer to the first. The keystone to complete the arch, which began with flexible scheduling and Lloyd Trump's staff utilization project, is probably the availability of materials designed specifically for the individual.

It was just such questions as these that prompted the Institute for the Development of Educational Activities, a project of the Charles F. Kettering Foundation, to support a convocation of teachers and administrators from

SOURCE: Reprinted from *The "Bank" Concept: A Way to Facilitate Individualized Instruction,* Mimeographed paper, Anaheim, Calif.: I/D/E/A UNIPAC Bank, March, 1969, pp. 11, by permission of the author.

all over the nation. This convocation was held in May, 1966, in Garden Grove, California. Participants were drawn from most of the "innovative" schools across the country. When these educators were asked the key question, "What has been the major stumbling block to tailoring instruction to meet the needs of the individual?", they responded almost universally by identifying the critical need was for individualized materials. From this conference came general agreement that you needed to have flexibility in five basic areas in order to produce an environment conducive to individual instruction; flexibility of time, staff, facilities, evaluation, and materials.

There had been attempts at meeting the time need for individuals going back to the mid-fifties with various attempts at flexible scheduling. There had been additional attempts at organizing professional staffs to meet the needs of individuals as expressed through the staff utilization study of Dr. Lloyd Trump at Ridgewood and at other locations. Certainly, school architects had been attempting to build flexibility into school plants even longer than that. Experimentation in types of evaluation instruments more closely allied to assessing individual progress had been attempted in various locations. The fifth major area that had undergone little exploration was that of materials designed for individual use.

Several schools had begun the major task of developing, collecting, and using materials designed for individuals, but as there are an infinite number of individuals, the task was truly overwhelming. When this factor was presented to I/D/E/A and the Kettering Foundation, together with a proposal that a center be established for the collection and reproduction of these kinds of materials, the challenge was picked up and supported by the Foundation. Under the auspices of Mr. Edwin Vause, Executive Vice-President of the Charles F. Kettering Foundation, the Materials Dissemination Center of I/D/E/A became a reality in the fall of 1966.

The major goal of the Materials Center was to facilitate the development and dissemination of materials suitable for supporting individualized instructional programs. Mr. Gardner Swenson, formerly Principal of Brookhurst Junior High School in Anaheim, California, was chosen as Director of the Materials Center. Mr. Swenson had been long associated with attempts at individualizing instruction and is the originator of the Daily Demand Flexible Schedule. By early 1967, the goal for the Materials Center had been clearly defined. What remained ahead was to determine the best way to meet the challenge of attaining that goal. Several major questions needed answers. What should the design be of materials tailored for the individual? What are the necessary ingredients to these materials? What structure and format could best be devised to assist the exchange of these kinds of materials between teachers? What procedures could be devised for best assisting teachers in the development of materials for individualized instruction? In addition to these operational questions, there were three basic assumptions that needed testing.

1. Could teachers produce materials suitable for use by individuals?

2. Could youngsters learn from self-directed individualized materials?

3. Could one teacher employ materials developed by another teacher?

During 1967 and early 1968, many of the operational questions were answered through a series of workshops conducted under the sponsorship of the Materials Center of I/D/E/A. Preceding and concurrent with these workshops, a search was conducted for the best model to follow in developing these materials. Paramount in consideration was the desire to involve experts from the practitioners' level; that is, those who had been foremost in the experimental programs leading to individualized instructional materials. The model that eventually developed draws its tap roots from much of the work done by Benjamin Bloom, Hilda Taba, John Goodlad, and others. It also draws much of its strength from the philosophies expressed by Dr. Lloyd Trump and Eugene Howard. Initial design credit, however, must go to Dr. Glen Ovard, Coordinator, Educational Experimental Programs, Brigham Young University and Dr. Philip Kapfer, Director of Research, (Ruby Thomas Elementary School), Clark County Schools, Clark County, Nevada.

As the Materials Dissemination Center took form, it established a basic philosophy from which it has not varied in the subsequent months. The central theme was to establish the Center as a "Curriculum Bank" whereby those who contributed materials to the Center would in turn be eligible to withdraw similar materials. It was felt that if these instructional materials were to facilitate individualized instruction, they should be readily available to those participants who were attempting to implement an individualized instructional program. The initial collection of materials into the "bank" began in mid-1967 and continued until July of 1968 at which time the "Curriculum Bank" began distribution of the materials collected. The developmental period of 1967 and early 1968 answered the first basic assumption to be tested: Yes, teachers could produce materials designed for individualized instruction. The second assumption as to whether youngsters could learn from this material was still to be explored.

During the summer of 1968, a pilot program was conducted in Carmel, California, co-sponsored by the I/D/E/A Materials Center and the Carmel Valley Unified School District, using a portion of the Materials Center's collection. Using a summer school program of an experimental nature, approximately 450 elementary youngsters participated in a voluntary program employing these materials as the major instructional device. The results of this pilot program answered in the affirmative the second assumption. Indeed, youngsters could learn by the employment of this kind of material as their major instructional device.

From the experience gained in the previously mentioned workshops and this pilot program, the model for these materials has undergone careful revision. As the model underwent refinement, it became apparent that "new" terminology had to be devised to avoid preconceived notions associated with currently used materials that were designed for class-paced instruction. As this "model" evolved, the materials fell somewhere between what most educators thought of as a "resource unit" and that which was considered a "package" of materials. In fact, because the materials under development were a "new breed of cat," the terminology of UNIPAC eventually evolved, the term UNIPAC being developed as a reference to something other than a "unit" but yet something other than a "package."

At the present time the Materials Center has approximately 1,500 UNIPACS in the collection. These 1,500 UNIPACS represent various stages of development from the preceding 18 months. One of the prime considerations that is central to the philosophy of the Materials Center is that these materials should be viable; they should reflect the experiences gained as these materials are developed and used. The materials received today are far better examples than those formerly admitted into the collection. And certainly, and hopefully, the materials admitted 18 months from now will be an improvement over what is developing at the present time. The current rate of dissemination from the Center of approximately 100 UNIPACS per day tends to indicate we are well on the way toward testing the third basic assumption. With each UNIPAC distributed an evaluation-response sheet is included for the prospective user to react to the success of the materials that they employed. Preliminary "feedback" indicated an affirmative answer to the assumption and teachers can use materials developed by other teachers.

To facilitate the distribution of UNIPACS, two systems have been instituted. The first involves the usual "catalog" type of distribution. Presently, the third master list is in the developmental stage utilizing a computer printout of all the available UNIPACS. This will mark the first complete listing of all available UNIPACS in all subject areas for all performance levels. Previous lists have been in the nature of "trial balloons" in order to gain experience as to the best methods to categorize UNIPACS. The second system involves the distribution of UNIPACS using the National Cash Register Company's photochromatic micro-imagery system (PCMI). It is through this microform system that the Materials Center hopes to make available for examination by potential users the actual UNIPAC in total rather than a catalog listing system whereby only limited information is available. The initial output through the PCMI system has consisted of two 4 × 6 microform transparencies containing approximately 200 Mathematics and Science UNIPACS (over 5,000 pages). In the succeeding months transparencies will be produced containing UNIPACS in other areas of the curriculum. It is through NCR's PCMI system that education can take advantage of the advances in technology in order to expedite the effective employment of individualizing instructional materials. Although the PCMI system is not in widespread usage, it offers significant advantages in the quantity of material it is able to store, and certainly in the ease of retrieval. NCR has developed and will soon market the equipment necessary to retrieve, in "hard copy" form, the UNIPACS stored on the transparencies.

Several major school districts in the United States have established regional UNIPAC Centers in cooperation with the Materials Center of I/D/ E/A. These Centers are interim steps necessary to fill the gap while educational practice catches up with the available technology. These regional Centers will also give further backup data regarding the third basic assumption of whether teachers in one area can use these individualized lesson plans developed by other teachers. This assumption, however, may not be fully tested until there is an adequate supply readily available for teachers' immediate access.

The future holds still more unanswered questions, but plans are proceeding to provide some of the answers. In addition to utilizing the computer to store information regarding available UNIPACS, planning is now underway to design a system whereby feedback relative to the merits and/or application of any individual UNIPAC can be stored and retrieved as needed. It may not be too far fetched to think about the possibility of querying the computer as to what UNIPAC has been most successful in meeting the needs of any given youngster. If an eligible member of the "bank" has diagnosed a need, this need, in turn, could be fed into the computer and a listing of UNIPACS found most successful in similar situations could be provided that teacher.

The Materials Center was established in an attempt to assist schools in fulfilling one of the five basic requirements for optimum furtherance of individualized instruction. Certainly, materials are not the sole "road" toward individualized instruction, but for those schools and educators who are making the attempt to move along all fronts leading toward individualized instruction, it does provide one essential ingredient. The UNIPAC alone is not the answer, just as flexible scheduling, team teaching, or "folding walls" are not the answer. But for the school that is attempting to provide time for the individual to work, and evaluation for the individual, the UNIPAC may fill that need for materials that the individual can use to attain meaningful progress. In the meantime, for those schools that have not made a beginning in one or any of the five areas, the UNIPAC may provide the starting point, and even within a traditional setting, could better meet the needs of an individual youngster than the present-day class-paced materials.

UNIPAC DATA SHEET   March 25, 1969

To: Teachers and administrators concerned about teacher prepared self-instructive curriculum materials.

From: The I/D/E/A UNIPAC Bank
                    730 North Euclid Street/Suite 304
                    Anaheim, California   92801
                    (714) 776-9930

SUBJECT: UNIPAC WORKSHOPS THAT WILL PROVIDE
                    OPPORTUNITIES FOR TEACHERS TO WRITE SELF-
                    INSTRUCTIVE CURRICULUM MATERIALS.

Levels: Kindergarten, primary, elementary, junior high, high
                    school, special education, and in-service for adults.

Content: Art, Business Education, Counseling, Driver Education,
                    Foreign Language, Home Economics, Industrial Arts,
                    Language Arts, Library Science, Mathematics, Music,
                    Science, Social Science, and In-Service.

Duration: Motivational Workshop — 1 day minimum
                    Production Workshop — 3 days
                    Evaluation Workshop — 1 day

Pre-Planning: Decision on workshop program at least 3 weeks before
                    workshop and materials for teachers, 2 weeks before
                    workshop.

Participants: 20 minimum and 160 maximum

UNIPACs: 1,700 UNIPACs in the Bank available to "bank"
                    members.

Users: 2,300 teachers in 46 states, Canada, and Mexico use
                    UNIPACs and represent contact with approximately
                    70,000 learners.

Universities: 15 teacher-training institutes require future teachers to
                    produce UNIPACs.

Distribution: 5,000 UNIPACs distributed to 222 individual schools
                    in 25 states during the past 6 months.

Cost: 9 different sources of financial support have worked
                    with the Materials Center in sponsoring and financing
                    workshops for teachers; i.e., Title III, N.S.F., University
                    Course Fees, and In-Service Funds.

Inquiries: 2,000 requests for UNIPAC materials received and
                    processed by the Center.

CHARACTERISTICS OF A SUCCESSFUL *UNIPAC* PRODUCTION WORKSHOP

There are effective ways to organize and to conduct UNIPAC Production
Workshops. The following criteria have been identified from experience in
organizing and conducting over 200 successful workshops:

  I.   Instructional materials and written guidelines are distributed
       to participants for study at least two weeks prior to the first
       session of the workshop.

 II.   The workshop facilities contain spaces for large group
       presentations, small group meetings, and resource centers
       containing a library, resource material, audio-visual aids, and
       listening center facilities.

III.   The participants are selected on the basis of the following
       criteria:

       A. The participants recognize a need for curriculum
       materials that will facilitate an individualized instructional
       program in the classroom.

       B. The participants have the potential and desire to write a
       UNIPAC.

       C. The participants are granted released time from
       instruction and other classroom responsibilities during the
       workshop sessions.

       D. The participants are able to make decisions regarding
       the selection of appropriate learning activities and time
       available during the workshop.

       E. The participants are emotionally and intellectually
       prepared to work with other participants on a common
       UNIPAC if they so desire.

 IV.   The number of meetings and the length of the workshop
       sessions are based upon the need to effectively present each
       ingredient of the UNIPAC. In addition, the schedule of the
       workshop allows for independent consultation between the
       participant and the consultant as well as time for independent
       study. Usually, six sessions, four hours in length, with a week
       between sessions has been found to be very effective in
       meeting the objectives of the workshop.

V.   The most effective participant ratio is less than 20 participants to one consultant.

VI.   Depending upon local factors, the cost per consultant, including expenses and fees, varies between $200 or $300 per workshop day.

VII. Nationally-known consultants with expertise in one or more of the UNIPAC ingredients are selected. In addition, they are recognized as having the ability to relate to participants of the workshop.

VIII. Consultants provide an environment at the workshop sessions that facilitates individualized UNIPAC production.

IX.   The format of the workshop provides for constant and timely evaluation of both the participant product and the effectiveness of the workshop for the participants.

X.   The workshop structure provides time for field testing of the UNIPAC and acceptance by the Materials Center Bank.

Chapter 14. THE LEARNING PACKAGE IN THE HIGH SCHOOL

AN INSTRUCTIONAL MANAGEMENT STRATEGY FOR INDIVIDUALIZED LEARNING

Philip G. Kapfer

A frequent goal of the administrator is to integrate the essential components of instruction—the teacher, the learner, and that which is to be learned. The problem of integrating these components for the purpose of individualizing instruction is the central concern of this paper.

An instructional management strategy developed at Valley High School, Las Vegas, Nevada, is potentially effective for any school whose staff is attempting to individualize instruction, regardless of the type of schedule being used. To be genuinely effective in the school for which it was designed, however, the strategy was developed within the context of the four phases of instruction which have been advocated by innovators such as Bush, Allen, and Trump. These phases include large-group instruction, small-group instruction, laboratory instruction, and independent study.

SOURCE: Reprinted from *Phi Delta Kappan*, Vol. 49, No. 5 (January, 1968), pp. 260-63, by permission of author and publisher.

Educators should cease to be concerned primarily with the technical problems of team teaching and flexible scheduling. Rather, they should get to the heart of the matter—the opportunities to individualize instruction *provided by* these innovations. The reader may or may not feel that the technical problems of team teaching and flexible scheduling have been solved; yet progress has certainly been made toward their solution. Agreement can be reached, however, that the problems of individualizing instruction have *not* been solved.

One key to providing for individualized instruction is the preparation of individualized learning units or packages. Such learning packages are the major elements of the instructional management strategy proposed here, and will be discussed following presentation of the strategy.

ASSUMPTIONS

If a strategy for individualizing instruction is to be effective, it should begin with the currently existing program as perceived by teachers and pupils. In devising the strategy used at Valley High School, several assumptions were made concerning the perceptions of teachers and pupils, and concerning the schedule.

The first assumption, that *the pupil's responsibility is to learn and the teacher's responsibility is to make available to the pupil that which is to be learned,* places responsibility for the teaching-learning process where it belongs. The teacher does not cover a course, but rather uncovers it; he does not need to cover—or talk about—everything that is to be learned by the pupil.

A second assumption concerns the individuality of the pupil. *The subject matter of a course must be appropriate to the learner* with reference to 1) the pace of instruction, 2) the level of difficulty of the instructional material, 3) the relevance of the instructional material to reality as perceived by the pupil, 4) the pupil's level of interest, and 5) the individual learning style of the pupil.

Both the common and the individualized experiences of the pupil result from a third assumption which is related to the schedule: *The size of a group, the composition of a group, and the time allotted to a group should be appropriate to the purposes of the group.* The common experiences which every pupil in a given course should have are primarily a function of large-group instruction. Pupil-centered discussion of large-group presentations may occur in scheduled small-group instruction. Individualized, self-paced, quantity- and quality-monitored learning (that is, the use of learning packages with built-in self-correcting mechanisms) may occur in the laboratory phase of the course. In addition, the laboratory phase should include opportunities for student interaction and should provide directly for the independent study phase of the individualized instructional program.

A fourth assumption of the instructional management strategy is that *before truly individualized instruction can become a reality, learning packages are needed which will provide for self-paced rather than group-paced instruction.*

THE STRATEGY

The instructional management strategy is based on, but does not adhere strictly to, the principles of Program Evaluation and Review Techniques (PERT). In a PERT network diagram, an *activity* is a time-consuming element of a project which is represented on a network as a line between two *events*.

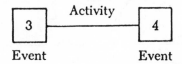

An event is a specific, definable accomplishment in the project plan, which is recognizable as a particular point in time when activities start and/or finish. An activity cannot be started until the event preceding it has been accomplished. A succeeding event cannot be accomplished until all activities preceding it are complete.[1]

The strategy is presented as a network diagram in Figure 14-1. The network is designed to show a sequence in which the pupil will attain an adequate *background* so that he is able to perceive problems and ask questions. The result of his questioning will be internal generation of a problematic *confrontation*. Through study and research the pupil will achieve *resolution* of the problem which he chose for investigation. Thus the sequence in the network is from achievement of *background* to problem *confrontation* to problem *resolution*.

Recycling, for some pupils and for some instructional objectives, may occur at various stages as indicated by arrows in the network. Thus, although the instructional management strategy may be thought of as a design for concept attainment through discovery or problem solving, it is not restricted to this interpretation. In the discovery interpretation of the strategy, the pupil might not be given a statement of the concept under study; rather, he would discover it for himself. In the presentation interpretation, a statement of the concept may be given to the pupil at the beginning of the learning package. In either case, the activities and events *following* Event 3 (see Figure 14-1) represent an inquiry approach. The activities surrounding Events 4 and 5, those involving minor and major quest, give the pupil the

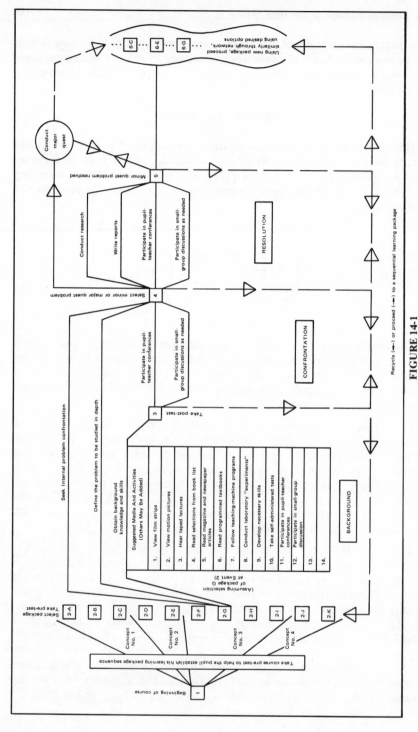

FIGURE 14-1

THE INSTRUCTIONAL MANAGEMENT STRATEGY NETWORK; DIAGRAM FOR SELF-PACED LEARNING

opportunity to become a researcher, and in the process of resolving problems the pupil learns information-seeking techniques. When the decision is made to proceed to a sequential learning package, options similar to those just outlined are available to the pupil.

PREPARING LEARNING PACKAGES

Learning packages usually include the following eight ingredients for individualizing instruction:

1.   *Concepts* are abstractions which organize the world of objects, events, processes, structures, or qualities into a smaller number of categories.

2.   *Instructional objectives* tell the pupil what he will have to be able to do when he is evaluated, the important conditions under which he will have to perform, and the lower limit or quality of performance expected of him.[2]

3.   *Multi-dimensional learning materials* of varying difficulty are cited from commercial sources, whenever possible, and include a variety of media which require use of as many different senses as possible.

4.   *Diversified learning activities* provide alternative approaches for achieving the instructional objectives, and include such activities as large group and small group instruction, field trips, model building, drama productions, games, laboratory experiments, role playing, pupil-teacher conferences, reflective thinking, and the like.

5.   *Pre-evaluation* is designed to assess the extent to which the pupil has already achieved the instructional objectives as a result of his earlier learning experiences. Pre-evaluation enables the pupil to invest his time wisely in areas in which he is weak.

6.   *Self-evaluation* is designed to assist the pupil in determining his own progress toward achieving the instructional objectives. Self-evaluation, the results of which indicate the pupil's readiness for post-evaluation, occurs after the pupil has used the multi-dimensional learning materials and participated in diversified learning activities.

7.   *Post-evaluation* is designed to assess the extent to which the pupil has achieved the instructional objectives as a result of his learning experiences.

8.   *Quest* includes problem confrontation, delimitation, research, and resolution. Quest is a pupil-initiated and self-directed learning activity.

Integration of the above eight curricular elements in the form of learning packages can serve as an important advancement in providing for self-paced learning through individualized instruction. An experimental course, *Human Relations—an Interdisciplinary Study,* which is currently under way at Valley High School, is based on the instructional management strategy. One of the learning packages developed for the course is reproduced below in the form in which it is available to students. Only the pre- and post-tests have been omitted here due to space limitations.

LEARNING PACKAGE TOPIC: STEREOTYPING[3]

I. CONCEPT STATEMENT

Stereotyping is a learned behavior which results in loss of individuality for members of a stereotyped group or institution.

II. INSTRUCTIONAL OBJECTIVES

A.   From his own experiences, the student will be able to define the term "stereotype" and give at least five examples of stereotyping. He will be able to explain how such thinking restricts his effectiveness in human relationships.

B.   Given six general headings and related terms, the student will write the response which he freely associates with each term. By looking at himself or at someone he knows, he then will be able to explain the degree of validity of his free association responses.

1. Physical appearance
   a. red hair
   b. blonde
   c. blue-eyed
   d. fat
   e. tall and dark

2. Geographical location
   a. Southerners
   b. Las Vegans
   c. New Englanders
   d. San Franciscans
   e. Westerners

3. Occupation
   a. doctors
   b. lawyers
   c. truck drivers
   d. musicians
   e. school teachers

4. Age
   a. teen-agers
   b. over 30
   c. over 65

      d. Old Shep
      e. kindergarten

   5. Socioeconomic level
      a. hicks
      b. snobs
      c. happy
      d. unhappy

   6. Racial, religious, and ethnic groups
      a. Pollacks
      b. Mormons
      c. Irish

III. LEARNING MATERIALS AND ACTIVITIES[4]

A. Scan—current news media.

B. View—"Common Fallacies About Group Differences," 15-minute 16 mm. film, McGraw-Hill.

C. View—"High Wall," 32-minute 16 mm. film, McGraw-Hill.

D. View—"None So Blind," color filmstrip with sound, Anti-Defamation League of B'nai B'rith.

E. Read—Robert P. Heilbroner, "Don't Let Stereotypes Warp Your Judgment," Anti-Defamation League of B'nai B'rith (pamphlet).

F. Read—Raymond W. Mack and Troy S. Duster, "Patterns of Minority Relations," Anti-Defamation League of B'nai B'rith (pamphlet).

G. Read—Earl Raab and Seymour Lipset, "Prejudice and Society," Anti-Defamation League of B'nai B'rith (pamphlet).

H. Read—William Van Til, "Prejudiced—How Do People Get That Way?" Anti-Defamation League of B'nai B'rith (pamphlet).

I. Read—Howard J. Ehrlich (ed.), *Theory Into Practice,* special edition, available from Anti-Defamation League of B'nai B'rith.

J. Read—William Peters, "Why Did They Do It?" *Good Housekeeping,* June, 1962.

K. Read—G. M. Morant, *The Significance of Racial Differences.* Paris, France: UNESCO, 1958, 47 pp.

L. Read—Arnold Rose, *The Roots of Prejudice*. Paris, France: UNESCO, 1958, 35 pp.

M. Read—David Westheimer, *My Sweet Charlie*. Garden City, N.Y.: Doubleday, 1965, 255 pp.

IV. SELF-TEST

A. Define "stereotype" and give at least five examples of stereotyping. Explain how the thinking represented in each of your examples restricts one's effectiveness in human relations.

B. List your free response to each of the following terms: blond, teacher, teen-ager, parent, Mexican, truck driver, farmer, fat, red. Are your responses accurate? Explain.

V. SELF-TEST KEY

Answers on the self-test will vary. After checking your performance with the objectives and discussing your answers with other students, if you still are in doubt about acceptability you should discuss the answers with one of your instructors.

VI. QUEST SUGGESTION

Select a common stereotype and describe the process of generalization by which this stereotype might have developed. Can you find any evidence to support or refute your description?

SUMMARY

The instructional management strategy is designed to assist teachers in establishing stepwise procedures for achieving individualized instruction. The important elements in the strategy are learning packages designed for use by individual pupils. Identification of the important concepts and instructional objectives which are to be taught by means of these packages will permit the establishment of hierarchical schemes around which the curriculum may be organized, K-12 and even higher. The packages may take many forms, but a common characteristic of each is the provision for self-pacing. As a result, the pupil is enabled to progress at his own best rate, thus avoiding the familiar difficulties of group-paced instruction.

NOTES

[1] *PERT Time Fundamentals* (Las Vegas, Nev.: Edgerton, Germeshausen & Grier, Inc., undated), p. 3.

[2] Robert F. Mager, *Preparing Instructional Objectives* (Palo Alto, Calif.: Fearon Publishers, Inc., 1962), p. 52.

[3]Charles A. Silvestri and Kathleen Harrell, *Human Relations—An Interdisciplinary Study* (Las Vegas, Nev.: Valley High School, 1967), unpaged.

[4]The student selects from the suggested learning materials and activities those which he needs in order to achieve the instructional objectives. He is neither restricted to these suggestions nor expected to use all of them.

Chapter 15. **THE LEARNING
ENVIRONMENT—
A SCHOOL DISTRICT**

LEARNING CENTERS: THE KEY TO
PERSONALIZED INSTRUCTION

E. Michael Brick

> *... It is in fact nothing short of a miracle that the
> modern methods of instruction have not yet entirely
> strangled the holy curiosity of inquiry; for this
> delicate little plant, aside from stimulation, stands
> mainly in need of freedom; without this it goes
> to wrack and ruin without fail.*

ALBERT EINSTEIN

The greatest problem facing educators today is one of preparing children
for a world that will exist in an entirely different form when they are

SOURCE: Reprinted from *Audiovisual Instruction*, Vol. 12, No. 8 (1967), pp. 786-92, by
permission of author and publisher.

responsible adults. Even though the last few years have been a time of educational research, reforms that might be expected have as yet only touched a small portion of our schools.

It is becoming conspicuous to practitioners, as well as observers, that our *electronic technology* is precluding the status quo in education. And yet, with the exception of the lighthouse districts across the nation, the facilities, teaching methodology, and content of instruction continue to resemble the classroom of decades ago. By comparison, stable business organizations have moved rapidly into the realm of putting theory into practice.

Perhaps the first casualty to the traditional theories and methods is the concept of teacher-centered instruction. An identifiable trend to shift from the *teaching* act to the *learning* processes is emerging in school districts that are attempting to personalize the instructional program. As a point of reference, the Aborigines have managed to exist for more than 20,000 years in a desolate environment. Anthropologists claim that their secret to survival has been teaching. They pass on to the young every shred of knowledge about how to find their way in a trackless desert. Such knowledge is conveyed to the young as being the way to behave, and any innovation is frowned upon.

The teaching process has provided the Aborigines with a way to survive in a hostile and relatively unchanging environment. Teaching and the imparting of knowledge make sense in an unchanging environment, but our society lives in an environment which is *continually changing*. We know that knowledge imparted in the area of physics will be outdated in a decade; that the so-called "facts of history" depend largely upon the current mood and temper of the culture; and that chemistry, biology, genetics, and sociology are in such flux that a firm statement might become outmoded by the time the knowledge is ready to be used.

The significance of this analogy is that education is faced with a new goal of *facilitating change and learning*. It is conceivable that the majority of our citizenry would accept the concept that the only man who is educated is the man who has *learned how to learn;* the man who has learned how to adapt to change; the man who realizes that only the process of *seeking* knowledge gives a basis for security.

Do we as educators know how to achieve this goal of *facilitating learning* in education, or is it a will-of-the-wisp which sometimes occurs, sometimes fails to occur, and as such offers little real hope.?

FOUNTAIN VALLEY SCHOOL DISTRICT POINT OF VIEW

The Fountain Valley School District has analyzed solutions for these perplexing problems to keep its program in step with a fast changing world and believes that the following questions must be answered to plan for the future:

Will the program be one that is life-oriented and therefore geared toward the development of problem solving, analysis, inquiry, and decision-making skills?

Is it one in which the student is actively and intimately involved as a participant rather than an observer?

Is it built on a student's successes as an individual rather than on his failure at a rigid norm?

Will it be in step with the requirements of the community and parental awareness of the need for innovation?

One of the innovations that the Board of Trustees and educators have established to resolve the questions presented is the *Learning Center concept*. The Learning Center functions as an *extension* of the regular classroom and operates as a teaching and resource learning center for a cluster of six or eight teachers, depending upon the building design. The educational process in these clusters is personalized through techniques of pupil *placement,* academic *diagnosis, prescription,* and continuous *evaluation.* The prime effort of the program is to integrate the classroom and Learning Center functions to cope with the knowledge explosion; to match students with necessary and appropriate materials, concepts, and people to provide for *individualized instruction.*

CLASSROOM PROGRAM

In order to understand the significance of the Learning Center, it is appropriate to describe the regular classroom program in that the processes involved are integrated.

Working in a nongraded school district, the teacher may be operating with single age level, flexibly grouped, or a multigraded class, but with multilevel books, basal systems, materials, reading labs, science labs, and electronic equipment.

1.   The *class grouping* arrangement allows the teacher to spend more than one year with the children in order to *expand* and *personalize* the instructional program. In the diagnostic process, children can be scheduled into the Learning Center for more individual work.

2.   Such *equipment* as tape recorders with headsets are used as "a second teacher" in the regular classroom to provide skill lessons in phonics or mathematics, spelling or enrichment materials. Tapes are prepared by the teacher for immediate skill needs, prepared by the District Curriculum Materials Center for more general needs, or purchased commercially.

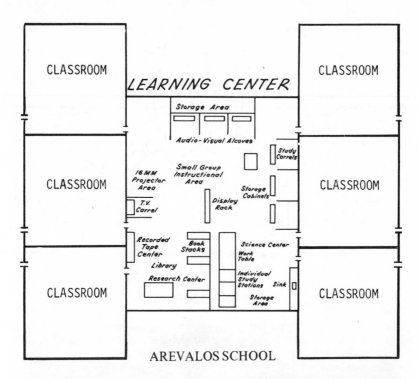

LEARNING CENTER

Storage Area

Audio-Visual Alcoves

16 MM Projector Area

Small Group Instructional Area

Study Carrels

Storage Cabinets

T.V. Corral

Display Rack

Recorded Tape Center

Book Stacks

Science Center

Work Table

Library

Individual Study Stations

Sink

Research Center

Storage Area

CLASSROOM
CLASSROOM
CLASSROOM
CLASSROOM
CLASSROOM
CLASSROOM

AREVALOS SCHOOL

This picture depicts the Learning Coordinator working with a group of children in the science center while the Teacher Aide, on the right-hand side, is checking out books with children from the library in an upper level (6th, 7th, 8th grades) Learning Center. (Arevalos School)

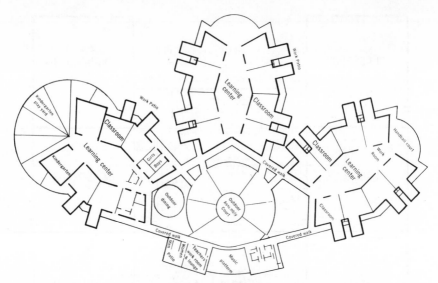

BUSHARD SCHOOL

This picture of a primary-level Learning Center shows the Learning Coordinator working with children from different classrooms in a math lesson. In the background, children are working on a specific phonics lesson with the tape recorder. To the right, children have been released from their classroom to go to the library to check out books independently and on the far right, children are practicing a play that they will be presenting to the rest of the children in the Learning Center at the end of the week. (Bushard School)

Film projectors designed as a self-contained projector and screen unit with headsets allow for additional individualizing of instruction. Students can take a self-selected or teacher-prescribed film or filmstrip to these projectors and view them in the classroom without disturbing the other children.

3. *Pupil-teacher conferences* are conducted during class time for the purpose of identifying academic successes or problems and to prepare a record for individual and small-group assignments or lessons.

These individual conferences permit personal evaluations and interaction for growth. These analyses are then converted into an ongoing profile for each child to continue effective personalized prescriptions.

This process is not only essential for individualization in the regular classroom but is also the foundation for scheduling of students into the Learning Center for individualized skill lessons and learning activities.

4. *Cooperative teaching* provides for additional grouping of children to capitalize on the teacher's strengths for in-depth instruction and encourages cross-fertilization of ideas and social maturation among students.

The Learning Center, because of its size and space arrangement, becomes an ideal location for special groups or classes to gather.

5. *Self-directed* learning activities include individual contracts for work at the student's level, self-selective reading with follow-up and evaluation by the teacher, small-group discussions with summary and evaluation, research, experimentation, creative dramatics, projects, and debate. These types of learning experiences place more responsibility for learning *with the individual student*. The Learning Center is completely integrated with these activities in such a way that many are conducted in the Center itself.

BUILDING PROGRAM

The educational program in Fountain Valley is one that utilizes everything under its control, even the building program, to facilitate the learning process. School buildings as such are not merely protective shelters; they are educational tools designed to provide the flexibility so precious to a diverse and creative instructional program.

The 11 schools in the district, all constructed since 1963, have reorganized the use of space so that six or eight classrooms are clustered about a core room called a Learning Center. The architectural firm of Carmichael-Kemp from Los Angeles has worked with the community, Board of Trustees, and educators in developing this concept to fulfill the instructional needs as indicated by professional staff.

In each building, provisions have been made for movable walls, sliding chalkboards in front of glass windows for control purposes into the Learning Center, vinyl-covered cork walls, movable desks, cabinets, and case work on

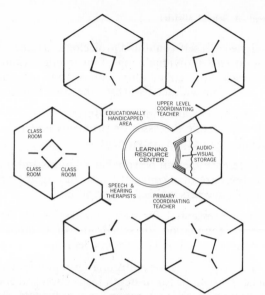

UPPER LEVEL
COORDINATING
TEACHER

EDUCATIONALLY
HANDICAPPED
AREA

CLASS
ROOM

LEARNING
RESOURCE
CENTER

AUDIO-
VISUAL
STORAGE

CLASS
ROOM

CLASS
ROOM

SPEECH &
HEARING
THERAPISTS

PRIMARY
COORDINATING
TEACHER

FULTON SCHOOL

The Learning Coordinator, in the background, is working with middle-level (3rd and 4th grades) children in a perception game. To the left, children are working on an assignment that has been prepared by the Learning Coordinator on tape. In the background, a group of children is viewing a film and another group has a study lesson utilizing the filmstrip. In the foreground, an 8th-grade level child is working in a math game with a group of younger children. (Fulton School)

casters to provide for flexibility in organizing special centers in both the classrooms and the Learning Center.

Learning Center: The Learning Center functions as a resource center for diagnostic materials, electronic teaching devices, tape banks, test banks, science centers, rotating library systems, use and storage of audio-visual equipment, and reference and resource materials.

It also operates as a teaching center supervised by a *Coordinating Teacher* who conducts individual, small-group, and cooperative teaching programs.

The Center is organized so that several activities can continue at once. In one corner of the room ten-year-olds might be working with microscopes analyzing and reporting on minute animal life; alongside, a group of seven-year-olds could be working on phonics with tape recorder and headsets; students from various classrooms are working independently in study carrels; in the back of the room, several children are watching a film about sets and numbers while another group watches an American Heritage presentation on educational television; other students are completing reading assignments in the library or checking out books from the Teacher Aide. At the same time, the Coordinating Teacher might be working with children to develop geographical concepts.

Coordinating Teacher: The Coordinating Teacher is selected on the basis of being a master teacher and an expert in interpersonal relations. Ten percent additional salary is paid for assuming this responsibility.

The Coordinating Teacher is not assigned to a regular classroom and works either in the Learning Center or with the teachers and children in the classroom cluster. The following is an outline of the Coordinating Teacher's major tasks.

1. Coordinating the use of the Learning Center with teachers as to materials, equipment, personnel, and programs.

2. Scheduling children for instructional purposes after planning sessions with the teachers.

3. Cooperatively evaluating the academic progress of the children with the teachers.

4. Developing and working in cooperative teaching programs.

5. Working on curriculum development projects independently or in planning sessions.

6. Conducting orientation for teachers to new methods and special programs.

7. Holding conferences with teachers individually or in teams for planning and problem solving.

8. Conducting in-service education programs.

The type of instruction the Coordinating Teacher provides in the Learning Center is based entirely upon a cooperative diagnosis of the specific needs and interests of each student. It is the Coordinating Teacher's function to fill the *prescriptions* and forward an evaluation to the classroom teacher regarding the effectiveness of the learning experience. This teaching includes requests for instruction in every area of the curriculum and is requested for students who range from gifted to slow in mental ability and academic achievement. *No ability group* or specific type of instruction is emphasized to the exclusion of others. This attitude prevails in that it is important for all children to have access to the opportunities provided by the Learning Center.

Regularly scheduled planning time for staff is important if the Learning Center is to function properly. While teachers may meet at all times of the day to handle problems as they arise, scheduled planning sessions are provided for through the use of paid Teacher Aides for lunch-time supervision and other large-group outside activities.

Building Educational Leader: The responsibility of the Building Educational Leader (Building Principal) for several Learning Centers at his school becomes one of assistance in the *teaming* sense and one of supervision in terms of suggesting the type of curriculum strategy to be developed. It is also his task to provide guidance for formal planning sessions with the Coordinating Teachers, and other special staff service with the classroom teachers.

A main concern of the Building Educational Leader is to provide direction so that the Center does not become a departmentalized situation which would lessen the responsibility of each professional to work with children on the basis of *diagnosis* of academic and social needs, *prescription* at individual levels, and *evaluation* to insure continuous pupil progress. The primary goal of this total team effort is to provide an atmosphere of cooperation, flexibility, good communication, and to promote the teachers' primary responsibility for the academic and social progress of students.

Auxiliary Personnel: Additional staffing for the Learning Center is the paid Teacher Aide who serves as a secretary and noninstructional assistant to the Coordinating Teacher and the regular teachers in the cluster. Her responsibilities include clerical work, filing, duplicating, circulating and retrieving materials, record keeping systems, and operating audiovisual equipment. Each Learning Center is staffed with at least one salaried Teacher Aide.

In addition to this Teacher Aide program is a volunteer group of approximately 1,000 parents who work in service capacities to the schools once a week for four hours.

1. The Curriculum Materials Center Aides fill requests from the Learning Centers and classroom teachers by making visual aids, teaching devices, and instructional media using hand tools.

2. Library Aides devote time by assisting in the central library with such tasks as shelving books, filing catalog cards, checking books out, and circulating requested books to the Learning Center.

3. Health, Welfare, and Safety Aides assist the nurses at the school level with hearing tests, immunization programs, safety programs, and puppet shows for primary children.

DISTRICT PROGRAM

Special Services Staff: The special services staff offers a wide range of technical competency by providing direct service within the Learning Center and classrooms which aid pupils directly. The psychologist, teacher of the educationally handicapped, the speech therapist, and the nurse function as resources of diagnostic information, special materials, and techniques which contribute to the variety of instructional alternatives available to the coordinating and regular classroom teacher.

Curriculum Materials Center: In order for the classroom teacher and Learning Centers to meet the needs and interests of individual children, it is most important to have a centralized storehouse of ideas, materials, equipment, and available personnel. In Fountain Valley, the Curriculum Materials Center functions as a distribution center for these areas and also provides a laboratory in which teachers can work. It is staffed with technicians and coordinators (one of whom is a professional AV person) who work with the teachers at the Center and in each of the schools.

The Center provides for in-service programs directed by the district and universities, library services, audio-visual services, teaching aids, study prints, films and filmstrips, transparencies, tapes and records, and "idea" booklets. The full-time consultants provide specialized assistance to teachers in that their recommendations are assessed at weekly in-service education meetings.

SUMMER SEMINARS

Seminars are conducted each summer for new and experienced teachers. These separate seminars are designed to explore the practical and theoretical application of new teaching techniques and methods. The emphasis for these programs is placed in five major areas:

1. The mechanics of a classroom organization and planning to individualize instruction

2. Use of materials and audiovisual equipment in individualizing instruction

3. "Theory to practice" of how children learn

4. Organization and techniques for cooperative teaching

5. Use of the Curriculum Materials Center, service personnel, functions and use of the Learning Center.

A 12-month school year with two four-week summer sessions also provides an opportunity for new teachers to observe demonstrations given by regular classroom teachers.

Fountain Valley's Board of Trustees, teaching staff, administration, and community hold for their children's education a *total* commitment to placing proven educational theory into practice. Research studies have gathered together a large amount of data concerning the individuality of the *learner,* the prominent role of the *teacher,* and the necessity for the development of a *total curriculum* to meet the individual learner's needs and interests. These educational processes do not take place in a vacuum but demand an extension to the classroom—the *Learning Center.*

The desirable input areas, when put into practice, are most conspicuous in that the Learning Center concept is really an extension of teaching space, instructional materials, electronic equipment, and teaching and supporting personnel.

Chapter 16. THE LEARNING ACTIVITY PACKAGE APPROACH AT NOVA

THE MULTI'S AT NOVA

Jan McNeil
James E. Smith

The Nova staff is organizing an instructional program that will permit each student to work at a pace and level commensurate with his ability and interest. The decision to organize an individualized instructional program is based upon certain well accepted assumptions. Six of these assumptions are:

Each student is a unique human being, with combinations of aptitudes, knowledges, achievement levels, interests, learning styles and needs, which differ from that of any other student.

Grouping students by ability has proven to be a convenience to teachers but has not resulted in individualized instructional programs.

Teacher-centered instruction, by definition, must be directed towards the "perceived average" of a given group.

A teacher is only one (an important one, yes) of the many resources with which the student should come in contact.

SOURCE: Reprinted from *Educational Screen and Audiovisual Guide,* January, 1968, pp. 16-19, 43, by permission of the authors and publisher.

Each student can become increasingly more self-directed by being given opportunities to make decisions relative to *what* and *how* he is to learn.

A student receiving individual and small group teacher assistance probably will become more highly motivated.

FOUR MAJOR IMPLEMENTATION FACTORS

To implement this unique program of instruction the Nova staff is considering four fundamental issues. The first three of these issues are how to properly organize the instructional staff to facilitate the individualization of instruction; how to schedule students, teachers and facilities to best facilitate the individualization of instruction; and, how to organize facilities, furniture and other physical resources so as to facilitate the individualization of instruction.

The fourth issue under consideration is that of how to best develop curricular materials that are geared to the individualization of instruction. At Nova these materials are referred to as Learning Activity Packages. The Learning Activity Package is defined as a broadly programmed set of materials that provide each student with alternatives of how, what, when and where to learn while utilizing efficiently a wide range of learning resources. The student literally works his way through a series of learning activities that are most relevant to him at any given time and at a pace and level unique to him. The package is organized around behaviorial objectives. Students are provided opportunities for self-assessment as well as teacher evaluations. The package contains required and optional in-depth learning opportunities utilizing a multi media, mode, content and activity approach. The Learning Activity Package is the curricular vehicle to help facilitate the individualization of instruction. (Figure 16-1.)

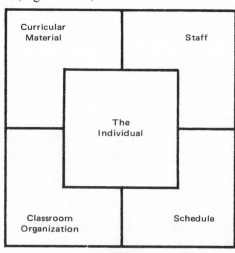

FIGURE 16-1

In most classrooms throughout the country "teaching" is characterized by these three criteria: (1) All students work through a similar set of learning activities. (2) All students work through the set of learning activities at the same pace level. (3) The learning activities revolve primarily around teacher-led lectures and discussions, the text book and paper and pencil.

The pattern for the above criteria is diagrammed as illustrated in Figure 16-2.

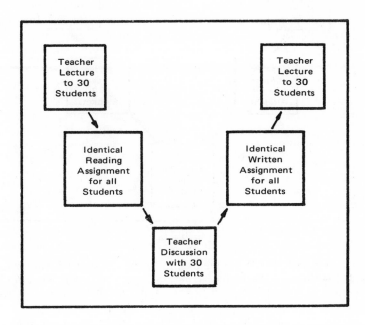

FIGURE 16-2

THE "MULTI" APPROACHES

The most creative teacher introduces into this pattern the use of the "Multi's"—that is multi media, mode, content and activity experiences. However, all students continue to work through a similar set of learning activities at the same pace and level and being directed at all times by the teacher. This pattern is diagrammed in this manner. (Figure 16-3.)

In the Learning Activity Package approach the advantages of the "multi's" can be utilized to a much higher degree. For example, the student

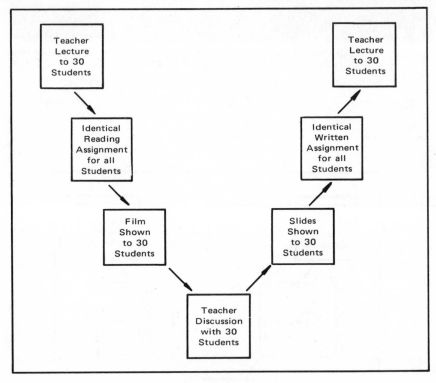

FIGURE 16-3

can work at a pace that is unique to him through a pattern similar to that above. If the lecture could be placed on video tape, the ready student merely is directed in the package to go to a "wet" study carrell, one with a video tape monitor and dialing equipment, and to dial the prescribed lecture. After viewing the video lecture he proceeds to the written assignment. When he is ready to see the film, he reports to an audio-visual area where every twenty-five minutes a film is shown. Upon completing the viewing the student may place his name on the board or sign up sheet. When twelve or fourteen students have placed their names on the board or sign up sheet, the teacher will conduct a small discussion with the set of students who are prepared for the discussion, that is those that have, at their own pace, seen the lecture on video, written out the assignment and viewed the film. After the small group discussion the student goes to the audio visual area, checks out a slide projector and set of slides, and views them. The student continues "through" the activity package participating in a variety of learning activities characterized by the "multi" approach. In this example each student continues to work through a like set of activities at a like level of sophistication, but at his own pace.

In the approach described above opportunities are still missing for the student to participate in alternate activities which: might be more interesting to him; are geared to an appropriate level for him; are more matched with his individual learning style; or provide him with the opportunity to make decisions that affect his own education. Therefore, a variety in activities is also provided for in the package approach.

One pattern of "multi" option that is provided for in the package is diagrammed as illustrated in Figure 16-4.

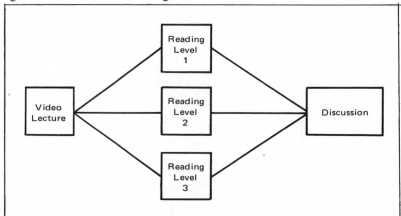

FIGURE 16-4

In this situation the student views the lecture on video tape, then decides, on his own or in consort with his teacher, to read about a given concept from any one of three sources depending upon his reading level. Following the reading assignment the student would participate in a discussion. Each has the reading background required for the discussion.

To provide additional alternatives from which the student can select, a pattern such as this might be appropriate. The student can now literally work his way through a set of learning activities that are indeed unique to him.

The student may select any one of several other sets of learning activities geared to his particular needs and interest. (Figure 16-5.)

IMPLEMENTATION REQUIREMENTS

One of the obvious implications for the Learning Activity Package approach is an appropriate environment for its implementation. At Nova High School the facilities have been organized to accommodate this type of learning environment, one of which has been designated as the laboratory.

In the minds of many educators the term laboratory connotes an appropriate place for biological and physical science curricula only. Indeed,

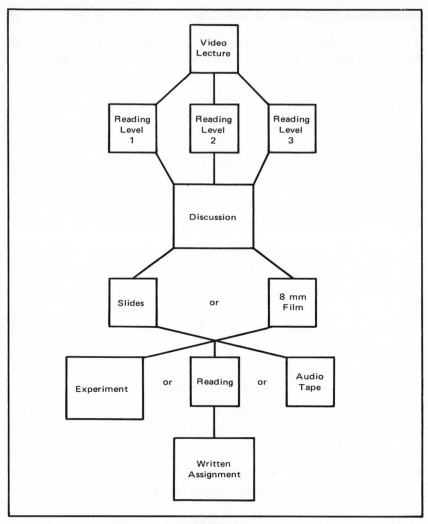

FIGURE 16-5

the *American College Dictionary* defines the laboratory as "a building or part of a building fitted with apparatus for conducting scientific investigation, experiments, tests, etc."

Science laboratories, yes; but, in addition, Nova has laboratory areas in social studies, mathematics, English, foreign languages, physical education and the fine and practical arts. A concerted effort has been made to equip these areas to encourage a student, or group of students, to engage in physical, as well as mental activities, in the above subjects.

Below is a description of what a particular laboratory is like at Nova. By no means is this picture intended to be the ultimate or to place any limits on the reader's creative ability. Rather, it is intended to serve only as an example, as a point of departure. You are limited only by your own creativity and the ability of your respective school system to finance such creativity.

HOW THE LABORATORY IS SET UP

The example is a laboratory shared by social studies and English. This particular laboratory is a suite of rooms. The main room is a large, spacious area which can accommodate one-hundred students comfortably. It is divisible with sliding vinyl doors. Across the hall are two conference rooms, each capable of handling fifteen students, which are used for small group discussion, tutorials, and individual or committee-type project work. The students also have immediate access to a resource center located in the center of the same building where books, periodicals, video and audio tape carrells, copying machines, and microcard readers are located. In addition the students may be directed to one of several other resource centers where one-of-a-kind type of audio-visual equipment and materials are located.

In the laboratory, flexible-type furniture is used. The observer would find different shaped tables and chairs, some regular student desks, and individual study carrells. The conference rooms are equipped with tables and chairs. There are two large television monitors used almost exclusively for video-taped lectures of an enrichment or motivational nature. This is completely congruous with individualized instruction, since they are not aimed at a specific idea or concept but are generally applicable to a larger segment of the scope and sequence. This suite also contains ample storage space for materials such as sets of multiple texts, audio-visual materials, etc.

This laboratory is staffed with three teachers and one para-professional. The teacher-aide takes major responsibility for attendance procedures, checking out materials, administering tests and assisting students with routine questions. This frees the three teachers to work individually with students or in small groups.

A simulated laboratory situation, something approaching the ideal, might be described as follows. One might find various types of furniture and materials. Perhaps individual study carrells would be available for students wishing to study alone. Each carrell would be wired for sound to enable students to hear tapes that have been prepared commercially or by their own teachers. Each carrell could have several tape channels allowing the student his choice of a number of pertinent tapes. Each carrell might have several drawers so that each student could have one place in the laboratory to call his own. One might find tables that can seat two or three students who might wish to work together, while other furniture would be of the lounge variety for reading purposes. Book and magazine cases as well as tape drawers and programmed materials files might be located conveniently throughout the room. The indexed card catalog, a duplicate of those found in the various resource centers, might be available to allow students to know immediately what books, film strips, microfilms, etc., can be found elsewhere. A rear projection device could be available for viewing, as well as a preview room for films and slides. Teaching machines for programmed material, either commercially or locally prepared, may be available for review work, drill, or even advanced work in a particular need or interest area. Computer terminals would be available for immediate information and media retrieval and for computer assisted instruction. This is just one simulation; others might vary in terms of hardware and/or software. Certainly a business education laboratory or a home science laboratory might have kinds of equipment peculiar only to that particular subject.

WHAT'S IN A L.A.P.?

The opening portions of this article dealt briefly with *(a)* the assumptions underlying and *(b)* the description of the Learning Activity Package. Consideration was also given to inclusion, as an integral part of the package, the use of the "multi's." There has been no haphazard approach to the inclusion of the multi's in these curricular materials at Nova. The ideas were carefully formulated and developed. A task force searches out, and attempts to include a variety of experiences utilizing the "multi's" in each Learning Activity Package that is developed.

As examples, excerpts from three Nova Learning Activity Packages are included. They have been "lifted" from the larger framework of a package, but will show the relative importance that the multi's play.

From a social studies package entitled "Man and His World in the 20th Century" a set of instructions which states to the students:

> The activities listed in the study guide below are designed to help you meet the objectives for this section of the L.A.P. Proceeding through them in the sequence outlined will be of greatest benefit. Be sure that you have done the required *readings, viewed either of the following films*—"People by the Billions" or "The Population Problem", and *viewed the video-taped lecture* entitled "People and Technology" prior to beginning the learning activities.

This depicts the reading and viewing types of multi's used as a background information gathering technique.

From a technical science package entitled "Hardness" a behavioral objective which states to the student:

> Given an assortment of materials, select four (4) and with the *aid of a hammer and/or file, place* in a hardness order the four

materials selected by arrangement of the samples in a sequence of increasing hardness.

This demonstrates the doing type of media and describes a terminal behavior based upon learning activities which included an audio tape and a reading.

From an English package entitled "Hedonism" a set of instructions for small group discussion which states to the student:

> You will *listen* to various brief pieces of music which in turn will be *matched* with short pieces of poetry in the attempt to match mood, or style, or sensual appeal, or structure. The technique will be: *Playing and listening* to the music, briefly *matching* the poems, *oral comments* on the appropriateness of the results.

This defines the parameters for a small group using a media presentation to stimulate discussion.

We could cite examples from science and mathematics Learning Activity Packages as well but space does not permit. The total staff at Nova does, however, subscribe to the notion that a variety of learning experiences, with the use of the multi's as options, does provide for a more meaningful, more well-rounded means of reaching a larger segment of the school population. The Nova staff is firmly committed to the ever expanding use of the multi's utilizing the Learning Activity Package as the curricular vehicle to individualized instruction and the laboratory as the learning environment for its implementation.

Chapter 17. A SAMPLE *LAP* DEVELOPED AT NOVA

SAMPLE PREPARATION FOR MICROSTUDY

A. V. Rapp

(LAP pages shown in parentheses)

RATIONALE: The need for preparing samples for microanalysis.

Man learned long ago that there were many things which he could not see, but which controlled the environment around him, and thus must exist.

Based on the effects of these unseen quantities and misassociations, he developed many strange practices and superstitions to control or affect these causes.

Early technology is steeped in such strange practices; such as in the making of the still famed Damascus sword. The arms makers of this city believed that the cause of their superior sword was due to the practice of cooling the blade rapidly by sticking it into the belly of a fat, male slave. This process was to have transferred the male soul of the slave to the blade of the sword and thus give it supernatural powers.

SOURCE: Reprint of a mimeographed LAP as used in the Nova Schools, Ft. Lauderdale, Florida.

Of course, today we know that the same results could have been achieved by cooling the blade in an oil and that the heart of their quality product was not only in the cooling process, but in the process of making steel which they had discovered quite accidentally and were not really aware of.

In order to better understand these unknown quantities which control the material and products of our technology, man has over the years developed techniques which allow insight into the hidden alcoves of the past.

One such set of techniques is the preparation of metals so that when viewed under the microscope we will be able to see the peculiar and distinct patterns of that metal, and thus get insights into the causes of its properties.

It is the purpose of this package to introduce you to the equipment, techniques and total process of preparation of a microanalysis specimen.

Turn to the next page and read the objectives.

(LAP page 2 starts here)

OBJECTIVES:

1. Given the terms cut-off machine, mounting press, handimet grinder, low-speed polishing table, metallurgical microscope, you will be able to:

    a)   Identify verbally or in writing visual representations or the actual item,

    b)   State orally or in writing the purpose of each item,

    c)   Demonstrate and state orally or in writing the correct procedure for using each item.

2. Given specific metal samples you will be able to demonstrate, or orally, or in writing describe:

    a)   The preparation of the samples for etching,

    b)   The selection and use of a correct etchent and etching time for each sample,

    c)   The setting up and viewing of the samples with the metallurgical microscope.

If you think you can meet the objectives of this package, turn to page 3 and take the self-test.

If you think you cannot meet the objectives as stated on this page, turn to page 4 and begin the package assignments.

(LAP page 3 starts here)

SELF-TEST

QUESTION 1: Directions: With your instructor go into the testing lab. There you are to identify and explain the purpose and how to use the following items by oral statements and demonstrations: cut-off machine, mounting press, handimet grinder, low-speed polishing table, metallurgical microscope.

When you have completed this, have your instructor initial the acceptable or unacceptable spaces.

_____ acceptable   _____ unacceptable

QUESTION 2: Acquire a metal sample from your instructor and prepare it for etching by polishing. Have your instructor check it as acceptable or unacceptable.

_____ acceptable   _____ unacceptable

QUESTION 3: In the space below list the type of metal you are using and the etchent you will use. Have this checked by your instructor.

_____ metal   _____ etchent

_____ acceptable   _____ unacceptable

QUESTION 4: From your instructor acquire the etchent you have decided upon. Etch your sample and set it up in the microscope for viewing. Have your instructor check this and initial the appropriate space.

_____ acceptable   _____ unacceptable

(LAP page 4 starts here)

In order to do a micro study of specimens we must have a working knowledge of the techniques, materials and equipment which are used in this process.

The following objectives and assignments are designed to aid you in achieving this competence.

Objective: Given the terms cut-off machine, mounting press, handimet grinder, low-speed polishing table, metallurgical microscope, you will be able to:

a) Identify verbally or in writing visual representations or the actual items,

b) State orally or in writing the purpose of each item,

c) State orally or in writing the correct procedure for using each item.

Select one of the following assignments. Your selection should be based on which assignment will best benefit you and the availability of the materials needed for the assignment.

After reading through all the choices, indicate your selection by placing a check mark in front of the assignment you have selected.

( ) Assignment 1a—Read the information sheets (pages 7 to 22). Then proceed to assignment 2.

( ) Assignment 1b—Arrange with your instructor for a group demonstration of the purposes and procedures in using the metallurgical equipment. There must be a minimum of three (3) in the group and you must arrange the formation of the group; i.e., you will have to find at least two other members of the class who are at the same point as you and who want the demonstration. Then arrange for the demonstration with your instructor. Following the demonstration, proceed to assignment 2.

( ) Assignment 1c—View the video tape on "The use of the metallurgical equipment and preparation of a sample." 402 Cut 1 Then proceed to assignment 2.

Assignment 2—Return to page 3 of this package. There you are to do Self-Test Question No. 1 only. When you have completed this question, return to the next page and do the next assignment.

─────────────────────────────⟶ Turn to page 3.

──

(LAP page 5 starts here)

⌐ Upon return, start here

⌐→Now that we have some knowledge of the equipment and its use in preparing samples, we must arrange this knowledge into an orderly sequence (procedure) so that we can achieve a desired result, namely a polished specimen which may then be etched and viewed under the microscope.

Objective: Given specific metal samples, you will be able to demonstrate and orally or in writing describe:

a) The preparation of the samples for etching,

b) The selection of and use of a correct etchent and etching time for each sample,

c) The setting up and viewing of the sample with the metallurgical microscope.

Select one of the following assignments. Your selection should be based on which assignment will best benefit you and the availability of the materials needed for the assignment.

After reading through all the choices, indicate your selection by placing a check mark in front of the assignment you have selected.

( ) Assignment 3a—Read the information sheets (pages 7 to 22). Then proceed to assignment 4.

( ) Assignment 3b—Arrange with your instructor for a group demonstration on the procedure in preparing and polishing a metal sample for etching. There must be a minimum of three (3) in the group and you must arrange the formation of the group; i.e., you will have to find at least two other members of the class who are at the same point as you in this package and who want the demonstration. Then arrange for the demonstration with your instructor. Following the demonstration proceed to assignment 4.

( ) Assignment 3c—View the video tape on the use of the metallurgical equipment and preparation of a sample. Then proceed to assignment 4.

Assignment 4—Return to page 3 of this package. There you are to do the Self-Test Question No. 2 only. When you have completed this question, return to the next page and start the next assignment.

————————————————————————→   Turn to page 3.

_____

(LAP page 6 starts here)

⌐Upon return, start here

⌊→ With our samples now polished, we must in most cases etch the sample to reveal the various grains and constituents which make up the metal. The selection of this etchent is of great importance if the desired results are to be obtained.

Select one of the following assignments. Your selection should be based on which assignment will best benefit you and the availability of the materials needed for the assignments.

After reading through the choices, indicate your selection by placing a check mark in front of the assignment you have selected.

( ) Assignment 5a—Read information sheets (pages 23 to 25). Then proceed to assignment 6.

( ) Assignment 5b—Arrange with your instructor for a group demonstration on the selection of etchents and how to use them. There must be a minimum of three (3) in the group, and you must arrange the formation of the group; i.e., you will have to find at least two other members of the class who are at the same point as you in this package and who want the demonstration. Then arrange for the demonstration with your instructor. Following the demonstration proceed to assignment 6.

( ) Assignment 5c—View the video tape on the use of the metallurgical equipment and preparation of a sample. Then proceed to assignment 6.

( ) Assignment 6—Return to page 3 of this package. There you are to do the Self-Test Question No. 3 only. When you have completed this question, return to the next page and start the next assignment.

————————————————————→   Now turn to page 3.

(LAP page 7 starts here)

┌─ Upon return, start here

└→With the etchent selected, we have only to go through the process of etching and view under the microscope to see the results of our work.

Select one of the following assignments. Your selection should be based on which assignment will best benefit you and the availability of the materials needed for the assignments.

After reading through the choices, indicate your selection by placing a check in front of the assignment you have selected.

( ) Assignment 7a—Read information sheets (pages 19 to 22). Then proceed to assignment 8.

( ) Assignment 7b—Arrange with your instructor for a group demonstration on the proper use of the etchent and use of the microscope. There must be a minimum of three (3) in the group and you must arrange the formation of the group; i.e., you will have to find at least two other members of the class who are at the same point as you in the package and who want the demonstration. Then arrange for the demonstration with your instructor. Following the demonstration proceed to assignment 8.

( ) Assignment 7c—View the video tape on the use of the metallurgical equipment and preparation of a sample. Then proceed to assignment 8.

Assignment 8—Return to page 3 of this package. There you are to do the Self-Test Question No. 4 only. When you have completed this question, you have completed this package. Return to this page and ask yourself the following question:

┌─ Upon return, start here

└► "Can I now use the metallurgical equipment to process a sample to the point of viewing it under the microscope?"

If your answer is "yes," have your instructor O.K. your use of this equipment.

If your answer is "no," have a conference with your instructor.

(LAP page 8 starts here)

INFORMATION

The Preparation of Metals for Microscopic Examination

The end purpose of preparing a metal for microscopic examination is to allow us a view of the solid state of a metal which is not normally visible to the naked eye.

This microscopic view, which shows specific physical characteristics of the structure, permits us to relate these characteristics to physical properties, thus providing a clearer understanding of the material, what happened to it and how it will react in specific situations.

Let us begin by saying that there are many ways in which we can achieve the desired result—getting a sample ready for microscopic examination. However, in this package we are going to deal with only one method—mechanical hand polishing.

As you enter the Test Lab you will find to your right the equipment which is used to prepare and observe the metal specimens.

Item 1 is the mounting press. It is used to embed a sample too small to normally handle with your fingers. The sample is placed in the mold with a plastic granule and, through heat and pressure, the finished embedded sample is produced.

(Ref.—for operating instructions see page 10)

Item 2 is the abrasive cut-off machine. This is used to cut off pieces of material which are to be polished. This machine uses blades made of various abrasive materials.

(Ref.—for operating instructions see page 13)

Item 3 is the "Handimet Grinder." This apparatus is used for the hand grinding of samples, which is the major step in the polishing procedure.

(Ref.—for operating instructions see page 15)

Items 4 are the two polishing tables. Polishing table 4a is a low-speed table on which a diamond paste is used as the abrasive. Table 4b is a high-speed table on which a gamma alumina is used as the abrasive. These two polishing tables will be used for your final polishing.

(Ref.—for operating instructions see page 17)

Item 5 is the metallurgical microscope. This instrument is used to observe the structures making up the sample.

(Ref.—for operating instructions see page 18)

Now let us consider the operating instructions for each of the specific pieces of equipment.

(LAP page 9 starts here)

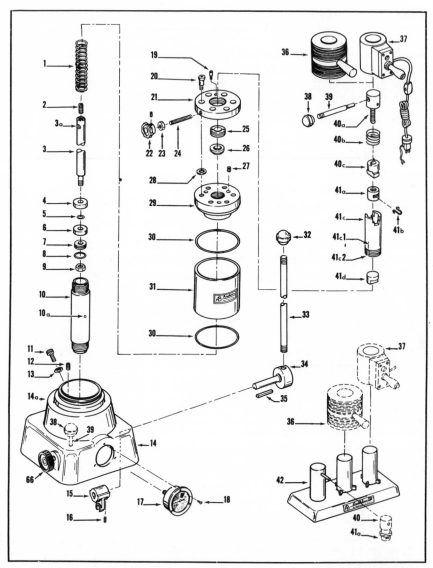

Courtesy: Buehler Ltd.,
Evanston, Ill. U.S.A.

FIGURE 17-1
NO. 20-1301 AND NO. 20-1302 AB SIMPLIMET ® PRESS

Mounting Press Operating Instructions

1. Close the release valve hand wheel (66—Figure 17-1).

2. Pump mold base (41d—Figure 17-1) midway up the mold cylinder (41c—Figure 17-1). This is accomplished by a series of strokes on pump handle (33—Figure 17-1).

3. Remove mold closure assembly (40—Figure 17-1). This may be accomplished by twisting handle (39—Figure 17-1) and lifting up.

4. Place automatic heater (37—Figure 17-1) over mold (41c—Figure 17-1).

5. Plug in heater to 110 V. A.C. outlet and turn switch to on position.

6. Allow entire system to preheat for 25 minutes.

7. With care (these parts are now hot) remove ram and closure assembly (40a—Figure 17-1).

8. Now pump mold base (41d—Figure 17-1) to the top of the mold.

9. Carefully position specimen with its flat surface on the mold base.

10. Open the release valve (66—Figure 17-1) and the mold base and specimen will drop to the bottom of the mold cavity.

11. Rapidly, insert 50 grams of thermosetting bakelite powder.

12. Replace mold closure assembly (40—Figure 17-1) and lock into place with a twisting action.

13. Apply 4,200 lb/in. pressure to mold by pumping handle (33—Figure 17-1).

   Note—We are using a 1″ mold.—4,200 lb/in. is read on the gauge on the base of the press. The inside red dot indicates a pressure of 4,200 lb/in. (See Figure 17-2.)

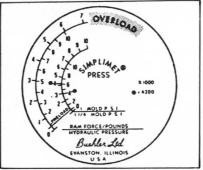

Courtesy: Buehler Ltd., Evanston, Ill. U.S.A.

FIGURE 17-2

GAUGE ASSEMBLY DIAL FACE

Warning: *Do Not Allow Pressure to Reach Overload Range*

14. Release the pressure (4,200 lb/in.) immediately.—This is done by opening the release valve.

15. Close release valve and reapply pressure of 4,200 lb/in.
16. Release again and then reapply. It will now be maintained for the duration of the melt and curing cycle.
17. Leave the pressure on the sample for a period of 5 minutes.
18. Put on gloves and safety glasses for the following operations.
19. Release pressure.
20. Carefully remove mold closure assembly.
21. Close release valve and pump mold base up in order to force molded sample out.

Warning: Great care should be taken during step 21. On occasions gases are trapped in the plastic and can cause the sample to blow apart. You should be wearing safety glasses.

22. Remove sample from mold base.
23. Place sample in a safe place to cool to room temperature.
24. Remove any flash or adherent cured molding material from mold base, ram, and around mouth of cylinder.
25. Recoat parts with silicone mold release fluid if finished samples tend to adhere to molding surface.

(LAP page 12 starts here)

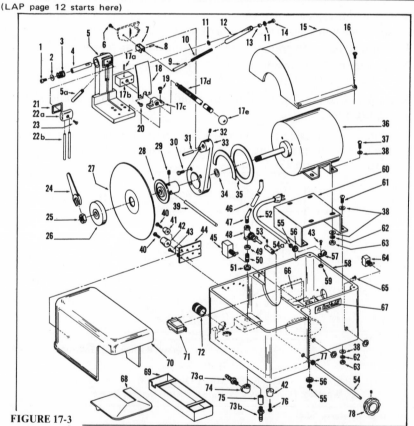

FIGURE 17-3

NO. 10-1114 AB CUT-OFF MACHINE   Courtesy: Buehler Ltd., Evanston, Ill. U.S.A.

(LAP page 13 starts here)

CUT-OFF MACHINE OPERATING INSTRUCTIONS

The cut-off machine is used in those cases where a section of material must be removed from a longer piece of stock. It will produce smooth parallel faces and add little, if any, distortion to the surface of the sample.

Step 1—Determine the nature of the material which is to be cut (type and hardness). A hardness test may be useful in this determination.

Step 2—Select the correct cutting wheel for your material. (see chart)

No. of Wheel	Cut-off Wheels Chart Uses
10-4110	For extra hard steel and other metals, and for large samples
10-4112	For hard steel, Rc 45 to 60
10-4114	For medium hard metals and for general use
10-4116	For medium hard steel, Rc 30 to 45
10-4118	For soft steel and for general use
10-4120	For soft steel, Rc 20 to 35, and all Rb
10-4122	For tubing and small stock
10-4124	For non-ferrous materials, including uranium, titanium and zerconium

Step 3—Unplug cut-off machine.

Step 4—Raise wheel hood (70—Figure 17-3).

Step 5—Carefully remove tray (68—Figure 17-3).

Step 6—Lock motor shaft by inserting Arbor pin (39—Figure 17-3) into hole in Arbor.

Step 7—Remove nut (25—Figure 17-3) with Arbor wrench (24—Figure 17-3) by turning clockwise (left hand threads).

Step 8—Remove flange (26—Figure 17-3) and place cut-off wheel on the shaft against the arbor.

(LAP page 14 starts here)

Step 9—Replace flange and nut.

Step 10—Tighten nut. *Important:* Do *not* over-tighten; excessive pressure may damage wheel, flange and nut.

Step 11—Remove arbor pin.

Step 12—Close wheel hood (70—Figure 17-3).

Step 13—Loosen vise (17—Figure 17-3) by turning vise handle (17d—Figure 17-3) counterclockwise.

Step 14—Place material to be cut (capacity of this machine is 1/2 inch diameter) in the vise.

Step 15—Adjust stock so that cut-off wheel will hit the stock where the cut is desired.

Step 16—Tighten vise jaw securely by turning handle (17d—Figure 17-3) clockwise.

Step 17—Make sure that the stock is firmly held in the vise. If the stock should move during the cutting operation, damage will occur to the wheel and machine.

Step 18—Turn on water by rotating control handle (78—Figure 17-3). This will provide water for cooling during the cutting operation. Make sure you have a steady flow before proceeding.

Step 19—Start the cutting wheel motor by turning on motor switch (45—Figure 17-3).

Step 20—To cut through sample apply a steady downward pressure on vise handle (17—Figure 17-3). *Warning:*   Do not force the stock through.

Step 21—Listen to the sound as you cut through the metal. A drop in the sound level usually means you have cut through the sample. *Never lift cover (70—Figure 17-3) to check if sample is completely cut while the motor is running.*

Step 22—Now that you have cut through the sample, shut off the motor.

Step 23—Shut down the water flow.

Step 24—Unclamp and remove stock and sample.

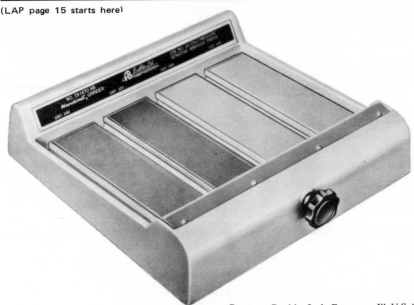

Courtesy: Buehler Ltd., Evanston, Ill. U.S.A.

NO. 39-1470 AB HANDIMET GRINDER ®

OPERATING INSTRUCTIONS FOR THE HANDIMET GRINDER

The handimet grinder is used for the rough grinding phase of sample preparation.

The following operating procedure should be used when grinding with this apparatus.

1. Check your sample to see that the ends are parallel.

2. Check the abrasives on the four plates of the grinder. There should be successive grits of 240, 320, 400 and 600. If these are worn or torn, inform your instructor and he will replace them for you.

3. See that the intake water hose is connected to faucet securely.

4. Turn black flow control knob in front of grinder slowly, until a uniform flow of water occurs over the abrasives.

5. Select a sample and hold it between your thumb and middle finger, then place your forefinger on top of the sample.

6. Holding the sample as described in Step 5, place it face down on the 240 abrasive and push it away from you.

7. Repeat the strokes several times, then rotate the sample 90° and repeat strokes again.

8. Continue on this abrasive until specimen appears smooth, then proceed to the next step.

9. Continue as you have on each successive abrasive through 600.

10. When you have completed the 600 grit step, shut off the faucet first then close the flow control.

(LAP page 16 starts here)

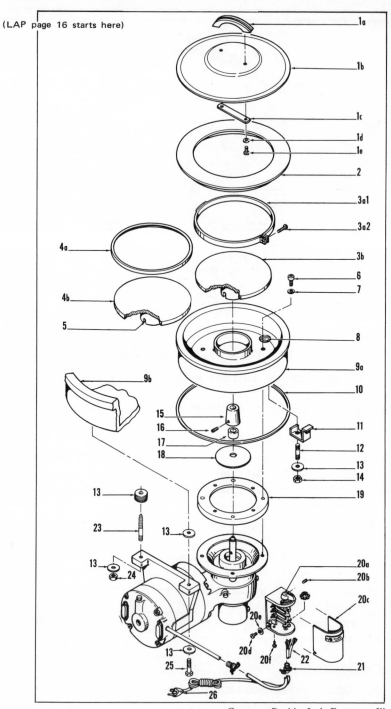

Courtesy: Buehler Ltd., Evanston, Ill. U.S.A.

FIGURE 17-4

(LAP page 17 starts here)

OPERATING INSTRUCTIONS FOR THE LOW-SPEED AND STANDARD POLISHER

The following instructions apply to both low and standard polishers. The difference between the machines is the speed at which the tables will rotate. It is recommended that you use the low speed in your early attempts at polishing samples.

1. Your sample has been prepared through the final steps of grinding by using the handimet grinder. You are now ready to polish the specimen.

2. Attach a nylon cloth (8″) to the wheel (3b—Figure 17-4). Stretch the cloth carefully before tightening screw (3a2—Figure 17-4).

3. Apply a one inch ribbon of No. 40-6162 AB metadi, 6 micron, to the cloth. Spread over polishing cloth with a clean finger. Moisten with metadi fluid or automet lapping oil.

4. Turn on motor to desired speed. (Both have two speeds, high and low).

5. Holding the sample face down between thumb and fingers, press down firmly against rotating wheel. Let the back edge hit first then bring sample slowly forward until all of the face is in contact. (See Figure 17-4.)

6. Move sample around the wheel in the direction opposite to the rotation of the wheel.

7. Polish until all fine grinding scratches are removed.

8. Wash sample and hands.

9. Repeat procedure steps 2 through 8 using microcloth as the wheel cover material, gamma alumina as the abrasive and distilled water as the lubricant.

10. When polishing is complete, clean bowl area of machine and table surface around polishing tables. Replace cover lids to protect tables.

11. You are now ready to etch your sample.

(LAP page 18 starts here)

UNITRON
INSTRUMENT COMPANY — MICROSCOPE SALES DIV.
66 NEEDHAM STREET, NEWTON HIGHLANDS 61, MASS.

Instructions for UNITRON Metallurgical Microscopes, Models MMU and MMA

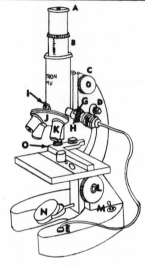

A. Eyepiece
*B. Graduated drawtube
C. Coarse focusing control
*D. Fine focusing control
E. Illuminator plug
F. Illuminator condenser unit
G. Filter slot
H. Iris Diaphragm
I. Lever to adjust angle of glass reflector
J. Revolving nosepiece
K. Objective lens
*L. Stage height focusing control
M. Switch to change light intensity
N. Plano-concave mirror
O. Accessory metallurgical mechanical stage

*Starred components are absent from Model MMA

FIGURE 17-5

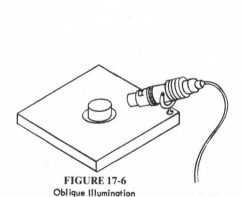

FIGURE 17-6
Oblique Illumination

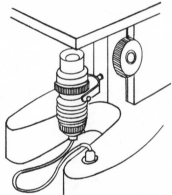

FIGURE 17-7
Transmitted Light For Transparent Specimens

INSTRUCTIONS FOR UNITRON METALLURGICAL MICROSCOPES,

SERIES MMU AND MMA
(Letters in parentheses refer to labelled illustration)

UNPACKING: The keys to the carrying case will be found tied to the handle of the microscope. A flat "coin-type" screwdriver is also attached. Open the microscope cabinet, remove any internal racks, accessory boxes, and interior packing. The microscope itself is bolted to the bottom of the case by means of screws, fastened to the base. Tilt the microscope cabinet to provide access to the underside of the cabinet. Using the

Ed. Note: At this point, detailed manufacturer's operating directions are included in the LAP but are not reprinted here.

(LAP page 23 starts here)

INFORMATION SHEET FOR METALLOGRAPHIC
SPECIMEN PREPARATION AND VIEWING

The following procedure is that which should be followed in preparing a specimen. The steps should be followed in the order given here. It should be noted that some steps may be omitted depending on the sample and its condition. The steps which may be omitted will be indicated.

Step 1. Cutting the specimen. If the specimen is part of a large piece of stock, it will most probably have to be separated; i.e., a small section cut.

For cutting the stock there are two acceptable ways:

a) Cut the section on the power hack saw, then face both ends on the lathe.
b) Cut the section using the abrasive cut off wheel (see ref. page 13). *Be sure the correct wheel* is on the machine before using it.

*This step may be omitted if the stock is already a convenient size, at least 1/2″ long and 1/2″ in diameter.

Step 2. Embedding the specimen—Some specimens may require embedding in plastic, to either protect them or make them easier to handle during the grinding and polishing stages.

For this operation, the embedding press is to be used. It requires about a half hour, including preheat for this operation so allow yourself enough time. (See ref. page 8 on the use of the embedding press.)

*This step may be omitted if the sample is 1/2″ long and 1/2″ in diameter.

Step 3. Grinding. The initial stage of surface preparation is the grinding stage. Its purpose is to remove deep surface scratches and deformations caused in earlier steps. The handimet grinder will be used for this operation (see ref. page 15). Care should be taken to use sufficient water during the grinding operations, and to take enough time in each step to gain the maximum value of that step. Time invested in grinding may save you time in polishing.

Step 4. Polishing. In the polishing stage the scratches left from grinding are removed to make a scratch-free specimen.

There are two (2) stages in the polishing step. First, the coarse polishing which is done with the standard polishing wheel (see ref. page 17) and a diamond abrasive and second, the final polishing which is done on the low speed polishing wheel (see ref. page 17) with a gamma alumina.

As you go through the first and second steps of polishing, wash your sample with alcohol so that you do not contaminate the wheel and so your sample will be properly clean for etching.

(LAP page 24 starts here)

Step 5. Cleaning before Etching. When you have finished the final polishing step, clean the specimen in alcohol. Be careful not to touch the polished area with your fingers as this may ruin the surface.

When the specimen is clean, dry the specimen in a stream of compressed air. The specimen should be completely dry. It is a wise practice to observe the unetched specimen under the microscope (see ref. page 19 and step 8 page 25). In some instances a specimen does not require etching to reveal its grain structure and in all samples an initial examination provides a reference to the quality of the polishing and may indicate imperfections which could later be misinterpreted as grain structure.

Step 6. Etching. In the etching operation we attempt, through a chemical reaction, to distinguish the grain patterns of the metal.

Select the etchent to be used from the following chart:

Etchent	Metal	Time
#1-50% Conc HCl	Zinc	
#2-Alcoholic FeCl$_3$	Most Copper Alloys	30 sec.
#3-Aqueous FeCl$_3$	Copper Alloys, Tin and Antimony	30 sec.
#4-Ammonia/Hydrogen Peroxide	Copper Alloys	3 sec.
#5-Keller's Etch	Aluminum Alloys	10 sec.
#6-Nital 2%	Steels and Irons	10 sec.
#7-Kalling's Reagent	Austenitic and Ferritic Stainless Steels	10 sec.
#8-Marble's Reagent	Reveals structure of Stainless Steels	10 sec.

Note: <u>You Must Wear Safety Glasses When Etching</u>

Acquire a small quantity of the etchent in a beaker and an eye dropper from your instructor. Place your sample on the glass plate by the sink and follow these steps:

Step 1. Check surface for dirt and oil. If any, clean with alcohol.

Step 2. Place sample face up on glass plate.

Step 3. Determine the time of the first etch. Suggested times are offered in the "Etchent Chart." However, these are for the first etch only and are averages of many samples.

Step 4. Note by recording on paper the time and apply the etchent to the entire face with the eye dropper.

(LAP page 25 starts here)

Step 5. Turn on water in sink.

Step 6. When the proper time has elapsed, flush the sample clean under the water flowing in the sink.

Step 7. Do not touch the surface that has been etched, but carefully dry the sample in a stream of compressed air.

Step 8. When and only when the sample is completely dry, take it to the microscope and observe the results (see ref. page 19).

Step 9. Should the structure not be revealed enough, repeat steps 4 through 8 until you achieve the desired results.

Special Note: Usually the time will decrease as the sample is additionally etched.

If you have followed through the procedure for polishing a sample and have gotten positive results you are promoted to the rank of Metallurgical Lab Technician.

Chapter 18. A TEACHER-MADE GUIDE FOR INDEPENDENT STUDY

VACUUM TUBES: PART I

James W. Hargis

Name_____ Class_____

TO COMPLETE THIS INSTRUCTIONAL PACKAGE IT WILL BE NECESSARY TO PERFORM EACH OBJECTIVE AS INDICATED.

OBJECTIVES:

1.   Be able to write the three basic functions of vacuum tubes.

   HOW TO LEARN:

   1.   INFORMATION SHEET NO. 1

   2.   Tape/Slide sequence: *Electronic Tubes.*

SOURCE: Adapted from a mimeographed self-instructional module as used at the Occupational Skills Center, Union High School District No. 5, Milwaukie, Oregon, by permission of author.

2.   Given a symbol of triode vacuum tube, be able to identify and explain the function of each element of that tube.

HOW TO LEARN:

1.   Information Sheet No. 1

2.   Tape/Slide sequence: *Triodes, Tetrodes, Pentodes*

3.   Self-Test Step No. 1, Step No. 3.

3.   Be able to label the pins of a tube in the accepted order from the bottom.

HOW TO LEARN:

1.   Information Sheet No. 1

2.   Self-Test Step No. 2

4.   Be able to list the filament voltage for five or six given tube numbers using correct units.

HOW TO LEARN:

1.   Radio Servicing; Marcus P. 148

2.   Self Test Step No. 4

5.   Be able to relate the B + voltage and the grid to the flow of electrons.

HOW TO LEARN:

1.   Information Sheet No. 3

2.   Self Test Step No. 5, Step No. 6.

INFORMATION SHEET NO. 1

In a radio receiver, vacuum tubes essentially do three things: (1) amplify electrical signals; (2) rectify alternating current (changes it to pulsating D.C.) and (3) serves as an electrical oscillator.

This package is concerned primarily with basic vacuum tubes and how some act as amplifiers. The other two functions, rectification and oscillation, will be taken up in later packages.

The Heater (Filament)

In some vacuum tubes the heater emits (gives up) electrons when heated. In other tubes, such as those built in our program, the heater simply serves as an element which heats the cathode, which in turn emits the electrons.

The Cathode

The cathode, when heated by the heater, emits electrons which produce an electrical current. Whenever heaters are connected to an AC source, cathodes must be used to prevent serious hum.

The Plate

The plate collects the electrons emitted by the heater or cathode, and sends them along their way to the remainder of the circuit.

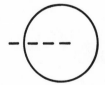

The Control Grid

The control grid regulates the amount of electrons flowing from the cathodes. The weak incoming signal is connected to this element and controls the stronger electron flow coming from the cathode. All amplifier tubes have a control grid. This grid is located adjacent to the cathode.

INFORMATION SHEET NO. 2

Numbering The Pins

Each element inside the tube is connected to a particular pin outside the tube.   A tube manual will indicate which element is connected to a particular pin; however, it is beyond the scope of this package to show the use of a tube manual at this time.

If you look at the bottom of a miniature tube, you will find seven pins evenly distributed around the bottom. However, there will be one space larger than the rest. The numbering begins in a CLOCKWISE direction from the first pin located to the left of the larger space when the tube is held in the position shown in the figure below.

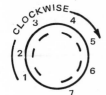

Looking at the bottom of the tube, the pins are numbered clockwise beginning at the largest space.

Although many special types of sockets are used, most of the vacuum tubes used in electronics require one of the eight sockets illustrated below.   One method of classifying tubes is according to the socket required.

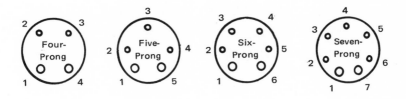

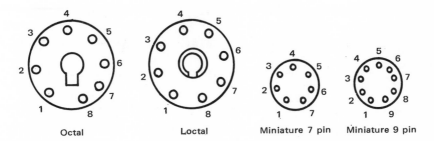

Octal   Loctal   Miniature 7 pin   Miniature 9 pin

INFORMATION SHEET NO. 3

A major function of tubes is amplification, to increase in strength a small input AC signal. A large voltage across the cathode and plate causes the electrons emitted from the cathode to flow toward the plate. A grid controls the amount of current flowing from the cathode to the plate. A small AC grid voltage causes a large change in the cathode plate current. A triode tube has the effect of amplifying the input signal.

A basic requirement for the operation of a vacuum tube is the B+ voltage causing the current to flow from the cathode to the plate. Although the filament heats the electrons off the cathode, the B+ voltage is necessary to force electrons to the plate. The cathode-plate current must exist so that the tube can amplify the input signal.

SELF-TEST

1. Label and state the function of each element of the triode tube.

A._____

   Function_____

B._____

   Function_____

C._____

   Function_____

D._____

   Function_____

E._____

   Function_____

2. Label the pins of the following tube in the accepted order.

3. A triode tube has the effect of _____
   the input signal.   (one word)

4. List the filament voltage correctly for at least five of the six given tube numbers using correct units.

A._____ SY3GT

B._____ 6BA3

C._____ 2AS2

D._____ 1AD2

E. _____ 11726

F. _____ 50C5

5. Circle the letter of the sentence describing the effect of the B+ voltage on current in a triode.

A. The B+ voltage causes current to flow from the cathode to the plate.

B. The B+ voltage causes current to flow from the plate to the cathode.

C. The B+ voltage causes current to flow from the control grid to the plate.

D. The B+ voltage causes a potential difference between the filament and grid.

E. The B+ voltage causes current to flow from the cathode to the control grid.

6. Circle the letter of the statement describing the accepted purpose of the grid in a triode in terms of the cathode-plate current.

A. The grid in a triode controls the capocitance between the cathode and plate.

B. The grid in a triode amplifies the input signal.

C. The grid in a triode controls the amount of current flowing from the plate to the cathode.

D. The grid in a triode holds the cathode and plate apart.

E. The grid in a triode controls the amount of current flowing from the cathode to the plate.

Chapter 19. INDIVIDUAL OPTIONS THROUGH THE UNIT PLAN

MEADOWBROOK JUNIOR HIGH SCHOOL: WITH FOCUS ON THE INDIVIDUAL

Ernestine R. McDonough
Maurice H. Blum

GOALS

It is the purpose of the Meadowbrook Junior High School:

. . . to help each student learn how to take charge of the development of his own potential, and to understand that only he, in the long run, is responsible for his learning.

> Agency

. . . to help each student become personally involved in his learning—to be free to actively explore his own resources and those of the school and the larger environment.

> Motivation

SOURCE: Adapted from mimeographed literature prepared by Meadowbrook Junior High School, Newton Public Schools, Newton, Mass., by permission of the authors.

... to help each student develop enough confidence in himself and in others to be able to think imaginatively and explore openly ideas, values and relationships. | Creativity |

... to help each student find true satisfaction in learning, and to understand that the subject matter skills acquired are not only useful in themselves, but are tools with which to meet situations and solve problems. | Scholarship |

UNIT AND UNIT TEAM

Meadowbrook Junior High is organized into four groups called Units: Alpha, Beta, Gamma, Sigma. Each unit contains approximately two hundred and twenty-five students of all ages, ability levels and interests. Within the Unit the student operates as an individual and as a member of a class.

Twelve House Advisors and a guidance counselor devote their time to one Unit Team. House Advisors represent the major subjects of most students: English, mathematics, social studies, science, foreign language, as well as fine and applied arts.

Although the four Units follow the same goals and curriculum, each Unit Team uses the teaching techniques and materials they feel will best meet the needs of the students. The teachers of each Unit plan the order in which subject content will be presented, and establish the schedule every twelve weeks.

The Unit Team focuses the attention of the staff on the individual and his needs. Weekly meetings of the Unit Team are held to pool the resources of the team members in an attempt to understand each student and make appropriate plans to help him.

HOUSE AND HOUSE ADVISER

Meadowbrook Junior High places the student in an active role in the learning process. He is continually in need of clarifying his goals and evaluting his progress in relation to them. The House and House Advisor provide the place and personnel for this important task.

Not more than twenty students and a teacher make up the House group. First, second and third-year students are represented in each House. Meetings are scheduled five days a week, giving the House Advisor opportunity for group activities and for frequent conferences with the individual students. The House provides the student with time to think and work as an individual and as a member of a small group, focusing attention on the goals of the program.

The House Advisor serves as a catalyst, a guide and a resource person. He helps the students to understand the goals of the program and to assess himself in relation to them. He guides each member of his House in making schedules, choosing subjects and evaluating academic and social progress.

As one of the twelve members of the Unit Team, the House Advisor represents his students in each team meeting. He is responsible for reporting the student's progress to parents and other teachers.

DECISION MAKING AND COMMITMENT

Meadowbrook Junior High is built on the premise that *the most meaningful learning takes place when an individual makes a personal commitment to and becomes involved in his own education.*

To become involved in his own learning, a student needs opportunities for choice. He needs a chance to consciously look at alternatives, with appropriate guidance, and to make decisions. He needs an environment which permits him to feel the satisfaction that comes when he makes decisions that are appropriate for him and to learn from inappropriate decisions.

With these needs in mind, Meadowbrook Junior High provides opportunities:

For choice of units of work in literature, social studies and science;	Choice
For choice of activities within a unit of work;	
For choice in specific areas of foreign language and math;	
For choice of electives in the many areas of special opportunities;	Decision Making
For choice of when, where, and with whom part of his school time is spent;	
For help in learning to take responsibility by making an agreement;	
For help in developing mutual trust and respect among students and teachers in classes and group activities;	Commitment
For help in growing in ability to make decisions and to take responsibility for his own education.	

SUBJECT OFFERINGS

Meadowbrook Junior High School recognizes that students differ in their educational needs. Within the subjects required of all, English, mathematics, social studies, science and physical education, many different units and levels are offered. Other subjects are offered to fulfill individual needs and interests. Each student, with guidance, selects a program of study which is appropriate for him.

The following subjects are offered:

ENGLISH

Units in:
Literature
Composition
Grammar and English Language

SOCIAL STUDIES

Units in:
History
Geography
Economics
Anthropology
Political Science

LANGUAGES

Courses in:
Latin
French
Spanish

MATHEMATICS

Courses in:
Basic Mathematics
Preparation for Algebra
Modern Algebra
School Mathematics Study Group
(S.M.S.G.)
Illinois Mathematics
(U.I.C.S.M.)

SCIENCE

Units in:
Chemistry
Biology
Physics
Earth Sciences

PHYSICAL EDUCATION. . . .INDUSTRIAL ECONOMICS. . . . . . . .THEATRE ARTS.

. INDUSTRIAL ARTS. . . .MUSIC. . . . . . .TYPING . . . . .ART. . . .HOME ECONOMICS

. . . . READING SKILLS . . . . . . .GENERAL ECONOMICS AND PRODUCTION.

CENTER TIME

Meadowbrook Junior High provides each student with some time in the school day to work and study according to his own interests and needs. Each day, the student chooses the subject, the teacher, and the materials with which he wants to work. Data processing makes it possible for the student to obtain his choice. He may choose to concentrate on one subject for several days or divide his time among many subjects. A teacher may request the presence of a student who needs additional help and is not seeking it on his own.

Resource centers and laboratories are established in all subject areas. Centers and laboratories are equipped with materials for research and enrichment. One or two teachers are present to assist the student. They may act as tutors to help with a problem, as resource experts to suggest materials, as evaluators of completed work, or as leaders of small groups. In addition to teachers, centers have a teacher aide who is called a Center Director.

In center time, students may choose—

. . . resource centers in the following areas:

English
Mathematics
Science
Social Studies
Foreign Language
Art
Music
Typing
Industrial Arts
Home Economics

. . . a resource center which contains library and audio-visual materials— books, tapes, filmstrips, records and films. Instruction in audio-visual equipment is given by an experienced teacher.

. . . a resource center which contains a twenty-station laboratory with recording and listening facilities.

. . . a resource center which includes a science laboratory and science materials.

. . . a resource center which specializes in enrichment materials. Experts on current affairs, lecturers or films on specific topics of interest, and individuals and groups from the performing arts are often available.

EVALUATION

Consistent with the goals of Meadowbrook Junior High, evaluation is concerned with helping the student look at himself realistically, set educational goals, and become involved in learning activities that will help him reach these goals.

The Study Plan is used by student and teacher for planning work and evaluating progress in a unit of study. The student makes an agreement with the teacher to complete a piece of work to the best of his ability. Specific tasks, adjusted to the individual, are listed on the Study Plan and are signed off with comments by student and teacher as they are completed. When the agreement is fulfilled, a summary is made indicating accomplishments and weaknesses. Emphasis is placed on the quality of the work rather than on the number of Study Plans completed.

Pupil Conferences are the major means by which the House Advisor helps the student to evaluate realistically his planning and progress.

Parent Conferences are called by the House Advisor at least twice yearly to discuss in detail accomplishments and needs of each student. Conferences may be initiated by the parent if necessary.

Evaluation Forms are sent home at the end of each twelve-week term, with special emphasis given to the goals of Meadowbrook Junior High School.

The Test Profile shows how each child compares with other Newton or Meadowbrook students on standardized tests. These are interpreted to both students and parents, and serve as one of many ways by which a student can evaluate his strengths and weaknesses, know what to expect of himself, and the areas on which he needs to work.

Chapter 20. INDEPENDENT STUDY FOR SELECTED STUDENTS

THE FUTURE—NOW !!

H. Eugene Hollick

The current knowledge explosion has aroused public curiosity concerning both formal education and the school's function. The school's obligation increasingly has become that of preparing students to learn outside the environment of the school and the teacher.

The learner must be more than an acquirer of knowledge—he must be a contributor to the explosion.

The variance within an individual may be 80% greater than that within the group with which he is associated. It becomes all too evident that educators must do more than recognize the existence of these individual differences. They must design "individualized learning systems" which will permit dealing with these differences effectively.

SOURCE: Reprinted from *Educational Television,* June, 1970, pp. 11-15, by permission of author and publisher.

One format designed to accomplish this is the individualized learning system now functioning in the Coatesville Area School District of Coatesville, Pennsylvania.

WHO PARTICIPATES

In the "Coatesville Project" during the academic year 1968-69, 250 students participated in one to four different disciplines: mathematics, English, social studies, and journalism. There were five courses of mathematics, two of English, three of social studies, and three of journalism.

In 1969-70, there are 500 students participating in the last two years of the Senior High School whose student body totals 1,050 for those two years. We have also added three more subject areas: secretarial practice under the department of business education, descriptive physics for college preparatory students not anticipating a career in science, and accelerated physics for exceptionally adept students.

Last year, the I.Q. range of the students in the mathematics program was from 84 to 137, and the average I.Q. of this group was 107. The students in American Studies II were of a similar I.Q. range, but with the significantly lower average I.Q. of 101. Students in the program were selected only on the basis of their desire to be there.

I did ask teachers to look over the names of those who had elected to take the program and then provide us with a list of students whose past behavioral patterns indicated they were *not* well suited for the program. From this list, we arbitrarily took half and placed them in the program. We succeeded only in proving conclusively that we do not have any valid criteria for student selection; therefore, this year all students who requested this program were admitted to it.

HOW THE PROGRAM WORKS

As an example, let us take a student in American Studies II. For his unit on the rise of business in the United States, the student leaves a conference with his teacher carrying a packet containing the following material: a flow chart (see Figure 20-1), a statement of the objectives of the teacher outlined on the chart and expressed in behavioral terms, work sheets to accompany the audio and video programs included in the unit, evaluation devices, and answers to these evaluations.

A student proceeding through the learning tasks directed by the sample flow chart in the illustration would be introduced to the unit "Rise of Business" through a television program titled "America Goes Industrial." To receive this program, he would go to a student carrel, find the associated dial number on the daily program sheet, and dial that number. His next activity is a programmed reading which he finds in his packet of materials.

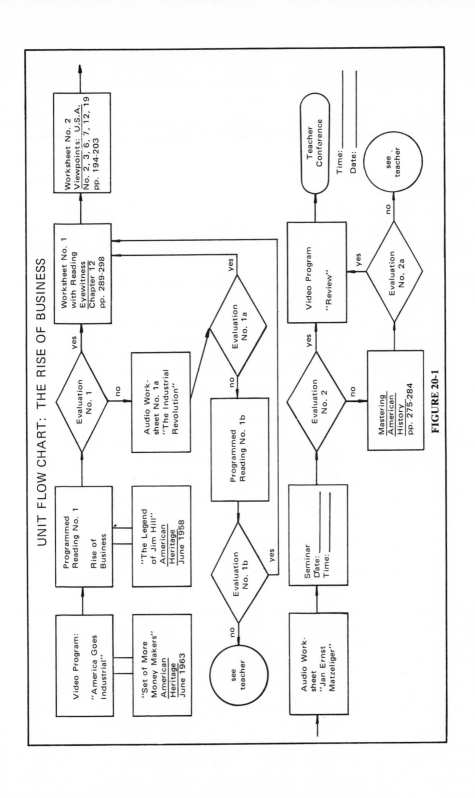

UNIT FLOW CHART: THE RISE OF BUSINESS

FIGURE 20-1

He then completes and does his own correction of the first evaluation exercise in his packet.

At this point, he must make a decision concerning his own success. If he considers himself successful, he proceeds along the linear portion of the flow chart via the "yes" route. If he was unsuccessful, however, he follows the "no" route through the branched circuit. Only *he* need know the path travelled, so he need not be concerned about being considered "dull" by his associates.

At each evaluation step of the branched circuit, success will direct him back into the "mainstream," or linear portion of the program. Each branch circuit has as its final attempt at assuring success a student-initiated teacher conference. The termination of each flow chart is a student-teacher conference. This is set up as an appointment with the teacher during the initial conference when the student receives the packet.

Through the course of the flow chart, the student encounters steps at which enrichment exercises are provided. They are indicated within a square which has arrows entering and exiting from and to the same rectangle—e.g., "Set of More Money Makers" from *American Heritage,* June 1963 (see Figure 20-1).

He may also encounter steps labeled "seminar" (bottom line of Figure 20-1) for which a specific time is indicated. These seminars provide an opportunity to discuss either the materials covered in the flow chart to that point, or special topics assigned for discussion. The seminar may or may not be attended by the teacher. Both types are used—the earlier ones attended more regularly by the teacher.

At the final conference, the student may expect an in-depth discussion over the content of the unit. As a result of this conference, his concepts of the unit content will be well understood by his teacher, and he can expect to receive help in seeing other viewpoints and/or in correcting erroneous ideas. He knows that there will be no "class" to hide behind if he is unprepared, and that the quality of his preparation for this conference will make the difference between a pleasant, helpful experience or one not quite so pleasant.

THE ROLE OF THE TEACHER

A student studying in this program is not assigned to classes or study halls, but to a teacher or a team of teachers who guide him through appropriate learning tasks designed to meet his individual needs. In this system, the teacher's job becomes one of educational diagnostician and prescriber to fit individual needs. The teacher is available full-time to meet students when they need him.

Students gather in areas with multiple media facilities available to them

Student dialing program after consulting his flow chart and schedule

A school *can* afford to provide this type of time for its professional staff by allowing educational technology to take over some of the duties they traditionally performed, such as presentation of material. These duties previously occupied a major portion of the teacher's time.

For this kind of program to be successful, the teacher must be available full-time to meet the student, in both student-initiated and scheduled conferences. It is therefore extremely important that the teacher have no other assignments such as classes, study halls, etc. The student's contact with his teacher is primarily in an individual conference or seminar of from two to ten.

DIAL ACCESS

In this type of program, students are not all studying the same thing at one time. The variations in position along the curriculum continuum may be rather high because of significant differences in student abilities and interest. Ability affects the linear progress through the defined curriculum much more than it does in a traditional program. It may take a student longer, but the facility is provided for success if he wishes to exert the effort.

A good example of this was a Junior girl who had been extremely weak in math, apparently because just as she was beginning to understand the material, her class would move on to a new topic. Under the new setup, she had that extra two or three days she needed to comprehend the material, and she became a very successful student in math. One of the teachers involved in the math program commented that many of his students who were considered weak had this same problem—they just could not grasp the material as quickly as had been required. Under the new program, although these students were not "covering" as much material as those in traditional classes, everyone agreed that they comprehended the material they did cover to a much greater depth than before.

We have also observed that the student's desire to succeed significantly and obviously increases as a result of being successful. A good example was one of the boys in the English program. He came into it merely hoping to find an English course different from the ones he already had failed or nearly failed. For three weeks he was lost. A failure notice was sent to his parents, resulting in a parental conference. Within six weeks, this student was doing B work. By mid-term he was surprising even himself. Although an industrial student who was completely uninterested in school, the program gave him the impetus to progress from the lowest group in English to the top. He said that he read more in that one year in the individualized program than in all his previous years in school. He is now enrolled in a trade school, after earning a three-year scholarship.

Although variance in the linear position is quite high, the bulk of the students function within a three-unit interval of each other. This, of course, affects the programming for the dial access system.

Requirements for dial access, of course, are totally dependent upon the educational requirements for which they are designed. Our experience would indicate that to place students on an individualized learning system for their entire curriculum would require approximately one carrel for every ten students. We currently have 107 carrels, 80 of which are video. Our current ratio of audio to video programs is four to one, and that seems fairly close to appropriate. Obviously, the number of carrels needed is related to the number of students only when all students are taking all their subjects this way.

Since the program capacity of a system is limited by its financial resources, one needs to provide the program capacity to deliver approximately three successive units in each subject area covered. The number of program sources is thus related to the number of courses offered and not to the number of students involved in each course. We need about one video and four audio programs per week for each subject unit. However, since the bulk of students is spread over a three-week period, this means that each course requires three video and twelve audio programs (three audio decks).

In addition, some program capacity must be available for providing for the needs of those students who, because of their rapid or slow progress, are not within the three-unit interval, but are working on other flow charts whose programs are not dial accessible. These students receive their programs by contacting the technician in the operating center who then manually provides them with their requests. A student must be able to signal the master control, not only for needs of this kind, but also to report technical difficulties when they occur.

Every classroom in our building is equipped with a monitor and dial plate. If a school is entirely on an individualized learning system, there is obviously no more need for classroom monitors than there is for classrooms. Even in a traditional format where classrooms are used, the monitor is important, but dial accessibility is totally unimportant if there is an intercom connection between the classroom and the central operating center.

The need (or lack of it) for dial accessibility of classroom monitors is related to the type of use they get. Since teachers use a program as part of a presentation, a request for that program requires only one setup and manual patch. Subsequent to that setup, a call for that same program requires only the pressing of the "play" button on the recorder. This can easily be done manually by the operator in the center. Such is not the case with carrels, however, because the program requirements for them vary drastically from one time to another. They need dial accessibility.

MATERIALS, PERSONNEL, AND EQUIPMENT

The success of this type of program depends heavily upon the materials used. The video and audio programs must be carefully designed for their specified learning tasks. A school district provides for such materials by giving teachers time to produce and/or plan the necessary programs. Although different arrangements have been tried, the only successful one we have found is using teachers during the summer, or whenever they have no other responsibilities and can devote full-time to producing the needed materials.

Not only must time be made available for the teachers. Special service personnel and certain physical facilities must also be provided. A visual and materials production center is imperative. There must also be a person who can implement the objective specified by the teacher who is working on either an audio work sheet or a video program. The studio needs a production staff to operate the equipment and provide the teacher with help in planning a video program by acquainting him with the capabilities and limitations of the equipment in the studio facility. Then, too, personnel are needed to type, duplicate, and assemble materials for the unit packets the students use.

Although an elaborate studio is unnecessary, the basic equipment in it should be of excellent quality. The technical quality of the programs used in any dial access system is obviously no better than that of their point of origination.

The facilities required for an individualized learning system have implications in the choice of courses offered as well as for the content of existing courses. For example, the traditional journalism program has taken on a new dimension. Our new program provides students with such experiences as writing and editorializing; production of visuals (such as

Industrial arts student receives help in brazing while teacher is busy

Student watches tape on operation of a mimeograph while using machine

lettering) and special materials for advertising; program planning and sequencing; audio taping, duplicating, and editing; sports writing, photography, and sportscasting; darkroom techniques; directing, technical directing, floor managing, and camera operations; videotaping and the techniques of integrating tape portions with live programming; audio control and lighting; announcing; silent and sound film preparation, editing, and use on television.

THE SCHOOL DAY

If asked where a student is at a particular time, school personnel must admit they don't know. He may be in the library writing, reading, using a carrel, researching 'back issues of a publication on microfilm, watching a filmstrip, or just meditating. He may be in a small-group room discussing an issue with his associates, using a calculator, a carrel, or programmed text materials. He may be in the room where his teacher is holding conferences, using reference material, or conferring with his teacher. He may be in the laboratory inquiring into the relationships between variables in a problem posed in a video program, or investigating some research project he has chosen on his own. He may be with a group of friends in a "classroom," viewing a dial-accessible video program they all want to see. He may be in a practice room pursuing a programmed keyboard exercise prepared by his music teacher, or listening to a dial-accessible stereo tape. Or he may be in the student commons having a soda, talking, or playing chess.

The student's whereabouts may not be known, but *he* is known. His teacher knows him as an individual with certain strengths and weaknesses. His academic effort is better understood than ever before.

A good example of this specialized knowledge of the individual is the experience of one of the girls who took part in the English program last year. She did not like the regular English course because she did not read well. When she entered the individualized program, her reading deficiencies were very evident, and now through individual diagnostic efforts, her teacher was able to give her prescribed methods to improve her reading. For three months she used the tachistoscope every day and, although she was not required to do so, also did the regularly assigned work in English. Her reading ability increased significantly and she began to really enjoy her English program.

Equally important to the teacher's knowledge of the student is the student's knowledge of the teacher. The student knows him as a person who cares. He no longer fears his teacher, nor does he view him as somebody on a pedestal to be revered. The teacher becomes a friend and counselor who is there when help is needed.

EFFECTS ON THE STUDENTS

Even though we may not be able to tell in advance who will profit from the individualized learning program, we have found no student whose academic achievement has decreased as a result of his participation. For example, almost all the students who took part in the individualized learning system in English appear to have progressed to some extent beyond what they might have learned in a regular classroom, and approximately 40% seem to have made significant gains beyond what would have been expected in a first-year program.

One boy was admitted to the English program during his Senior year because he wanted the "freedom" associated with the system, and because the guidance department felt that this program might be his only salvation. Everybody who knew him expected him to drop out of school any time. His grades in previous years, especially those in English, had been dismal. In the individualized program he really became independent—he seemed to enjoy working by himself, probably because he did not have the background or skills to work successfully with better students. He talked to his teacher and wrote his thoughts about his work. By mid-year, he was sitting in on seminars with the best students. By the end of the year he would discuss literature—or any other material—with them. This expected dropout is now attending a junior college.

The above-average student also profits from the individualized learning program. Approximately 10 of the 95 students in the English system were much brighter than the others. This group's final seminars were conducted entirely by the students themselves—the teacher helped only to plan the discussion. He did not even have to appoint a discussion leader. These students agreed that, after 12 years, they had learned how to learn.

I do not know whether this technique teaches students to think. Some of the examples of student response to the program, however, seem to indicate that this may be true. In my opinion, the inquiry approach, which can be used either in a traditional or an individualized learning program, contributes more to students in developing learning techniques than any other method.

Our primary interest in this particular project is in student attitude. We have experienced a 25% decrease in our drop-out rate. The tabulation of response to an attitude questionnaire distributed at the end of last year shows the change in student attitudes as a result of this program. This questionnaire was answered by all the students in the four subjects of last year's program. On the whole, they found it a positive experience.

The effect of this system on those students not involved is varied. It affects all students in some way. For example, a student in an industrial arts shop, where numerous different activities are proceeding at once, may need help in one type of activity while his teacher is involved with helping another student with an entirely different activity. Traditionally, this resulted in the student's having to wait until his teacher was free to help him. Now his teacher tells him to call the center and ask for program so-and-so which will give him the instruction he needs for operating certain equipment.

Again, a student in the business department, traditionally, may learn to use a particular business machine by watching a demonstration by his teacher. If he is fortunate, he has a front-row seat and can see the demonstration well. He may not have any occasion to use that particular machine until six weeks, or even six months, later. Now he can receive his instruction when his motivation is at its peak—when he needs to use the machine. He simply signals the center and requests a program of instruction for the machine in question, and watches that program while actually using the equipment.

OTHER EFFECTS

Perhaps the most noticeable effect on the students, both those involved and those not yet using individualized learning, comes through the change in outlook. The assumptions at any secondary school must change drastically when it institutes a program of prescriptioned education. No longer can it be preoccupied with late bells, hall passes, library passes, and all the other trivia which, unfortunately, take up the time of the educator in the traditional setting.

The school must concern itself with the student's progress through the educational continuum, with his development of responsibility, with his happiness and willingness to express his opinions, with his scrutiny and assessment of both published and non-published material, with his desire to remain in school, and with his desire to make a contribution to his society.

STUDENT REACTIONS

This tabulation summarizes student response to some of the questions asked about the individualized learning system in a questionnaire distributed in May of last year. Of the 260 students responding, 23 were enrolled in journalism, 93 in English, and 72 each in social studies and mathematics.

Most questions were answered by checking any of several responses. For this table, because of space limitations, we have compressed the response categories and indicated only the substance of the questions instead of giving them in full.

Percentages are computed on the number of answers received (given in parentheses after each question), not on the number of students who filled out the questionnaire. Some students did not answer some questions; other questions received more than one answer from some students.

1. When compared to courses of similar content you have taken in the past, in the course you are taking by individualized instruction what is your:

    In-depth comprehension? (258)

           Greater --- 73%   The same --- 20%   Less --- 7%

    Rate of progress? (258)

           Faster --- 67%   The same --- 23%   Slower --- 10%

    Interest level? (254)

           Higher --- 75%   The same --- 19%   Lower --- 6%

    Relationship with your teacher? (276)

           Positive --- 93%   Negative --- 7%

    Academic relationship with your other classmates? (251)

           More stimulating --- 85%   Less stimulating --- 15%

2. Would you elect to use the individualized system again? (258)

        Yes --- 80%   No --- 12%   Not sure --- 8%

3. Do you have enough opportunity to interact with your classmates regarding the course material? (255)

        Yes --- 84%   No --- 16%

4. Should a student take only one course via this method? (244)

        Yes --- 16%   No --- 84%

5. Did this method help you better budget your time? (255)

        Yes --- 84%   No --- 11%   No change --- 5%

6. Was the time allowed to complete work sufficient? (253)

        More than enough --- 57%   About right --- 31%   Not enough --- 12%

7. Should other courses be made available through this method? (254)

        Recommend yes --- 70%   Maybe --- 26%   Recommend no --- 4%

8. Concerning the technical quality in the carrels, how was

    The audio? (257)

        Good --- 55%   Fair --- 30%   Poor --- 15%

    The video? (259)

        Good --- 25%   Fair --- 40%   Poor --- 35%

Schools at other levels will be similarly affected when individualized learning programs are undertaken in them. We expect such a result in one junior high school which this year will use this approach for its entire Seventh Grade. There will also be similar reactions in the four different elementary schools which are using pilot programs in four different subject areas this year. And the philosophic shift will become more marked in the High School as more and more students become involved. It is contemplated that within five years, the entire curriculum will be offered through individualized learning, and that between 95 and 100% of the students will be involved.

The use of the school building may also undergo some revisions. Many attempts to extend use of the school plant have failed because of interference with family traditions. With this sort of system, there is little need for a specific starting time for any student. The only need is a definition of how much attendance is required. The parents and students can work out the details of when that attendance will be. The randomness of selection could result in up to a 25% decrease in student population at any one time. This will also affect building needs and future construction of schools.

Audio and video tape take on new meaning in education. Educational television can no longer be viewed as a medium by which to provide supplement and enrichment. It must be recognized as a major contribution to carrying out the instructional program of the school. It is the mechanism which permits the teacher to function as the professional he can be.

Chapter 21. SELF-SELECTED STUDY IN AN OPEN SCHOOL

WILSON CAMPUS SCHOOL

Donald Glines

Wilson has a philosophy which says, "if schools are to be significantly better, they must be significantly different." We really believe schools are drastically in need of reform. The reason that the Wilson program has drawn attention is not because of our quality, but instead because of the commitment made in July, 1968, to dramatically retool the educational system—to change Wilson from a "good conventional school" to a school dedicated to innovation, experimentation, research, and evaluation.

Wilson houses students from age 3 to age 20 (nursery through seniors) under one roof on a college campus. The students are a fairly good cross-section of the city of Mankato; the school operates on a modest budget—about median for Minnesota. Nothing new is being tried at Wilson—we are just copying good ideas; but probably Wilson has gone further toward the implementation of the following concepts than most schools in America:

SOURCE: Reprinted from *Automated Education Newsletter*, Vol. 5, No. 2 (February, 1970), pp. 3-8, published by the Automated Education Center, Detroit, Michigan, by permission of author and publisher.

daily smorgasbord scheduling; self-selected student-planned curricula; elimination of all K-12 course requirements; optional attendance; individual progress rather than ABC report cards, even for seniors; and a great deal of freedom and responsibility for all students.

The current Wilson emphasis is on improved human relations and personalized programming—a program individually designed for each student. Teacher and student images of themselves, of each other and of their relationships are crucial ingredients now missing in most innovative programs built around team teaching, non-grading, and flexible scheduling; they are most certainly missing in most conventional programs. Positive motivation, daily success, and self-direction are more important at Wilson than the study of subject matter.

In matching perceptions, many of the old educational hangups are being eliminated. Students are now involved in designing their own relevant curricula—most actually self-select and plan their own learning; no "courses" in the traditional concept of teacher dominated classes are scheduled or taught. They choose the consultants (teachers) with whom they would like to work, in any area they wish to work; they choose their own teacher-counselors. As these matches are formed, skill, age, sex, and interest are factors as well as personality and perception, as related to both student and teacher. Kids need an adult to relate to, and they need to study relevant and meaningful material; thus Wilson is attempting to accomplish the old textbook preached, but until now seldom practiced, cliché of individual needs, interests, and abilities.

There are no required classes, even for the primary age children. Attendance is optional, an open campus policy is followed. Students can go home and sleep if nothing relevant is offered that day. Students come to school and visit the many centers of study that are available—still traditionally labeled as art, music, theater arts, mathematics, and eight others. Students may work in any of these 12 centers or in any combination of any interdisciplinary or multi-disciplinary approach they find of interest and value.

The student observes what is being done by others, looks at the materials, and has individual interviews with the consultants. If the consultant can help suggest a program which seems appropriate, if the student can suggest and devise his own, if a combination of student and teacher ideas seems to fit together, the student can start to work immediately. If nothing seems to jell, he can continue to window shop in that area or in any of the other areas. There are no maximum or minimum number of "courses" a student may take, nor is there a limit on the amount of time. He may take two courses in depth, or may be selective in ten. One pursuit may be followed for an exhaustive 4 weeks, or it may be scanned for 4 weeks; it could be investigated for 18, 36, or 66 weeks—the student pursues the inquiry until satisfied or until time and other interests lead him to quest elsewhere.

His progress is evaluated in terms of learning objectives set through conferences with his instructors and with the parents whenever they request information or involvement. Hopefully much of the insight is gained through chats with students at home, but when teacher perspectives are desired, they are readily available by merely mailing to the school a parent conference request form to request written or oral communication from the school. To be able to respond to the parents, the areas being pursued by the student are recorded by the teacher-counselor and are kept on file in the central student folder. Their studies are readily changeable; students may start or stop courses whenever it seems desirable—whether November or March or August. The curricula is self-developed on a continuous progress, self-paced approach; there are no magic semesters or quarters and obviously no final exams. And there are certainly no "4th or 7th grades." Students of many ages may work together. The appropriateness of the mix is the criterion, not the number of years spent in school.

Thus a program is individually diagnosed and prescribed by and for each student. These diagnosis/prescription elements take into account student, parent, teacher, counselor, and society inputs. Theoretically, a student may take, and many do pursue, "anything they want." There are no graduation requirements other than just a general goal of about the equivalent of 20 traditional one-year courses, or combination of mini or micro-mini courses equalling that number, usually over a 3-5 year period, but these are only guidelines and are tailored to fit individual students. Often in practical operation, the student choice is modified through parent influences, teacher and counselor suggestions, and some colleges and employers who demand a transcript showing a diploma with certain courses. If students follow traditional restrictions, it is their choice. They are told of the alternatives: they can gamble on a future job or college based on maturity and other factors; they can go to a junior college or vocational school; they can join the army or get married or make other personal choices. They are told many colleges no longer care about four years of English, three years of social, and two years of foreign language. But they are advised that some still do, and that if they want to be safe they should take all the "nice" courses. To graduate from Wilson though they can major in "basketweaving" if they so desire.

Younger students have the same choices and follow the same program. However, at all levels, if the school really feels the student is making a tragic mistake, the student can be required to take a certain "course." For example, a five-year old usually needs a great deal of motor development. Wilson tries to make the program attractive enough that all who need it will choose it, but if a poorly coordinated student does not choose motor development, and if the staff is fairly certain that this is an emergency crisis (the surgeon may make a decision about an unconscious dying patient)—the school will step in and operate.

Most days students attending Wilson select from the daily smorgasbord schedule. It tells what foods are available on the menu for that day—what fruits are in season. Many activities on the smorgasbord are student planned. Because all activities are optional, the daily program for the student is, in most cases, determined by the individual student. The only reason for a "schedule" at all is to let students know if any special events are being offered, or if any areas are closed, or if a consultant would especially like to see them, or to indicate that a group has been scheduled to meet for some specific purpose. The schedule is developed daily by three or four persons; students can help schedule, but usually these are teachers and paraprofessionals who serve about three days a month each on a rotation basis; it normally takes them about one or two hours a day to construct the schedule for 600 students. There is a part-time clerk and a part-time teacher coordinator to handle on-going schedule problems.

Wilson features individualized learning and phase teaching. Once a student has chosen art as part of his personalized program, he individualizes his pursuits within the field of art, or by interrelating with other fields. About 85 percent of the day the student follows his own individually chosen schedule. One of the five phases of "instruction" at Wilson is the 1-1 tutoring or conference between student and instructor. This can be scheduled by the student and teacher whenever both are free and does not appear on the "master" schedule for that day.

The second phase involves open laboratory. This simply is active involvement by the student in some phase of his study (painting his picture). When this type of opportunity is available, which is usually 95-100 percent of the day, the schedule merely reflects open lab under the "art center" column—the student can go there whenever he desires. Closely related to open lab, but of less active physical involvement, is the third phase, that of independent study (an example would be reading in the resource center or listening to a tape in the automation center, or reading poetry in the English center). This is usually open to all students in all areas most all day; occasionally there may be some type of conflict which would close this possibility for some part of the day, but other areas are always open as alternatives.

The fourth phase is small group. Groups still play a role at Wilson but are only scheduled when students or teachers feel a need. A small group to discuss the topic of student unrest might meet when background study or interest indicates that such a session might be of value for those who would choose to attend. No groups are automatically scheduled to meet so many times each week at some specific time. The fifth phase, large group, is of the common treat variety and is an example of the specials on the daily schedule. Perhaps a well-known artist is in town and agrees to discuss his art form and demonstrate some general techniques to a group of interested students for a short period of time during the day.

Thus the daily smorgasbord schedule—a little ham, a little turkey, lots of roast beef, several salads, lots of milk, blueberry pie, and others—is offered each day or on some days for students to select. It is rather embarrassing, by the way, if no one selects the music pie designed by Mrs. Jones. It usually indicates problems, and Mrs. Jones often offers herself right out of a job. Attendance still remains optional; if there are no students, there is no position for Mrs. Jones.

To operate such a program, a great deal of team planning and less but essential amounts of team teaching must occur. Teachers must talk with teachers about kids or the entire program collapses. An attractive physical environment is of value, too. Wilson has carpeted some rooms, has plants and animals in some, and has brightly colored red, purple, green, orange, yellow, and blue walls in many.

Wilson tries to operate on a modified differentiated staffing pattern—doctors, nurses, nurses' aides, and candystripers. The school program is available on a volunteer 7:30-5:30 plan—teachers and kids come and go as they desire each day; no one is required to spend that amount of time in school, although many do—and not just the athletic teams. Wilson is trying to become a community school, open 24 hours a day, seven days a week. Rigidities found in the state college system prevent this at present, but the school does operate on a 12-month basis now, always open for study except for two weeks of winter vacation, one week of spring vacation, two weeks of summer vacation, one week in the fall. These match college contract periods.

The 12-month idea is one of the most successful. Students are encouraged to attend 170 days during the 12 months for purposes of state aid, but otherwise can come and go as they please. They can take vacation in November or January or August. There is no reason for students to attend school only from September to June. Some parents can best take their vacations in January if they work in summer trades or tourist areas, or if father is low in seniority on his job. Some families never get a good vacation together because of traditional schools and their insistence on September to June enrollment. Wilson students have a continuous, self-paced individualized program, so nothing is missed if they are absent; they are encouraged to go duck hunting with Dad, even on a "school day."

The foreign language program at Wilson has great potential. Students are encouraged to take 3-6 hours a day of Spanish and/or International Studies. Immersing oneself in the language over a short period of time seems to make sense. As many as possible go to Mexico for six weeks or more each year. Spanish is difficult to learn in Mankato, Minnesota. Plans are now underway for similar programs in other areas of the world.

Students should be outside the school walls as much as possible. Therefore, Wilson students take their psychology class by working three 40-hour weeks at the state mental health hospital; they work in local offices; they take social studies while on vacation trips with their parents; they study by working in local city government offices—all these not for pay but for "course completion."

The five year olds are in school all day long and self-select on the daily smorgasbord as do all other students. The three- and four-year-old programs are limited again by lack of state financial support, but Wilson has one-half day programs for each, merely by taking the money out of the former high school allocations. There are no elementary, middle, and high school divisions. Wilson is just one non-graded school. The various learning centers house students traditionally PreK-12. It is not possible to really intelligently separate so-called "5th graders" from "6th graders" or "9th graders" from "10th graders," so no attempt is made to determine such false distinctions.

Research and evaluation were weak in the first year of operation at Wilson. During this second year extensive horizontal and vertical studies of both short- and long-range duration are being carried out. A Research Systems person is now on the staff. The College Office of Institutional Research has taken charge of outside evaluation. A research committee for the school has been formed. Graduate students will do their thesis studies at Wilson. A Ph.D. in psychology has been hired to work with Human Relations and Evaluation. Studies in the affective, psychomotor and cognitive will be undertaken, with emphasis on the first two of these three. Hopefully by the end of 1970 and each year after that, some significant research and evaluation results will be available as a further contribution to the changing educational scene.

The school administratively operates through a Design Team. One person is responsible for Future Planning; another for Learning Resources; another for Student Services; and another for Human Relations. These four are full-time autonomous persons who make decisions. If a "veto" is ever needed, it is wielded by the person in charge of Future Planning (traditionally the Director). Three part-time positions—Special Projects, Dissemination Programs, and Research Systems—complete the seven-man Design Team. These persons make decisions in their areas, function as a coordinating group for the entire school, and work with the various learning teams in small groups. Large group faculty meetings are almost non-existent. In the meantime, the learning teams make daily decisions at the student level as related to programs, and students make individual decisions about their studies and group decisions through several types of student organizations. Parent, faculty, and student advisory teams complement the entire design. Parent involvement in the school program is greatly desired. But even more necessary is student input. Students help to make decisions at all levels, not just about Saturday night dances. They operate the student center; they have no dress codes; they are encouraged to protest. Student involvement is one of the keys to success in changing schools.

Chapter 22. DIAGNOSIS AND PRESCRIPTION FOR THE INDIVIDUAL LEARNER

THE P.E.P. APPROACH TO LEARNING DIAGNOSIS

Phyllis Green

How does a child learn best? What factors tend to mold the learning characteristics of childhood? How can we as educators identify these factors, in an economically feasible setting for public school systems to handle? These are a few of the probing questions the Bucks County Schools' Intensification of Learning Project is attempting to answer, with the aid of federal funds, within the short span of 2 1/2 years.

A child's learning style is directly influenced by his total development. All components of his development must be evaluated for clues to his unique style of learning. For this reason, the team approach to diagnosis offered the most inclusive means of identifying learning characteristics.

SOURCE: This paper first appeared in *P.E.P. Capsules,* Vol. 2, No. 1 (July, 1968), and in more complete form in *Intensification of the Learning Process,* Report No. 1, Bucks County Public Schools, February, 1970. Reprinted by permission of author and publisher.

The P.E.P. (Personalized Education Prescription) diagnostic team consists of a psychiatrist, a clinical psychologist, a social worker, the school principal and a master teacher. All contribute diagnostic information which is the basis for the resultant learning prescription for each child.

The social worker provides information gained from an in depth two-hour family interview centering on the parents' interpretation of the physical and behavioral development from birth to the present time.

The psychiatrist summarizes his impressions based on a 45-minute interview and neurological screening.

The psychologist presents the results of a thorough clinical psychological evaluation touching on intellectual, personality and neurological areas.

The school principal offers early school history dealing with previous and present teacher observations, test scores, medical history, and home environmental relationships of which he is aware.

The master teacher provides the results and interpretations gleaned from the Gesell Developmental Test and the Illinois Test of Psycholinguistic Abilities, which she can administer, and the Getman Vision Screening test administered by the school nurse.

The diagnostic information is then interpreted, within the total team conference, by the curriculum specialists (language arts, mathematics, social studies and science) into a personalized learning prescription for that child. Specific individually prescribed recommendations for materials and activities to be used in the content areas are cited, plus suggestions as to the behavioral approach of the teacher to the child, the defenses to support and those to discourage, the interests of the child, and recommendations for a parent conference.

The total team conference is under the direction of the associate project director who guides and contributes toward a total team approach.

The Project not only offers the opportunity to discover and highlight the learning characteristics of children but it also provides the chance to compare the expensive diagnosis obtained from the social worker, psychiatrist and psychologist with the more economically available information obtained by the principal, school nurse, master teacher or guidance specialist, and the classroom teacher. Can our educational evaluative procedures compete favorably with an in-depth, clinically specialized diagnosis?

The source of the highest correlation with the expensive means of diagnosis appears to be the Gesell Developmental Test with the Kindergarten and Primary Grade Teachers' observations plus the Illinois Test of Psycholinguistic Abilities also correlating highly in that order.

The Gesell test offers a surface screening in the developmental areas of personality, communication skills, neurological growth, intellectual capacity range, interests, social and emotional behavior. The Gesell diagnosis consistently correlated with the family and psychiatric interviews and the psychological evaluation. The latter offered a much more penetrating analysis, however; and a caution must be heeded that the Gesell test is limited in depth of analysis and is only as good as the examiner, thus demands a thorough training program strengthened by an experienced understanding of child development.

The insightful Kindergarten and Primary Grade Teacher can become an extremely proficient diagnostician of learning characteristics. Many teachers, however, though able to identify these traits, tend to look at the child in relation to the group, neglecting to make use of the child's unique learning patterns to intensify his progress.

The Illinois Test of Psycholinguistic Abilities provides an inclusive overview of the child's expressive and receptive facility in the areas of communications. The sub-test scores help to diagnose the learning modalities most preferred by the child, whether it be oral, aural, visual or motor or a combination of these.

Thus the diagnostic techniques being used in the P.E.P. Project to evaluate the children are undergoing appraisal themselves. The results will help to yield a more economically possible diagnostic program without sacrificing quality or quantity of the information obtained. The ultimate diagnostic goal of the P.E.P. Project is to discover the learning style of the student rather than restrict pupil diagnosis to the limited and temporary state of his learning achievement.

A process was established whereby the diagnostic team reviewed all of the diagnostic data on a child, and wrote prescriptions related to the classroom activities of the child in such a way that the learning of this child could be intensified. The following list includes all of the areas that have been studied regarding each of the children in the project. This listing includes the person or persons responsible for the initiating or gathering of the information:

Diagnostic Data	*Person/Persons Responsible*
1. Physical Examination	School Doctor
2. Visual Screening	School Nurse
3. Speech and Hearing Evaluation	Nurse and Speech and Hearing Consultant from the County
4. Teacher Anecdotes	Classroom Teacher
5. Cumulative Folder	Principal
6. Gesell Developmental Test	Master Teacher

Diagnostic Data	*Person/Persons Responsible*
7. Achievement Test	Classroom Teacher, Curriculum Specialist, Principal and Master Teacher
8. Illinois Test of Psycholinguistic Ability	Speech and Hearing Staff, County
9. Wechsler Intelligence Test for Children (W.I.S.C.)	Psychologist, Einstein Medical Center (Contracted Services)
10. Bender-Gestalt Test of Performance Visual Motor Gestalt Function	Psychologist, Einstein Medical Center (Contracted Services)
11. Dr. Mark Ozer Neurological Test	Psychiatrist, Einstein Medical Center (Contracted Services)
12. Psychiatric Interview	Child Psychiatrist, Einstein Medical Center (Contracted Services)
13. Developmental History	Psychologist, Einstein Medical Center (Contracted Services)
14. Pupil Observations	Master Teacher, Classroom Teacher, Principal, Curriculum Specialist, Child-Youth Study Director
15. Visual Perception Screening	Nurse
16. Gross Motor Skill Screening	Physical Education Teacher

LEARNER'S RESPONSE TO A VARIETY OF STIMULI

I.   Problem: One of the objective tasks of P.E.P. is the need for identifying and developing multi-level learning activities which by their nature allow pupils at all ability levels to learn effectively. The problem which arises from this task involves:

a)   Identifying the student's preferred learning stimuli;

b)   Providing a variety of media;

c)   Evaluating the child's response to the various instructional activities.

II.   What is being done now to solve the problem?

   a)   The P.E.P. diagnosis contributes information pertaining to the identification of student preferred learning modalities: visual, oral, aural, kinesthetic or tactile. The designated preference evolves from an analysis of the psychological, psychiatric, I.T.P.A., Gesell Developmental and the teacher observation data.

   b)   A variety of instructional stimuli are then provided by the teacher, the curriculum specialists, and the diagnostic team in the form of materials, activities, or equipment. The learning purpose determines the setting and length of exposure. The Instructional Media Center provides the resource center for most of the materials and equipment.

   c)   The child's response is evaluated in terms of his voluntary use of the media, his affective behavior when involved with each particular type of stimuli and his overall state of learning in relation to past achievement. The teacher is in the best position to evaluate these areas both from an observational and test appraisal point of view. However, the evident difficulty is in the organization and documentation of individual evaluations for a classroom full of children.

III.   P.E.P. Team recommendations:

   a)   Early identification of the student's preferred learning modality would benefit both student and teacher. Thus, an evaluation should be done as early as possible in his initial schooling experience. Some suggested appraisal techniques would be the I.T.P.A., the Gesell Developmental and the Pupil Description Worksheet based on teacher observation. For a more inclusive evaluation, a psychological examination could be administered. The P.E.P. Project afforded an opportunity to compare the quantity and quality of the data obtained from all of these sources and it was not evident that a psychological examination be given in order to determine the preferred learning modality.

   b)   The larger the variety of media available to a teacher, the more readily she can establish a motivating and successful learning atmosphere. In order to conveniently acquaint teachers with the types of materials, equipment, and activities available in all curriculum areas, an accessible learning resource center must be developed. Ideally, each school should provide this type of service but financially a district or county center would be more feasible. In conjunction, the services of curriculum specialists could also be made available on a district or county level. A curriculum coordinator within each building could conceivably handle both diagnosis and curriculum guidance. This is more applicable to the elementary program than the secondary level.

c)   In evaluating pupil response to stimuli, it is important that the learning program be well organized for best control of the evaluation techniques. The teacher should include periodic appraisals both written and oral. Check-lists for equipment are valuable and convenient methods for quick evaluations of how often a piece of equipment is used and by whom.

The teacher aide can be of great value in providing the services needed for a well-organized evaluation program. She can see that the children are "checked out" on the equipment, make note of affective pupil response, mark materials done independently, offer guidance to small groups doing project work and generally relieve the teacher of the clerical duties involved in the organization which a multi-media approach demands.

The children should have the opportunity to explore all types of stimuli and not be restricted to the student's preferred modality diagnosed in the prescription. This diagnosis is primarily to afford the teacher with a motivating avenue for instructional purposes. The child should be given the opportunity to select the learning activity he prefers, guided in discovering it as a purposeful learning tool rather than a toy.

The teacher can be aided by the students in appraising the multi-media by simply asking them to indicate their preferences and explaining the reasons for their selections.

The P.E.P. Project has shown that when children are exposed to a variety of stimuli, generated by a multi-media program, their response reflects their preferential modality for learning and helps to strengthen those areas which indicate a developmental weakness. More importantly, student affective behavior was viewed as one of the enjoyments in the learning process.

INTENSIFICATION OF
THE LEARNING PROCESS

Division of Curriculum and Instruction Services

PUPIL DESCRIPTION WORK SHEET

Purpose

The following statements are intended as a guide for describing a child in a classroom situation. They attempt to give a picture of what a child is, how he learns, and how he reacts to learning situations. They do not cover the amount or kind of factual content the child may have learned, but only the pattern of his learning. No attempt has been made to make these statements all inclusive; they are intended to describe some aspects of learning that can make a difference to a teacher in her handling of a classroom situation. This may occur through her understanding of a child's strengths and weaknesses, the suggestion of potentially successful approaches, or the warning of areas of difficulty. In general, only extremes of conduct or ability are indicated; we are not attempting to describe the "average" child in these areas, on the assumption that such a child does not need attention. Thus, any child may be sometimes shy; it is the one who is extremely shy or fearful that stands out needing to be helped.

PUPIL DESCRIPTION WORK SHEET

A. Receptive Learning Modalities

      1. LEARNING SKILLS in VISUAL situations or materials are GOOD.

SOURCE: This paper is adapted from various pupil description materials provided by the staff of the Division of Curriculum and Instruction Services, Bucks County Public Schools, Doylestown, Pennsylvania, George E. Raab, Superintendent. Permission for their use was granted by Raymond Bernabei, Assistant Superintendent.

2. LEARNING SKILLS in VISUAL situations or materials are often of POOR quality.

3. LEARNING SKILLS in LISTENING situations are GOOD.

4. LEARNING SKILLS in LISTENING situations are often of POOR quality.

5. LEARNING SKILLS in MANIPULATIVE activities are GOOD.

6. LEARNING SKILLS in MANIPULATIVE activities are often of POOR quality.

B. *Expressive Learning Modalities*

7. PERFORMANCE SKILLS in coloring, cutting, pasting, and handwriting show FACILITY.

8. PERFORMANCE SKILLS in coloring, cutting, pasting and handwriting often show CLUMSINESS.

9. SKILLS in the GYMNASIUM and playground, in hopping, skipping, etc., are PERFORMED EASILY.

10. PERFORMANCE SKILLS in the GYMNASIUM and playground, in hopping, skipping, etc., often show CLUMSINESS.

11. QUALITY OF SPEECH (tone, loudness, diction, etc.) is usually EFFECTIVE.

12. QUALITY OF SPEECH is often inadequate and shows POOR ARTICULATION.

13. QUALITY OF SPEECH is often inadequate and particularly shows EVIDENCE OF SLURRING.

14. Often USES FACIAL EXPRESSIONS or gestures to extend verbal communication.

15. FACIAL EXPRESSIONS or gestures are NOT USED to extend verbal communication.

16. Shows HIGH DEGREE of physical CAPACITY for continuous STRENUOUS MOVEMENT.

17. LACKS the physical CAPACITY for continuous STRENUOUS MOVEMENT.

18. Uses WORDS EFFECTIVELY to express himself.

19. Tends to be ARTICULATE and to VERBALIZE FEELINGS easily.

20. Tends to be very INARTICULATE and UNABLE to VERBALIZE FEELINGS.

C. Orderliness in Work/Play Habits

21. ABILITY TO ORGANIZE own activities is CONSISTENT.

22. ABILITY TO ORGANIZE own activities is INCONSISTENT.

23. RIGID in APPROACHES to different methods of LEARNING.

24. Can SWITCH from one method of LEARNING to another with no apparent difficulty.

25. Relies heavily on having a SAMPLE PATTERN OR MODEL to follow in performing a task.

26. Sees most things in terms of BLACK OR WHITE, right or wrong, with NO SHADINGS.

D. Concern with Where He Is in His World

27. Continually REQUIRES DETAILED DIRECTION from teacher in performing activities.

28. BODY ORIENTATION (left and right sides, legs, arms, etc.) shows CONFUSION.

29. WORLD ORIENTATION (names of days of the week, months, seasons, etc.) shows CONFUSION.

30. Makes MATURE HUMAN FIGURE drawings.

31. Makes IMMATURE HUMAN FIGURE drawings.

32. Draws HUMAN FIGURES as DIFFERENT or STRANGE.

33. RESPONDS well to CONSTRUCTIVE CRITICISM.

34. VOLUNTEERS to RECITE but then has INCORRECT ANSWER.

E. Intrinsic or Extrinsic Responses

35. REASSURANCE is frequently NEEDED for motivation.

36. Shows need for PROMPT REWARDS.

37. REQUIRES PRESSURE to get work accomplished.

38. Applying PRESSURE brings a POSITIVE RESPONSE toward getting work accomplished.

39. Applying PRESSURE makes little or NO DIFFERENCE in work accomplished.

40. Applying PRESSURE has an ADVERSE EFFECT on work accomplished.

41. Tends to do MORE THAN REQUIRED.

42. Tends to PROCRASTINATE or do incomplete work.

43. Is STIMULATED BY COMPETITION.

44. Tends to AVOID COMPETITION with others.

45. Tends to GIVE UP when the going gets difficult.

46. PERSEVERES even in the face of difficulty.

F. Emotional Maturity

47. Is NOT PROGRESSING EMOTIONALLY.

48. Tends to become ATTACHED to INDIVIDUAL adults.

49. Frequently reverts to INFANTILE BEHAVIOR such as crying, using baby talk, imagining illness, etc.

50. OCCASIONALLY tends to ACT YOUNGER than his age.

51. Adapts to CHANGE with DIFFICULTY.

52. Often REACTS IMPULSIVELY and with a lack of self-discipline.

53. Is VERY SELF-DISCIPLINED.

54. Hampered in activities by FEAR OF MAKING MISTAKES.

55. Exhibits a STRONG PUSH toward maturity.

56. Shows PROVOCATIVE, DEFIANT behavior and tends to FIGHT easily.

57. His PROBLEMS tend to be of SHORT duration and RESPOND quickly to REMEDY.

58. Tends to be STUBBORN in the face of AUTHORITY.

59. Seems ARRESTED in FORWARD DEVELOPMENT.

60. Seems to be SLIPPING BACKWARD in DEVELOPMENT.

G. Self-Concept

61. VACILLATION shown in DECISION-MAKING.

62. Tends to show concern because BODY DEVELOPMENT seems SLOWER than normal.

63. Is concerned because BODY DEVELOPMENT seems to be MORE MATURE than for average of class.

64. INDEPENDENT.

65. DEPENDENT on others.

66. Often seems OVERLY DEPENDENT on ADULTS.

67. Gives an appearance of LOW SELF-ESTEEM.

68. Covers LACK OF SELF-CONFIDENCE with a show of CONCEIT.

69. SHY and fearful.

70. OUTGOING, EASY MANNER with no feelings of timidity.

71. Seems UNAWARE of the NEGATIVE effect his behavior has on OTHERS.

72. TOO SENSITIVE.

73. An AGGRESSIVE child.

74. Appearance indicates an occasional OVER-CONCERN with CLEANLINESS.

75. Often appears in class in an UNKEMPT AND DIRTY condition.

76. At times behaves in STRANGE ways WITHOUT apparent cause or REASON.

77. Appears WITHDRAWN and stays WITHIN SHELL during school activities.

H. Preference for Others

78. Tends to PREJUDGE OTHERS, who may be different, on the basis of incomplete understanding or bias.

79. Prefers the COMPANY OF OLDER PEOPLE.

80. Usually PLAYS or works with YOUNGER CHILDREN.

81. PREFERS the company of children of the SAME SEX.

82. PREFERS the company of children of the OPPOSITE SEX.

83. INSENSITIVE to others.

I. Performance in Groups

84. Tends to be SET APART from OTHER children.

85. Tends to have LIMITED SUCCESS in FRIENDSHIPS.

86. PERFORMS well when WORKING ALONE.

87. PERFORMS well when WORKING in ONE-TO-ONE relation.

88. PERFORMS well when WORKING IN A SMALL GROUP.

89. PERFORMS well when WORKING IN A LARGE GROUP.

90. PERFORMS well in ANY SIZE GROUP.

91. Tends to be LOST and relatively uninvolved when working IN A LARGE GROUP.

92. Takes an ACTIVE PART IN LARGE GROUP activities.

93. Even in SMALL GROUPS, remains relatively UNINVOLVED in activity.

94. Takes an ACTIVE PART IN SMALL GROUP activities.

95. Appears to be RELUCTANT to work COOPERATIVELY with others.

96. WELL-LIKED by peer group.

97. NOT LIKED by peer group.

98. Generally PLEASANT and LIKABLE.

J. Participation

99. A little TOO AGGRESSIVE for a GIRL.

100. A little TOO PASSIVE for a BOY.

101. Frequent and effective CONTRIBUTOR OF IDEAS in LARGE GROUP discussions.

102. Frequent and effective CONTRIBUTOR OF IDEAS in SMALL GROUP discussions.

103. Shows an EAGERNESS TO LEARN.

104. Desires ACTIVE PARTICIPATION in learning.

105. PASSIVE in approach to learning.

106. RELUCTANT to PARTICIPATE in activities that might result in PHYSICAL INJURY.

K. Leadership

107. Exhibits LEADERSHIP QUALITIES.

108. Often CHOSEN AS A LEADER by his peers.

109.   Often tries to DOMINATE or over-control PEOPLE or situations.

110.   Is RARELY SELF-ASSERTIVE even when such action is legitimate.

L. Attention

111.   Frequently INATTENTIVE.

112.   Shows a tendency to DAY-DREAM.

M. Distractibility

113.   EASILY DISTRACTED when not under close supervision.

114.   A SOURCE OF DISTURBANCE in the classroom.

N. General Range of Intelligence and Achievement

115.   General range of ABILITIES is HIGHER than that of most children in this age group.

116.   General range of ABILITIES is LOWER than that of most children in this age group.

117.   Generally ALERT and RESPONSIVE.

118.   Generally UNRESPONSIVE.

119.   LEARNING FROM EXPERIENCE is PRODUCTIVE, allowing transfer and generalization to other situations.

120.   Unusually able to pick out RELATIONSHIPS TO ENVIRONMENT.

121.   General FUND of INFORMATION is LARGE.

122.   General FUND of INFORMATION is SMALL.

123.   Is able to PERCEIVE, identify, and be directed by GOALS.

124.   MEMORY skills are EFFECTIVE.

125.   MEMORY skills are INEFFECTIVE.

INDIVIDUAL PROFILE DRAWN FROM STUDENT "A"

002   LEARNING SKILLS IN VISUAL SITUATIONS OR MATERIALS ARE OFTEN OF POOR QUALITY.

003   LEARNING SKILLS IN LISTENING SITUATIONS ARE GOOD.

005   LEARNING SKILLS IN MANIPULATIVE ACTIVITIES
        ARE GOOD.

008   PERFORMANCE SKILLS IN COLORING, CUTTING,
        PASTING   AND   HANDWRITING   OFTEN   SHOW
        CLUMSINESS.

009   SKILLS IN THE GYMNASIUM AND PLAYGROUND, IN
        HOPPING, SKIPPING, ETC., ARE PERFORMED EASILY.

012   QUALITY OF SPEECH IS OFTEN INADEQUATE AND
        SHOWS POOR ARTICULATION.

013   QUALITY OF SPEECH IS OFTEN INADEQUATE AND
        PARTICULARLY SHOWS EVIDENCE OF SLURRING.

014   OFTEN USES FACIAL EXPRESSIONS OR GESTURES TO
        EXTEND VERBAL COMMUNICATION.

016   SHOWS HIGH DEGREE OF PHYSICAL CAPACITY FOR
        CONTINUOUS STRENUOUS MOVEMENT.

020   TENDS TO BE VERY INARTICULATE AND UNABLE
        TO VERBALIZE FEELINGS.

022   ABILITY TO ORGANIZE OWN ACTIVITIES IS
        INCONSISTENT.

025   RELIES HEAVILY ON HAVING A SAMPLE PATTERN
        OR MODEL TO FOLLOW IN PERFORMING A TASK.

026   SEES MOST THINGS IN TERMS OF BLACK OR WHITE,
        RIGHT OR WRONG, WITH NO SHADINGS.

027   CONTINUALLY REQUIRES DETAILED DIRECTION
        FROM TEACHER IN PERFORMING ACTIVITIES.

028   BODY ORIENTATION (LEFT AND RIGHT SIDES, LEGS,
        ARMS, ETC.) SHOWS CONFUSION.

031   MAKES IMMATURE HUMAN FIGURE DRAWINGS.

032   DRAWS HUMAN FIGURES AS DIFFERENT OR
        STRANGE.

034   VOLUNTEERS TO RECITE BUT THEN HAS INCORRECT
        ANSWER.

035   REASSURANCE IS FREQUENTLY NEEDED FOR
        MOTIVATION.

036   SHOWS NEED FOR PROMPT REWARDS.

037   REQUIRES PRESSURE TO GET WORK
        ACCOMPLISHED.

038   APPLYING PRESSURE BRINGS A POSITIVE RESPONSE TOWARD GETTING WORK ACCOMPLISHED.

042   TENDS TO PROCRASTINATE OR DO INCOMPLETE WORK.

044   TENDS TO AVOID COMPETITION WITH OTHERS.

045   TENDS TO GIVE UP WHEN THE GOING GETS DIFFICULT.

050   OCCASIONALLY TENDS TO ACT YOUNGER THAN HIS AGE.

051   ADAPTS TO CHANGE WITH DIFFICULTY.

052   OFTEN REACTS IMPULSIVELY AND WITH LACK OF SELF-DISCIPLINE.

056   SHOWS PROVOCATIVE, DEFIANT BEHAVIOR AND TENDS TO FIGHT EASILY.

058   TENDS TO BE STUBBORN IN THE FACE OF AUTHORITY.

059   SEEMS ARRESTED IN FORWARD DEVELOPMENT.

065   DEPENDENT ON OTHERS.

068   COVERS LACK OF SELF-CONFIDENCE WITH A SHOW OF CONCEIT.

071   SEEMS UNAWARE OF THE NEGATIVE EFFECT HIS BEHAVIOR HAS ON OTHERS.

073   AN AGGRESSIVE CHILD.

078   TENDS TO PREJUDGE OTHERS, WHO MAY BE DIFFERENT, ON THE BASIS OF INCOMPLETE UNDERSTANDING OR BIAS.

080   USUALLY PLAYS OR WORKS WITH YOUNGER CHILDREN.

081   PREFERS THE COMPANY OF CHILDREN OF THE SAME SEX.

083   INSENSITIVE TO OTHERS.

085   TENDS TO HAVE LIMITED SUCCESS IN FRIENDSHIPS.

086   PERFORMS WELL WHEN WORKING ALONE.

087   PERFORMS WELL WHEN WORKING IN A ONE-TO-ONE RELATION.

091   TENDS TO BE LOST AND RELATIVELY UNINVOLVED WHEN WORKING IN A LARGE GROUP.

093   EVEN IN SMALL GROUPS, REMAINS RELATIVELY UNINVOLVED IN ACTIVITY.

095   APPEARS TO BE RELUCTANT TO WORK COOPERATIVELY WITH OTHERS.

097   NOT LIKED BY PEER GROUP.

104   DESIRES ACTIVE PARTICIPATION IN LEARNING.

109   OFTEN TRIES TO DOMINATE OR OVER-CONTROL PEOPLE OR SITUATIONS.

111   FREQUENTLY INATTENTIVE.

112   SHOWS A TENDENCY TO DAY-DREAM.

113   EASILY DISTRACTED WHEN NOT UNDER CLOSE SUPERVISION.

114   A SOURCE OF DISTURBANCE IN THE CLASSROOM.

116   GENERAL RANGE OF ABILITIES IS LOWER THAN THAT OF MOST CHILDREN IN THIS AGE GROUP.

122   GENERAL FUND OF INFORMATION IS SMALL.

124   MEMORY SKILLS ARE EFFECTIVE.

127   IMAGINATIVE.

130   TENDS TO FAIL THE MAJORITY OF EDUCATIONAL OBJECTIVES.

132   BEHAVIOR TENDS TO FRUSTRATE TEACHER.

133   FREQUENTLY EVOKES A FEELING OF ANNOYANCE AND DISLIKE IN TEACHER.

INITIAL PERSONALIZED PRESCRIPTION FOR STUDENT "A"

A. *Interests*

1. Physical activities
2. Concrete math and computation
3. Cutting and pasting

B. *Suggested Groupings*

1. Small

    2.   Tutorial

C. *Behavioral Approach of Teacher*

1. Emphasize structure
2. Try to avoid a struggle with this student, if patience ends, send him to principal
3. Give close physical contact whenever possible, a pat or a hug
4. Praise, be warm and supportive. Teacher must counteract mother's approach

D. *Defenses to Support*

1. Encourage his general tendency to structure

E. *Defenses to Discourage*

1. Discourage the struggle with mother or teacher

F. *Language Recommendations*

1. Continue speech class
2. Many expressive activities
3. Listening skills
4. Ear barriers to aid concentration
5. Experience stories

G. *Social Studies Recommendations*

1. Advantage series
2. Project work to work through interest in cutting and pasting
3. Materials and activities to expose him to things outside of the family

H. *Math Recommendations*

1. Structured-programmed material
2. Records and tapes
3. Cuisenaire rods
4. Aluminum measurement activities
5. An interest area to work through but cannot demand too much depth

I. *Science Recommendations*

1. Science Primers
2. Basic Xerox program
3. Have him aid in developing kits
4. Easy models
5. Space study to broaden his horizons

6. Activities and discussion which will help him to develop better body image concepts. A puzzle made from a blown-up picture of himself or magazine pictures of people.

J. Recommended Approach to Parents

1. Suggest a thorough examination by an allergist
2. Suggest a thorough eye examination as a follow up to scissors accident and to check on problem of vertical pursuit in ocular motility.
3. Encourage parents to be consistent in dealing with Student A. Helping him to take responsibility for his actions rather than blaming on someone else.
4. Student A needs more outdoor play with other children. The opportunity to widen the boundaries of his home environment. Suggest the playground, swimming lessons, Y.M.C.A. or other day camping experiences and in the future, cub scouts.
5. Discuss with parents the possibility that Student A is not working up to his ability in school because of the home restrictions he must adhere to.

Chapter 23. INDEPENDENT STUDY AND TEACHER BEHAVIOR

TEACHING ROLES IN INDEPENDENT STUDY

Gary D. Lonnon
Richard J. Bodine

Independent study, as an educational program, has become a nebulous, all-inclusive title for all activities which take place outside formal classroom instruction. In general, most independent study programs found in the public schools are designed to structure the students' unscheduled or study hall time. Statements such as, "Your independent study assignment for tomorrow is . . .," are quite common. Such an assignment is hardly "independent." Rather, these assignments usually take the form of homework, projects, or contract agreements, depending upon the amount of time a student is expected to spend on them (homework—one day; project—one grading period; etc.).

The role of the teacher in relation to these "independent study" assignments might be generally described as "director of learning activities."

SOURCE: Reprinted from a mimeographed paper supplied by the authors, at Decatur-Lakeview High School, Decatur, Illinois, by permission of authors.

Assignments are given, assignments are checked, and grades are assigned by the teacher. In this respect, the teacher's role differs little from that of the teacher before the concept of independent study was prevalent.

Perhaps a chart would help clarify this. Below are listed these three common activities referred to as independent study and the characteristics of each. Note particularly the role of the teacher or the teaching team.

Variations at each level, of course, can be found in many schools. For example, students are often used in evaluating class work.

UNSCHEDULED TIME USAGE			
	Level I - Homework	Level II - Project	Level III - Contract
Student Role	Complete work by next class meeting	Complete work by pre-arranged date.	Complete work at own speed, within limits.
Independent Choices Allowed by Student	Perhaps, but not usually, a choice of topic.	Choice of topic within subject area and where study--lab, library, etc.	Choice of time pacing and choice of where to study.
Teacher Role	Direct learning and enforce assignments	Direct learning, suggest possible topics, arrange for freedom of movement by student, and enforce assignments.	Direct learning arrange for for freedom of movement by student, serve as consultant to student, and enforce the contract.
Evaluation	By teacher or team	By teacher or team	By teacher or team

It would be difficult to accept any of these three above-mentioned activities as examples of independent study in the strict sense of the word. Independence implies freedom—thinking or acting with a minimum of outside influence. Homework, project work, or contract work do not allow for, or even tolerate, freedom on the part of the student.

In most public school systems, the concept of student freedom is an extremely threatening idea—threatening to tradition, to the community, to the staff, and to the students themselves. It is at this point, the dealing with threat, that team teaching becomes a significant factor in an independent program.

What might a true independent study program look like? First of all, all work done by students is self-assumed. If the practice of giving and enforcing assignments persists in an independent study program, independence on the part of the students, which is an acquired skill, cannot develop. Secondly, the evaluation of the self-assumed work must be done by the student himself. If the teaching team insists upon retaining the right to evaluate, students will continue to look to the teachers for direction. Thirdly, the student must be given the freedom to schedule his own activities and time. Without these options the spirit of the program is violated.

The "threat" of an independent study program such as this is rather obvious. By asking a teacher or a teaching team not to give assignments, not to assign grades, and/or not to require class attendance, the common and traditional definition of "teacher" is changed. In the public schools, nothing is so threatening to a staff as change, particularly a change in its professional role.

Role change by one teacher, a teaching team, or an entire staff needs a supportive climate in order to progress. If teachers are to attempt any innovation, including independent study, they must feel comfortable in experimenting with the innovation and feel secure in knowing that if mistakes are made, the support will not be withdrawn.

A teacher working within a team is assured of support in attempting independent study if two conditions exist; first, if the program has been mutually planned by the team, and, secondly, if the principal is a working member of the team during the planning. In addition to the climate of support created by team teaching efforts in an independent study program, the individual teacher also benefits from the professional sharing of feelings and ideas with other team members, which is quite an innovation in itself.

There is no common definition of team teaching. Applications of the concept are as numerous as there are schools involved in such programs. It is difficult, therefore, to describe an ideal teaching team for an independent study program. If students are to be encouraged to do true independent study, as described earlier, in one subject area only, or at one grade level only, the size of the team and characteristics of the team members will vary greatly from those of a team which is encouraging independent study in all subject areas or on all grade levels.

Those independent study programs which cross subject lines and/or grade levels require interdisciplinary teaching teams. There tends to be more openness, freedom of discussion, and willingness to examine professional roles and practices in interdisciplinary teams than in those teams made up of only, for example, the 5th-grade teachers or the geometry teachers.

A change of professional role would not be necessary in an independent study program if the students involved were to follow the same lock-step pattern as is commonly required. Students who are expected to listen to a content presentation, complete assignments related to this presentation, and take tests on this "basic" material in order to legitimize achievement, need a system which is structure-oriented and content-oriented. Indeed, there are many students in the schools who will probably function best in this atmosphere (although this statement may well be a rationalization).

However, students in a true independent program do not need a structure-oriented or content-oriented environment. In fact, these serve as powerful sedatives to the development of independence.

How might a teaching team go about organizing an independent study program for a group of students? Experience has shown that students cannot be told on Friday that they have the opportunity to be independent and they will become so on Monday. Rather, independence must be approached in a sequential manner. Three basic steps should be considered by the teaching team:

1. Orientation of the students

2. Trial and error on the part of both students and team

3. Productivity

A more complete examination of each of these steps follows:

Orientation.   The first effort by the team should be to explain to the students *why* the independent program exists. This involves a sharing of educational philosophy with students from which challenging and stimulating discussions and exchanges usually follow. It is necessary for the students to understand the rationale of the program if they are to be working partners with the teaching team in the endeavor.

Once the students and the team have an adequate working understanding of the purpose of the program, the team should introduce the options which will be available to the students in the program. Remember, if the students *must* do a project or *must* produce a paper or any of the other *musts* which might be contrived, an independent program does not exist.

Some of the possible choices or options which a team might consider for the students are:

1. Acceleration—content and grade level

2. Changing of course sequence

3. Changing staff resources

4. Studying his own diagnostic data

5. Moving outside the content area

6. Guaranteed grades

7. Self-scheduling

Such a list of options could be limitless. The teaching team will be able to offer more options and combinations than can a single teacher, but this does not mean that one teacher cannot promote an effective independent study program alone.

The students should be allowed to offer options and should be encouraged to react to the list of options offered by the teaching team.

The final list of options available to students in the independent study program will be limited only by what the school system and the team feel can be tolerated. For example, a school district may not be willing to guarantee "A's" for independent work due to the external pressures of building class rank for college or selecting a valedictorian. In another case, the 7th-grade teachers are opposed to the idea. Regardless of the possible and inevitable problems which will occur, any teaching team can build an adequate list of options to begin the independent study program.

During the orientation phase of the independent program, the team will be called upon to establish a supportive climate for the students. This supportive climate will be of utmost importance during the Trial and Error stage to follow, but it must be firmly established during the orientation. The central idea is to make students feel at ease without constant direction and to be aware that they and the teaching team are partners in the program, equally sharing the successes and the failures. Establishing this supportive climate requires different professional talents from the team members and each member can be of professional assistance to the others.

Trial and Error. This phase of the program might better be called the "goof-off" phase. It is the step which produces the highest degree of threat to the teaching team and to the school. However, it is an essential step in the development of independence and *cannot* be by-passed.

During the trial and error phase the students will be experimenting with the options which have been offered and agreed upon by the team and the class. It is highly unrealistic to expect that a student will examine the list of possible options, select the one he wants to explore, and then move immediately to the productive state.

The early reaction of the students will be to do nothing, or more explicitly, "goof off." Of course, when the students are accused of doing "nothing," the statement is made relative to what non-program students are doing—homework, projects, or contract work. In these programs, achievement and progress can be measured quite easily. In an independent program, tangible "proof" of progress is not so readily determined. Other valuable learning experiences are taking place, however. Individual students will be examining personal goals, feelings, and aspirations. Also, it is at this stage that the students come to realize that the responsibility for learning belongs to them, and that if they do not "achieve" commensurate with their personal goals, it is their responsibility.

As this realization becomes an integral part of their value system, many will constantly pressure the teaching team for direction. In many overt and subtle ways they will ask, "What do you want us to do?" Of course, if the team succumbs to this pressure, a major purpose of the program has been defeated—the team is selecting the options for the student.

This is not to say that the team cannot offer possible alternatives or suggestions to the students. However, there is a fine line between suggestions and assignments, especially in the usual teacher-student relationship. Complicating the picture even more is the internal pressure the team will be feeling concerning the lack of productivity by the students. It would be so easy to simply tell the students what they ought to be doing.

Some students will move through the trial and error stage quickly—in perhaps four to six weeks, while others will work with this stage much longer. Most students will move back and forth between the trial and error stage and the productive stage many times during the school year.

A great deal of patience is required from the teaching team during the trial and error stage. Yet, the supportive climate has been established and the team can remain consistent with its philosophy, a new professional role has been learned and the independent study program is on firm ground.

Productivity. Once the orientation and trial and error stages have been experienced, students will move into productive activities, although all students involved will not make this move at the same time. For example, in a recent effort with independent study, one boy began productivity after four weeks. However, a girl in the same group struggled with trial and error stages for over eight months. It was extremely difficult for the teaching team to refrain from pressuring the girl by comparing her "achievement" to that of the boy. If this had been done, the girl would never have learned the self-discipline and independence which she now has.

The teaching team should be aware of and willing to accept the various types of productivity which will be evident. Traditionally, the only type of productivity accepted had to be tangible—a paper or a model. Other acceptable types of productivity might be:

1. Student attitudes have been improved.

2. Verbal discussion of activities have improved.

3. Self-direction or self-discipline is evident.

4. Student leadership has emerged.

5. Interest in a greater variety of topics is noticed.

These types of "products" cannot be readily measured by tests, so there is a strong tendency not to accept them as worthwhile of and by themselves without supportive, objective test data. Although most schools and teachers state that their goals include the teaching of self-discipline, improved attitudes, leadership, and verbal skill, they try to teach these in a content-oriented curriculum which tends to relegate the goals to a secondary position in favor of content achievement. On the other hand, a process-oriented curriculum, even though it not only embodies the above-mentioned goals but places primary emphasis on them, usually creates extreme levels of internal pressure, and is, therefore, avoided.

Do not interpret this to mean that content is not important. Of course it is. But in an independent study program, process must be granted equal importance. Interesting to note is that in a recent experimental independent program, the students in the program, like the one mentioned earlier, did better on a pre-post testing pattern (standardized testing) than did their control group, even though the experimental group were not required to attend class or take tests and were guaranteed grades over a two-year period.

It should be noticed that the relative abilities of students have not been mentioned thus far. There is a general feeling that independent study is only for better students. Ability is significant only in the productivity stage. The team will need to know a student's ability in order to make reasonable judgments about the quality of his products. But in the orientation and trial and error stages, relative abilities are not critical, and low-, as well as high-ability students can profit from the independent program.

Professional roles at the productivity level are relatively simple. The team becomes a manager of learning resources, including materials, staff, and community resources. It must see that all resources are readily available to the students. The team also serves the students as resource people, assisting, but not directing, the students in a variety of ways in their learning activities.

In summary, a review of the professional roles of a teaching team working with the independent study programs would be:

Orientation Phase:

1.   Establish a supportive climate for the program.

2.   Share the program philosophy with the students.

3.   Explain the administrative limitations of the program to the students.

4.   Build a list of options acceptable to the students, the teaching team, and the administration.

Trial and Error Phase:

1.   Continue to maintain the supportive climate, stressing that the "risk" will be shared by both the students and the team.

2.   Be sensitive to emotions from the students, the staff, and the community, *and* learn how to handle these emotions.

3.   Be aware that "goofing off" is a natural reaction and a necessary integral part of developing independence, and be willing to accept it as such.

Productivity Phase:

1.   Continue to maintain support.

2.   Become a manager of learning resources.

3.   Know the individual abilities of each student so that the quality of the products can be assessed.

4.   Be prepared to accept different types of behavior as evidence of productivity such as:

a)   Attitudinal changes

b)   Improved verbal discussion

c)   Evidence of self-direction

d)   Evidence of self-discipline

e)   Emergence of leadership

f)   Widening of interests

g)   Greater self-awareness

h)   Establishment of personal goals

i)   Deepening commitment to beliefs and societal concerns

j)   Other behaviors not measured by typical testing devices.

In order for the teaching team to maintain the professional role necessary for the success of independent study programs, each teacher must make behavioral shifts. The behavioral shifts necessary can be roughly classified into five behavioral and attitudinal changes. First, a shift from the position of "the fountain of knowledge" to "the consultant" in subject areas. This involves listening to the student, accepting his interests, and providing him assistance in pursuing his interests.

Second, the teacher must shift from the role of "director of learning" to a "resource person." Most important is the establishment of an "equality base" for student-teacher interaction. The professional will refrain from telling the student what to do but will assist the student to chart a course of action once the student decides what he wishes to pursue.

Third, the teacher becomes the "manager of learning resources" and relinquishes the role of "pacer of learning." The teacher must abandon the arbitrary time limits present in the school structure. The teacher needs to become familiar with the resources available in the school and the community. Of utmost importance, the teacher must be prepared to assist the student in the interpretation of resource material and in the integration of several resources into something meaningful to the student.

Also, the teacher needs to understand that "multi-talent development" rather than the more narrow "academic-talent development" is the goal of independent study. This involves the recognition that activities and pursuits not strictly limited to the "normal" school curriculum can be significant and worthy of the time spent.

Finally, the teacher relinquishes the role of "enforcer of coverage" in favor of becoming "an assistant in students' self-evaluation." To do this, the teacher must develop skill in assisting the student to establish evaluative criteria for his activities. The teacher must learn to accept the criteria established by the student and judge the product according to that criteria.

In order to be successful, the teacher must develop skills such as, listening, dealing with emotions, giving support, and developing individual rapport to a much greater extent than these skills have been developed, or at least practiced, by most teachers.

There are many questions left to be answered concerning independent programs beyond the level of contract activities. Although there is existing evidence for formulating answers, it is not conclusive. The "experiments" with independent study have been too few in number and too limited in scope to make convincing conclusions. But as more schools become interested and more teams within these schools do experimental work, the concept of independent study will become an integral part of the school curriculum rather than an "experiment."

Chapter 24. AN APPROACH TO INSTRUCTIONAL MANAGEMENT THROUGH COMPUTERS

AN INSTRUCTIONAL MANAGEMENT SYSTEM FOR CLASSROOM TEACHERS

Cleone L. Geddes
Beverly Y. Kooi

During the 1967-68 school year, a computer-aided management system was used to help first-grade teachers in two schools in Los Angeles manage the daily affairs of their classrooms. The teachers operated under the Instructional Management System, which is being developed jointly by the System Development Corporation and the Southwest Regional Laboratory for Educational Research and Development.

The Instructional Management System is designed to help the teacher monitor the progress of her pupils and make decisions on the pace of instruction, the grouping of children, the sequence of lessons, and the individualization of instruction. The system helps the teacher answer such

SOURCE: Reprinted from the *Elementary School Journal,* University of Chicago Press, Vol. 69, No. 7 (April, 1969), pp. 337-45.

questions as: "How fast should these children progress from one lesson to the next?" "Do I have my pupils grouped to allow the most efficient learning?" "Do my pupils know their reading vocabulary well enough for me to spend today on the more difficult skill of sentence comprehension?" "Exactly what kind of help should I be giving this particular child?" The Instructional Management System helps the teacher by providing information almost daily about each child's achievement and by suggesting specific activities to help the pupil when he does not learn what is presented in any particular lesson.

The Instructional Management System provides a framework for making decisions on classroom management at any grade level, but some one level had to be selected for initial development and demonstration. The project staff wanted to encounter and solve the most difficult problems during early design and development of the system. For this reason, we decided to work with first-graders. They cannot read instructions, are not accustomed to classroom instructional routines, and have almost no previous experience with tests.

Usually each class we worked with was divided into three reading groups so that the teacher could work more closely with a few children at a time. A ninety-minute period was generally reserved for reading; during this ninety minutes the teacher worked directly with each group of approximately ten children for twenty to thirty minutes. While the teacher worked with one group, the other groups pursued independent activities or did workbook sheets that followed up their reading.

The teachers were satisfied with the practice of moving the children from one small-group situation to another in the classroom, but realized that there were problems that needed attention. The children were grouped according to the teacher's best judgment of how well they kept up with the group, not according to their mastery of skills; lesson assignments were made to the group as a whole and were based largely on the teacher's intuitive judgments about what the children needed. There was little opportunity for individual instruction. Any regular information the teacher gathered about her pupils' progress depended on her. She could observe the children in class or grade lessons or give tests that she herself planned and assigned, but she had no help in planning her observations and assignments or in analyzing the results. Consequently, she could not use the data effectively to pace or sequence instruction, or to discover what help she should give any one child, if she found time to give it.

In developing a management system, the System Development Corporation has tried to provide the information teachers know they lack. No attempt is made to force immediate changes in classroom routines that seem satisfactory to teachers. By trying the Instructional Management System in classrooms, we are discovering what information and what assistance actually help the teacher help each child. When we provide that information and assistance, more flexible, individualized routines will follow.

The classroom that uses the Instructional Management System has carrells wired for sound. Otherwise it looks like a typical classroom. Many classrooms have listening centers with tape recorders or phonographs and headsets. Classrooms that use the Instructional Management System have adapted these teaching aids to present instructions for diagnostic tests that resemble regular workbook exercises. The children in one group work on the tests at individual carrells during their regular follow-up portion of the reading period while the teacher is working with another group.

The tests have a simple format of multiple-choice items. The children mark their responses in pencil directly on the test booklet. The tests are collected each day and taken to the System Development Corporation, where they are first checked for identification and extraneous marks, then processed through an optical scanner. Data from the scanner are put on a tape for insertion into the computer, and the computer evaluates the responses for correctness and achievement of teaching objectives. A report is printed out showing the results of the tests for the group as a whole and for each individual child. A sample of this report is shown below in Figure 24-1.

```
TEACHER  53     DATE  05/22/68     TEST  9928, WHITEHOUSE,
GRADE  B1       SUBJECT  READING   REVIEW  GROUP  1

A. GROUP REPORT
    GENERAL OBJECTIVES              SCORE   ACTIVITIES RECOMMENDED
    2 WORD RECOGNITION               87      R28-0203 R28-0204
    9 PARAGRAPH COMPREHENSION        94

       TOTAL SCORE                   88

B. INDIVIDUAL REPORT
                                            GENERAL OBJECTIVES***
                                    TOTAL     SCORE THIS TEST
    STUDENT NAME                    SCORE      2           9
       RUTH STERLING                 97        96         100
       CARLA REECE                   97        96         100
       DONNA PRENTICE                94        92         100
       CATHY WILTON                  91        89         100
       LORI MATTHEWS                 89        85         100
          203    (70) R28-0203
       DANIEL LARSON                 86        85          88
       DALE SCHULTZ                  81        78          88
          204    (62) R28-0204
       MICHAEL ROLLINS               72        71          77
          203    (60) R28-0203
          204    (62) R28-0204
          902    (66) R28-0902
```

FIGURE 24-1
TEST REPORT

The report is in the teacher's mailbox when she arrives at school the next morning. The first part of the report shows the group's achievement on the test; the second part shows scores for individuals.

When the performance of a group or a child is not up to standard, an activity, or "prescription," is recommended. The activities are designated by code numbers. In the report shown in Figure 24-1 the activities recommended include those assigned the code numbers R28-0203 and R28-0204. The teacher selects the lesson designated by the code number from her files and uses it for the day's instruction. The prescription may be given to the whole group or to a single child. When there is no prescription, the class can move to the next unit of work.

COMPONENTS

The first component of the Instructional Management System is the objectives. They define the goals of instruction. The items in each test are keyed to these objectives. The second component consists of the tests, which measure the children's achievement of the objectives. The third component is the system of reports prepared by the computer. The reports provide the most frequently used information on a daily basis and more detailed information as necessary. The fourth component is made up of the activities prescribed to remedy deficiencies.

OBJECTIVES

The instructional objectives were defined early in the development of the system; they were based on actual instruction in various classrooms rather than on what we, as educational psychologists, might believe appropriate. To describe a first-grader's progress (or lack of it) on an almost daily basis, we had to know what is expected of him on a daily basis—what the instructional goals or objectives are. For example, what should a child learn and be able to do after he has "covered" any particular story in his preprimers or primers?

To identify objectives that we could state in operational terms, we examined publishers' guides and city school curriculum guides, we observed first-grade classes, and we consulted teachers. From these sources we derived several general objectives in reading and mathematics. Though we defined objectives and wrote tests for both arithmetic and reading, the greater thrust was in reading. Only the reading system will be described here.

The general objectives for reading are broadly defined skills that can be associated with successive levels of content as they are introduced in first grade. For example, at the end of each reading lesson in first-grade the child should be able to pick out a reading vocabulary word from all others; he should be able to select a written word when he hears it pronounced; he should recognize the sounds or key letters in his reading vocabulary words; and he should understand the meaning of the words, the sentences, and the paragraphs in his reading lesson. Thus, the general reading objectives are visual discrimination, word recognition, phonic analysis, structural analysis, word comprehension, sentence comprehension, and paragraph comprehension.

Though these general objectives seem fairly specific, they are not specific enough to indicate what should be in a test question or what examples the teacher should use in teaching a lesson. Each general objective, therefore, must be translated into a number of specific objectives from which specific instruction and test items can be drawn. Some specific objectives tell exactly what content should be included; other specific objectives show what skills should be taught and tested. Take the general objective in phonic analysis: The child is to show that he recognizes the sounds of initial consonants. If the new vocabulary for a specific lesson includes the words *ride, Tom,* and *see,* the specific phonic objective for that lesson would include having the child recognize the sounds of *r, t,* and *s,* in a wide variety of words.

The structure used to teach reading emphasizes a few general objectives during a semester, and each general objective incorporates a list of specific objectives. The structure seems to fit most elementary-school subjects. We chose reading for our major effort because it seems to offer a greater variety of problems in definition and testing than most other first-grade subjects. The decision to use an area that had a variety of problems helped us build a system that can be generalized to other subject areas.

One reason why we constructed mathematics materials was to see whether this assumption about generalization was true—whether the system we developed to teach reading could be used to teach arithmetic and other subjects. We found that the system was easier to use in first-grade mathematics than in reading, for mathematics offers more limited content to be tested and a more clearly hierarchical structure than reading does. The system also seemed satisfactory to teachers who wanted to describe various courses at various grade levels.

TESTS

The tests were not standardized in large-scale trials but were improved by trying them out in small groups and revising them on the basis of the children's responses. We wrote twenty-eight reading tests—one for every three stories in the basal reading series for the first semester. Each test emphasizes the vocabulary of the three stories being tested, but also presents some vocabulary words from the previous stories and each item is associated with some specific objective. Eight reading readiness tests precede the reading tests, and sixteen tests were prepared to measure progress in mathematics. The arithmetic tests were prepared by teachers with the help of personnel from the System Development Corporation. Each test is about six pages long and requires about twenty minutes to administer. About ten formats are possible in placing items on test sheets, but the scanner limits the items to multiple choice. Many, though certainly not all, instructional objectives can be measured in a multiple-choice format.

REPORTS

The type of report most frequently provided has been described. Figure 24-1 presents an example. This report tells the teacher how groups and individuals achieved on general objectives and suggests remedial activities. It allows the teacher to teach lessons that remedy fairly global and recent deficiencies in the performance of a group or a child. In the beginning, teachers using the system were quite content to do little more than this, for the report provided more information than they were used to having. When the teachers became more familiar with the system, however, they were able to see its possibilities and use more information.

Several other reports or printouts were then provided. One of these is a standard weekly report that provides individual and group scores on all tests taken. With it the teacher can follow trends in the performance of groups and individuals. The standard weekly report also ranks the pupils' long-term performance and shows any sudden rise or drop in a pupil's achievement, so that the teacher can act on changes as soon as they occur.

Associated with this weekly summary are periodic individual profiles that show on a graph the trend of each child's performance. Figure 24-2 is an example of this type of report. The "0" base of each profile is the mean score of the child's group on each test. A series of marks above or below the "0" line shows how many standard deviations above or below the mean the child scored on each test. Often the teacher finds that a child performs above (or below) average on most tests. Sometimes changes occur that signal a need for special attention from the teacher. Figure 24-2 shows a change from above average performance to below average. At this point, the teacher should look for a change in the skills being tested or some prerequisite skill that the child failed to master.

Two final printouts, which are available to the teacher on request, are the most helpful for remedying the difficulties of an individual child. When the teacher wants to know what deficiency in skills is pulling down a child's score, she can request detailed individual printouts. From the more general report, she can answer such questions as: "Why doesn't this pupil read well?" "Is he having difficulty in recognizing the words, or is he having difficulty in understanding their relationship in sentences?" The printout tells the teacher how well the child has been performing on the general objectives in all his tests.

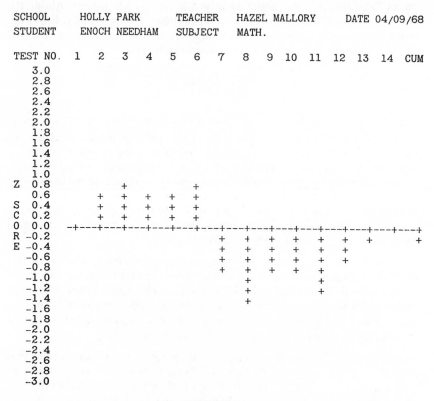

FIGURE 24-2

INDIVIDUAL PERFORMANCE PROFILE

The last printout tells the teacher exactly what kinds of items the child needs practice on. For example, the child whose performance is reported in Figure 24-3 consistently fails to associate the letter *l* with its sound in words and should receive instruction and practice on that skill.

These reports provide information that helps the teacher make classroom decisions. A knowledge of the most recent achievement of groups and individual children makes it possible for the teacher to answer such questions about her immediate lesson plans as: "Do my pupils know their reading vocabulary well enough for me to spend the day on phonics?" The reports also suggest activities to remedy deficiencies in recent achievement and to prevent the group from moving to the next lesson faster than it should. Information on long-term trends in performance makes it possible to group pupils efficiently and alerts the teacher to sudden changes. The reports on individual pupils provide information that can be used in conferences with parents, and this information makes it possible to give any child detailed help in overcoming a specific difficulty.

```
BUILDING    FRAZIER                          DATE 06/06/68
TEACHER     JANICE YATES

STUDENT     CATHY WILTON
SUBJECT     BI READING        TESTS 9914-9928
```

OBJECTIVE 2 WORD RECOGNITION

SPECIFIC OBJECTIVE	POSSIBLE ATTAIN-MENT	STUDENT ATTAIN-MENT	PER CENT
SAME LENGTH WORDS	4	3	75
INITIAL LETTER DISTRACTOR	47	41	87
FINAL LETTER DISTRACTOR	37	33	89
MANY LETTER DISTRACTORS	30	25	83

OBJECTIVE 3 PHONICS, INITIAL SOUNDS

SPECIFIC OBJECTIVE	POSSIBLE ATTAIN-MENT	STUDENT ATTAIN-MENT	PER CENT
INITIAL CONSONANT F	4	4	100
INITIAL CONSONANT B	4	4	100
INITIAL CONSONANT N	4	3	75
INITIAL CONSONANT W	4	4	100
INITIAL CONSONANT P	4	3	75
INITIAL CONSONANT L	4	2	50
VARIED CONSONANTS	12	12	100

OBJECTIVE 4 PHONICS, FINAL SOUNDS

SPECIFIC OBJECTIVE	POSSIBLE ATTAIN-MENT	STUDENT ATTAIN-MENT	PER CENT
RHYMING WORDS	12	10	83
SINGLE CONSONANT SOUNDS	18	14	77

OBJECTIVE 5 PHONICS, MEDIAL VOWELS

SPECIFIC OBJECTIVE	POSSIBLE ATTAIN-MENT	STUDENT ATTAIN-MENT	PER CENT
MEDIAL VOWELS	12	9	75

FIGURE 24-3

INDIVIDUAL DIAGNOSTIC REPORT: SPECIFIC OBJECTIVES

At first teachers may use the system only to maintain the group-paced structure. After they become familiar with the great amount of individual information that is available, they may want to expand their use of the system so that their programs gradually assume the characteristics of individualized instruction.

PRESCRIPTIONS

The final component of the Instructional Management System is the prescription—the remedial instruction suggested on printouts when achievement is below an acceptable level. Like other components of the system, prescriptions are patterned after needs the teacher currently recognizes. Prescriptions can be improved as new and better procedures and materials are developed.

Prescriptions for the first year were developed by two co-operating teachers during the summer, before school started. The prescriptions consist primarily of sheets of practice items, often borrowed from workbooks, each keyed to the objectives being tested. When a code number appears under "activities recommended," as in Figure 24-1, the appropriate sheets are used. However, the code number could designate some other activity, such as a group lesson, a programmed instruction sequence, or tutoring by another child who is proficient in the skill in question. Any of these activities could be described in folders that now contain only paper-and-pencil practice sheets. The development of alternative activities is now receiving primary attention in the improvement of the Instructional Management System.

CONCLUSION

The Instructional Management System, then, is a classroom management system that is being developed. The system uses the practical situation a teacher faces and offers help with information needs she recognizes. The system accommodates the typical, group-paced classroom. At the same time, by providing information on children's learning difficulties, the system encourages the teacher to undertake more individualization in her classroom. The Instructional Management System is planned to serve the teacher who wishes to use this information to make her own program completely flexible and appropriate for each child's individual needs.

The Instructional Management System is not a finished system. Each semester the staff of the System Development Corporation uses the regular collection of data on pupils' performance to evaluate and revise tests, materials, computer programs, and procedures. After such data have been collected for several semesters and the system has been revised on the basis of the data, plans will be made to use the system on a wider scale.

Chapter 25. COMPUTER-BASED INDIVIDUAL STUDY

THE STATE OF THE ART IN McCOMB

J. D. Prince

In computer-assisted instruction (CAI) such as the drill-and-practice mode developed by Patrick Suppes at Stanford University, educators are not yet dealing with an easily affordable, trouble-free, basic system which can be used equally well in all public schools—i.e., a CAI system as useful as the Model-T Ford.

The Model-T was the automobile which put America on wheels; it was cheap, dependable. If an American could afford $300 and had a Sears Roebuck catalog, he could dress this functional (but plain) auto up in any manner desired to suit his taste.

Today, CAI programs are more nearly like Duryea's first gas buggy—cranky, noisy, slow, undependable but nevertheless, with enough promise

SOURCE: Adopted from *Progress Report No. 3*, USOE Grant OEG-3-7-704721-5096, May, 1969, by permission of author.

that we can see that CAI can change education in our nation today just as Duryea's smoky, bulky buggy eventually replaced the horse.

How does a school district become interested in CAI and why could it have such an impact upon education in the future? The answer is quite simple. CAI individualizes instruction.

Southern school districts with high percentages of disadvantaged children have particular concern with educational systems which individualize instruction.

We are now convinced in McComb that computer-assisted instruction can individualize instruction. After a year of operation in McComb Municipal Separate School District, we found that significant educational difference existed between groups of children on CAI instruction and children in control groups.

Our findings in the second year of operation show there is little significance between groups of high income, high I.Q. children on CAI and regular instruction (if teachers are comparable in ability) but startling results are obtained in favor of CAI in Negro and low-income groups regardless of teacher ability.

If statistical results obtained in the McComb program can be replicated in other southern school districts, CAI drill-and-practice programs can make a significant difference in improving education in the South.

But first, this program must be practical in the sense that it can be easily attained in a poor school district before it can make a measurable educational impact. Is the program practical?

IS THE SUPPES' DRILL-AND-PRACTICE PROGRAM A VIABLE INSTRUCTIONAL SYSTEM?

1967-68 Results

Children learn mathematics skills using the CAI drill-and-practice technique remarkably well. During the first year of the program, 544 McComb children in grades 1-6 were enrolled in the experimental group and 515 children were matched in the control group. Pre-testing and post-testing were done of both control and experimental groups. Test conditions were rigidly controlled in all test situations.

In all six grades, results were statistically significant that the experimental group could achieve better on an achievement test measure in skill building than did the control group.

The Suppes' CAI program was not designed to develop skills in arithmetic concepts and arithmetic application. As you may note, test results showed there were three groups in these two areas where significant results were obtained and one group where negative results were obtained.

No effort is made to racially identify any of the first year test group in Chart 25-1.

These results were not sufficient, however. We asked these questions: How did the experimental and control children do when teachers were equally trained? How do children of different racial groups perform? What type of retention of skill building is retained over the summer vacation? These questions are but a few statements which we have put to statistical analysis. Some of these results are detailed below.

Teacher versus Teacher When Training Is Comparable

Does computer-assisted instruction influence performance on achievement tests when two teachers are equally trained yet one does not use the CAI technique? This question can be best answered by an experiment conducted during the 1967-68 year by two sixth-grade teachers at Westbrook School, Mrs. Mildred Long and Mrs. Odessa Holmes.

Both teachers attended the complete training school given at Stanford University in the summer of 1967. Both teachers have approximately the same number of years of experience in teaching, have comparable academic training, and are rated as two of the best sixth-grade teachers of either race in the school district.

Both teachers taught in adjacent classrooms. During this school year, this school had an entirely Negro student body, although the staff was integrated.

Mrs. Holmes, Negro, taught the sixth-grade experimental group of 27. Mrs. Long, Caucasian, taught the control group of 28 sixth-grade students. As Mrs. Long had had Stanford CAI training at the same grade level in another school (using the CAI drill-and-practice technique), she was quite familiar with the requirements and the expectations for Mrs. Holmes's experimental group. Mrs. Long made a determined effort to keep her control classwork equivalent to the training given by Mrs. Holmes. Mrs. Long used conventional techniques. Both teachers used identical texts.

A comparison of achievement test scores of the experimental and control groups (Table 25-1) showed Mrs. Holmes's sixth-grade experimental group able to achieve at a significantly higher level than Mrs. Long's sixth-grade control group.

Does the CAI Program Have Marked Effect on First Graders?

The South Central Region Educational Laboratory (SCREL) made a statistical study comparing experimental and control groups at the Universal Elementary School (all Negro first grade) as contrasted with the achievement

STATISTICAL RESULTS

Experimental VS Control Groups - - Suppes   (Stanford)   Mathematics   Drill and Practice

Location and Grades: McComb Public Schools, McComb, Mississippi, Grades 1-6
Dates: Pre-test September, 1967   Post-test May, 1968
Test: Stanford Achievement

		Mean Pre-test			N	Mean Post-test		Mean Post-Pre Test		Post-Pre Test		
	Grade	Control	N	Exp.		Control	Exp.	Control	Exp.	t - score	P	df
Arithmetic Computation	1	1.19	62	1.41*	52	1.47	2.55	.26	1.14	3.69	<.01	112
	2	1.96	54	1.99	25	2.80	3.37	.84	1.42	5.23	<.01	77
	3	2.76	56	2.82	22	4.04	4.85	1.26	2.03	4.64	<.01	76
	4	2.45	77	2.26	58	9.17	3.36	.69	1.10	2.63	<.01	131
	5	3.71	134	3.09	83	4.60	4.46	.90	1.37	3.43	<.01	215
	6	4.36	160	4.82	275	5.48	6.54	1.13	1.72	5.18	<.01	433
Arithmetic Concepts	3	2.97	56	2.83	22	4.26	4.78	1.29	1.95	3.01	<.01	76
	4	2.31	77	2.65	58	3.06	3.01	.74	.36	-2.25		
	5	4.00	134	3.42	83	5.24	4.78	1.29	1.37	.50		
	6	4.88	160	5.34	275	5.39	6.31	.52	.98	3.74	<.01	433
Arithmetic Applications	4	2.88	77	2.89	58	3.28	3.33	.41	.44	.22		
	5	4.12	134	3.56	83	4.73	4.33	.65	.77	.88		
	6	4.52	160	5.06	275	5.06	6.13	.61	1.08	4.09	<.01	433

* Grade equivalence in years and months

CHART 25-1

TABLE 25-1

				Results of Holmes vs. Long					
Mean	Pre-test			Mean	Post-Test			Mean Gain	
Cont.	N.	Exp.	N.	Cont.	N.	Exp.	N.	Cont.	Exp.
Computation (Arith)									
3.5	28	4.0	27	6.2	27	4.5	28	1.0	2.2
Concepts (Arith)									
3.0	25	4.7	27	5.4	27	4.5	25	0.6	0.7
Applications (Arith)									
3.2	25	4.1	27	5.3	27	3.9	25	0.7	1.2

of a matched pair control group drawn from the all Negro first grade of the Westbrook Elementary School. In this study the SCREL group ran a testing program independent of that conducted by the McComb-Stanford testing team. The purposes of this research study as stated by the SCREL staff in the summer of 1967 were:

A pre-test control group design will be used, employing both on-site and remote control groups. The remote control will consist of similar first-year pupils selected randomly from the elementary schools of the district.

Since the CAI component is of primary concern, multi-colored groups will be established to provide interpretable comparisons. These control groups will consist of: (1) the pupils in Section I not drawn to participate in the CAI, (2) the first-year pupils in Section II, and (3) the remote control group described above.

The digest of the SCREL statistical data is revealed in Table 25-2. These data indicate that the experimental group is able to function more successfully on an achievement test measuring arithmetic skills than in the control group. An interesting sidelight to the SCREL study is that the reading level of the Universal (experimental) group is also significantly higher than is the reading level of the control group.

Interpretation: The test results indicate that E1, those first-grade pupils in Universal School who received computer-assisted instruction, achieved significantly higher in arithmetic than the two comparison groups C2 and C4 who received traditional instruction. The E1 group also achieved significantly higher in reading than the C4 comparison group. C2 is a

TABLE 25-2

CALIFORNIA ACHIEVEMENT TEST				

Arithmetic Subtest

Group	N	X Gain	t	p
CAI (E 1)	33	25.12		
Non-CAI				
(C 2)	18	12.78	2.79	< .01
(C 4)	51	16.12	2.83	< .01

Reading Subtest

Group	N	X Gain	t	p
CAI (E 1)	31	19.97		
Non-CAI (C 4)	48	9.55	3.62	< .01

comparison class drawn randomly from Westbrook School. C4 consists of all other first-grade pupils in Westbrook School.

CAI and the Intelligent Child from the High-Income Home

Our results (Table 25-3) reveal that there is little statistical difference in performance on achievement tests in mathematics when children from high-income homes (with average or better I.Q.'s) are compared in the experimental and control groups. Also, we find (Table 25-4) no significant difference in retention over the summer between these children. The following tables give statistical comparisons between fifth-grade children from high-income homes at the Otken Elementary School compared with those from even higher income brackets from the Hughes Elementary School. The Otken group was the experimental group. The Hughes group was the control group.

Both classroom teachers are excellent teachers. Both used modern mathematics techniques. The teacher at the Otken Elementary School had been in the Stanford training program the previous summer.

Retention of Children from Low-Income Homes

In the tables below (Tables 25-5 and 25-6) clear indication is given that disadvantaged children in the experimental groups learn mathematics from the CAI technique (and retain what they learn) better than disadvantaged children in control groups. Universal School is the experimental group in this program in a very disadvantaged area. Westbrook is the control group in

TABLE 25-3

	N	Mean Gain Exp.	N	Mean Gain Cont.	Diff	Significant?
		OTKEN vs HUGHES SEPT. TO MAY*				
Computation	25	1.36	24	1.74	-.38	NS
Concepts	25	1.46	24	.60	.86	< .01
Applications	25	.68	24	.90	-.22	NS

TABLE 25-4

	N	Mean Gain Exp.	N	Mean Gain Cont.	Diff	Significant?
		OTKEN vs HUGHES SEPT. TO SEPT.**				
Computation	25	.79	24	.88	-.09	NS
Concepts	25	1.33	24	.65	.68	< .01
Applications	25	1.18	24	1.47	-.29	NS

*Testing date late September, 1967, to early May, 1968, seven months of actual instructional time.

**Testing date late September, 1967, to late September, 1968, a lapsed time between tests of twelve calendar months.

TABLE 25-5

	N	Mean Gain Exp.	N	Mean Gain Cont.	Diff.	Significant?
		UNIVERSAL vs WESTBROOK SEPT. TO MAY				
Computation	26	1.65	66	.60	1.05	< .01
Concepts	26	2.23	66	1.59	.64	< .01
Applications	26	1.33	66	.42	.91	< .01

an equally disadvantaged neighborhood. All children and teachers were Negro in this particular instance and were at grade level five.

TABLE 25-6

UNIVERSAL vs WESTBROOK SEPT. TO SEPT.						
	N	Mean Gain Exp.	N	Mean Gain Cont.	Diff	Significant?
Computation	26	1.04	66	.05	.99	< .01
Concepts	26	1.14	66	.04	1.10	< .01
Applications	26	.70	66	.00	.70	< .01

Notice in Table 25-6 above that concepts shows a marked gain over the summer. Refer to Table 25-3 and 25-4 and note that a similar concepts growth is found in the Otken-Hughes comparison. What does this indicate?

COMPARISON OF *CAI* RESULTS WITH DISADVANTAGED EXPERIMENTAL GROUP TO ADVANTAGED CONTROL GROUP

An interesting comparison can be made by comparing the performance of the experimental Negro group at Universal School as shown in Tables 25-5 and 25-6 with the white control group from the advantaged Hughes Elementary School as shown in Tables 25-3 and 25-4. This comparison is set

TABLE 25-7

UNIVERSAL vs HUGHES SEPT. TO MAY						
	N	Mean Gain Exp.	N	Mean Gain Cont.	Diff.	Significant?
Computation	26	1.65	24	1.74	-.09	NS
Concepts	26	2.23	24	.60	1.63	< .01
Applications	26	1.33	24	.90	.43	NS

forth in Tables 25-7 and 25-8 below. Tables 25-7 and 25-8 are a recompilation of Tables 25-3 through 25-6.

TABLE 25-8

	N	Mean Gain Exp.	N	Mean Gain Cont.	Diff.	Significant?
UNIVERSAL vs HUGHES SEPT. TO SEPT.						
Computation	26	1.04	24	.88	.16	NS
Concepts	26	1.14	24	.65	.49	NS
Applications	26	.70	24	1.47	-.77	.01

Tables 25-7 and 25-8 indicate very clearly that there is very little statistical difference between the educational gains of disadvantaged Negro children on CAI and advantaged white children in a control group taught by normal instructional techniques. This particular finding (which is replicated throughout our statistical results at other grade levels) is an indication that computer-assisted instruction may well be a technique suited for closing the educational gap which exists between the disadvantaged and children from more affluent segments of society.

An interesting observation is that the conceptual gain of the Negro students was greater at the end of the year's instruction than was the gain of the class taught by traditional instruction. An interesting sidelight is the significant gain in "applications" of the white group at the time of retesting in September, 1968.

Conclusions

Computer-assisted instruction is a viable educational technique. From analysis of data presented here we could be tempted to infer it is not as successful a teaching technique for children from advantaged homes as it is for children from disadvantaged homes. Further study of available data is imperative in this respect.

WHERE DO WE STAND NOW?

CAI is a viable educational system if the McComb Project is any indicator. CAI as a practical educational concept stands at the brink of a tremendous future, but this future is clouded by several rather severe problems which are faced by all CAI programs. These problems are: (1) expense of hardware, (2) lack of hardware compatible with existing software, (3) lack of sufficient programs, (4) a proliferation of languages in which the software is written and (5) lack of commitment of computer manufacturers to produce equipment tailored to educational requirements.

Our conviction as to the McComb experience with the Suppes' drill-and-practice mathematics program is that to deliver CAI as a viable school program here hinges about the possibility that hardware costs can be cut considerably and communication costs reduced by the use of a technique where a small computer is updated by a data processing computer. Locally we envision CAI as being delivered as a peripheral, or fallout, to a data processing program.

Our idea is to utilize the memory of the data processing computer (obviously it would have to be properly programmed to do this task) to update a "batch process" CAI program brought to the big computer from tapes generated on smaller peripheral computers. These smaller computers would operate independently of the big computer during the day—not connected by any real-time arrangement to the data processing computer by telephone line. The small computer will generate data on tape, which data is updated during night hours on the data processing computer, thus leaving the data processing computer available for full usage during prime time for school district data processing operations.

Our reasoning has been developed by this train of thought.

For CAI to be delivered at a reasonable cost, it must be delivered by a computer system which has more than one purpose and has no easily reached finite limitation on the number of pupils served.

Computer hardware available on the market at the moment is too expensive to deliver a program at a cost effectiveness which would be supported by a single local school district simply because the CAI mode is not adapted easily to real-time data processing equipment. The details of this arrangement are too complex to be set out in this short document, but we can suffice by saying that the switching demands of a terminal require so much computer memory that the number of real-time terminals which can be driven by any computer memory can quickly be reached by the number of pupils in any medium-sized district.

The obvious solution to this dilemma is to remove the switching function from the central processor and use the data processing computer as it is intended to be used—as a batch processor of information.

We have independently (and exhaustively) investigated all large commercial computer configurations technically capable of delivering CAI. We can state without equivocation that we could not afford to operate any of the systems that we have investigated without federal support.

Examined in detail in our investigation were nine different commercial computer configurations. This examination occupied an eight-month period of time in which we received detailed proposals from seven separate firms. Our efforts to find an "affordable CAI system" already on the market terminated in January of 1969.

As a result of our investigations, we have concluded that there must be a way to deliver an "affordable" CAI system, but rethinking the approach taken by commercial computer firms (used to dealing with well-financed businesses) was necessary before this goal could be reached for public schools.

A Satellite Computer System

To be "practical" CAI must be salable in even the smallest school districts. Being "salable" means a favorable cost effectiveness ratio. Such a ratio would be measurable in terms of educating pupils within the financial limitations of the district offering the program. We have set an arbitrary figure of $20 per pupil as a salable figure.

This figure of $20 per pupil would be within the same range as one-fifth of the mathematics cost per pupil per year in an average classroom.

We see two major costs in any CAI budget, outside of personnel.

The first is communication. Obviously all students in the school district cannot be handled at a point immediately adjacent to a central processing computer or a satellite computer. At distances beyond 2,000 feet, independent communication devices (either high-grade telephone line or microwave transmission) must become a part of a CAI network. The telephone line itself is a relatively inexpensive communication device. However, computer impulses (digital in nature) must be translated into an audio signal. This requires a relatively expensive data set at either end of the telephone line. This data set converts the digital pulse of the computer into an audio signal which can be transmitted over the telephone line. The audio signal must be reconverted to a digital signal at the other end of the line. The rental costs of these data sets run approximately $130 per terminal per month. With 40 teletype terminals in operation, data sets become an expensive part of a CAI budget. Circumventing this cost would require owning one's own data sets (purchase cost approximately $500 apiece) or the use of a microwave transmission tower, which system would run in the same cost range as a transmission system for educational television.

An alternate would be to design a system which would largely eliminate telephone lines or need for microwave communications.

The computer cost is the second immense factor in CAI. A factor limiting real-time systems is the number of terminal devices which can be driven by the computer. The simplest terminal available, the teletype machine, demands computer memory to attend to its mechanical needs. 32-K of 8 bit word memory can handle the necessary computations to perform CAI and drive only 28 teletype terminals without severe impairment of the program. One teletype terminal can handle approximately 45 children in a given day. Thus, using this rule of thumb measure, each 32-K (8 bit) memory can handle 1,440 students in a six-hour school day on a real-time basis. Using this figure, the finite limitation of a 256-K memory computer (a very large computer indeed) would be in the vicinity of 12,000 pupils per day using the relatively simple teletype terminal. The cost of this 256K computer per child is out of fiscal reach of any school district unless the school district has some outside source of funds.

An alternative approach would be to design a system in which the memory of the computer is not tied up by this switching function. In this case a satellite switching computer, not operated on a real-time basis but with sufficient memory and disc storage to operate programs for one day at a time can be updated at night by a relatively small data processing computer (24K of 8 bit words).

Conclusions

In April of 1969 the McComb District school board let a contract with a firm to develop a satellite computer system updated by a Honeywell 200 data processing computer. This computer configuration meets the requirements of the model described above. The location of smaller computer satellites in large elementary schools in some measure will cut communication costs. The data processing computer is free to do prime time educational data processing. The information necessary to drive the small computers will be updated at night by a batch processing procedure.

Hopefully the McComb School District will be able to produce a "practical" computer-assisted instructional program in drill and practice mathematics during the third year of its ESEA Title III project.

Part D

**Individualized Learning:
The Present in
Colleges and
Universities**

Introduction

Individualization has occurred in certain institutional contexts in higher education for many years. In courses such as practice teaching, music performance, or doctoral thesis it is obvious that the group process is likely to be out of place. In recent years, however, there have been efforts at individualizing certain courses that traditionally have been taught to large numbers of students organized in groups. It is not uncommon, for instance, to find that students studying the laboratory aspects of a course such as Instructional Media and Technology are now essentially "self-taught." This is accomplished through the extensive use of instructional packages, such as slide-tape-workbook combinations, that spell out desired terminal behaviors and provide for self-checks of the learner's progress.

In Chapter 26, S. N. Postlethwait describes such an audio-tutorial approach as it is used to teach a university level biology course. Then, together with J. Novak and H. T. Murray, Jr., he gives an example of the technique, including portions of tape commentary, objectives, and workbook exercises. The audio-tutorial method, it should be noted, has not alienated the students nor made the professor less humanistic, as signified by the fact that Professor Postlethwait was voted the year's outstanding professor award by the student body on his campus, Purdue University, after this method had been put into effect.

In Chapter 27, Benjamin Richason, Jr., describes a similar technique as it has been applied to quite a different subject—geography. It is important to note that not just a part, but the *whole* introductory geography course is taught in this manner at Carroll College.

A third report from higher education is that of J. Hugh Baird, W. Dwayne Belt and Lyal Holder, contained in Chapter 28. They describe an application of individualized learning that goes beyond a single course, constituting an

312

evolving teacher training program at Brigham Young University. The planned pattern of preservice studies is organized around behavioral objectives, a syllabus of learning activities, and tests to evaluate trainee performance.

In spite of these and other pioneering efforts, such as those at New York Institute of Technology, Oakland Community College, and a few other locations, there has been no widespread adoption, as yet, of individualization as a *modus operandi* throughout college level curricula. This seems ironic not only because of the leadership role that colleges and universities are supposed to play, but also because they, more than any other sector of education, are being pressed, even challenged, by their student body to become *relevant* and to consider the dignity and worth of the *individual*.

Chapter 26. **INDEPENDENT STUDY**
IN BIOLOGY

TEACHING TOOLS AND TECHNIQUES:
AN AUDIO-TUTORIAL APPROACH
TO TEACHING

S. N. Postlethwait

I. HISTORY OF THE AUDIO-TUTORIAL SYSTEM

The audio-tutorial system began in 1961 as an attempt to make some adjustment for the diversity of backgrounds of students in a freshman botany course. Students had attended a great variety of high schools so that some had received very excellent training and others relatively poor training. Students with equal capacities could not perform equally well because of this difference in background. To assist the students with poor background, it was

Source: This presentation was given before a group of educators at the University of Hawaii Communications Center on January 24, 1967. It was summarized in *Pacific Speech,* Vol. 1, No. 4, as a sample of the audio-tutorial or independent learning system of instruction. This excised version of the speech was edited by Richard A. Sanderson, Director, Communications Service Center, University of Hawaii. Slight adaptations were made for this text. Reprinted by permission of the author and publisher.

decided to make a special lecture on tape each week and file this tape with the language tapes in the Audio Visual Library. Students could go to this facility and hear the supplementary lectures thus enabling them to compete more effectively.

During the course of preparation of these lectures, it appeared that the students might well bring their textbooks along and open them to the appropriate pages so that the subject matter in the text could be related to the subject matter covered by the tape lecture. Later it seemed logical to add the use of their laboratory manual in the same pattern to relate to the subject matter in the text and to the subject matter on tape. Still later, it seemed feasible to provide the student with plants and experimental materials so that these too could be related to the laboratory manual, textbook, and tape lecture. Ultimately the discussion on the tape was no longer a lecture but rather was discussion on a one-to-one basis (one teacher-one student).

Learning events included a great range of experiences such as reading from the text, doing an experiment, collecting data, analyzing data, manipulation of a microscope, watching a time-lapse movie, observing plant specimens, charts, diagrams, photographs, and listening to brief lectures or discussions as appropriate. The success of the initial tapes encouraged me to run an experiment of 36 students for one semester which further confirmed the potential of the audio-tutorial system. At the end of the second semester of experimentation, I met with these students to restructure the botany course, disregarding all traditional limitation and placing total emphasis on student learning. All busy work would be eliminated and an attempt would be made to adapt the method of presentation to the nature of the objective. The first restructured course included one hour per week—General Assembly Session (GAS); 1 hour per week—Small Assembly Session (SAS); and ? hours per week—Independent Study Session. The Independent Study Session was the modification of the original audio taped tutorial.

In subsequent revisions of the system an Integrated Quiz Session (IQS) has been substituted for the Small Assembly Session. The IQS is a modified seminar and oral quiz. It involves eight students seated informally around a table with one instructor. The instructor is supplied with the various items which were included in the learning center the preceding week, and these items are used as a basis for student discussion. All students are asked to discuss items in their turn and are asked to do so in a specified pattern or format. First, the item is to be identified; secondly, the student is to tell its role in the week's work or objectives; and thirdly, the student is to explain how it fulfills this role. Each student has an opportunity to add comments concerning any item which he thinks may enlighten the group.

This session has been an effective feedback mechanism for informing us of the success or failure of any program sequence of experiments and often provides clues for improving our approach. It also helps to clarify the appropriateness of the communication vehicle used in attempting to achieve the objective. It turns into a miniaturized seminar and thus enables many students to see relationships and concepts which were not evident from the Independent Study Session earlier.

II. RESULTS OF THE AUDIO-TUTORIAL SYSTEM

Two questions most commonly asked concerning the system are: (1) Have we now eliminated the personal contact important for motivation? and (2) Is this now a "spoon-fed" type operation in which there's not opportunity for student discovery or inquiry? In answer to the first question concerning personal contact, we find personal contact is actually enhanced. We now have relegated much of the routine of teaching to a routine vehicle and teacher's time now can be devoted to meaningful personal contact. The opportunities for personal contact are as follows:

1. As in the conventional lecture system, the senior instructor is available at the General Assembly Session for this kind of personal contact (such as it is).

2. In the Independent Study Session an instructor is available to give direct attention to individual needs on a one-to-one basis for any problem requiring instructor assistance. Also in this session students may visit with instructors about any additional aspects of the subject matter which they find interesting.

3. The Integrated Quiz Session provides an opportunity for every student to become well known by at least one instructor in the course, and every student to know at least one instructor very well. Additional opportunity is available for every student to know many instructors well but there is no alternative but to become well acquainted with at least one instructor.

The second question concerning inquiry is also answered in the affirmative. First, let us define levels of inquiry. Inquiry occurs at various levels with the maximum or first level of inquiry represented by research. The second level of inquiry is the type of experimentation which can be completed in the span of a three-hour laboratory. The third level of inquiry is one in which the busy work of doing the experimentation is completed by the instructor and the student is asked to collect data from the results and analyze these data. The fourth level of inquiry is to provide the student with data and ask the student to analyze these data. The fifth, of course, would not be considered real inquiry but merely a demonstration. All of these levels of inquiry are feasible under the audio-tutorial system. At the first level of inquiry, our students are asked to do two miniature research projects—the first, we provide guidance throughout the project but the second is left totally to the initiative of the student. In the first project the problem is defined, the materials and methods are described, the student is told what data to collect and asked to analyze these data and write up the project in the format of a scientific paper. The second project is completed by those students who hope to make an "A" in the course and here the student is restricted only by the materials available to him. He defines the problem, decides on the experimental procedure, what data to collect, analyzes these data, and writes up his project in the form of a scientific paper.

At the second level of inquiry, a problem is defined for an experiment requiring two to four hours and is done in the ISS as well under the audio-tutorial system as under the conventional system. The subsequent levels of inquiry are also handled effectively in the ISS. The results of the audio-tutorial system have been positive from every point of view. Better instruction can be given with equal or less staff and space. Grades and student interest have improved at all levels. Costs are reduced for equivalent levels of instruction.

III. PHILOSOPHY OF THE AUDIO-TUTORIAL SYSTEM

It is sometimes said that "teaching is an art." This may be true; however, "education" should be a "science." The scientific method demands that one begin by defining the problem first. The "problem" in education, simply stated, is "learning must be done by the learner." While this is not a very profound observation, it stands to reason that if "learning is done by the learner," the educational system should provide activities which require student involvement. Both teacher and student alike should be concerned with the kinds of activities and situations which contribute to learning. If these activities and situations can be identified, the teacher is obligated to provide a course structure which will permit the student to engage in these activities and the student is obliged to perform them conscientiously. Let us list some of these activities and situations.

1. *Repetition.*   There is little question but that the nature of many objectives requires repetition for their achievement. However, repetition ought to be engaged in in an intelligent fashion and adapted to the individual needs of a particular student. In a course with 500 students the teacher cannot possibly make the adjustments in repetition for individual student needs. Only the student can determine intelligently how much repetition is necessary.

2. *Concentration.*   Most classrooms are not organized to permit students to concentrate during their study. Students are distracting to one another and other disassociated events which may be occurring tend to distract the student's attention from the subject at hand. The audio-tutorial system permits the student to isolate himself from the surrounding environment by covering his ears with the earphones and by the use of other media to reduce his awareness of his surroundings.

3. *Association.*   In a study of plant science the major objective is to learn about plants. It makes sense, therefore, that a study of plants should be conducted where plants are available for observation. Diagrams, charts, models, photographs, and other such devices should be a "means to the end" so that the students' attention is directed to the literal plant itself. The audio-tutorial system provides an opportunity for the student to have an object available at the time he reads about it, does experiments, etc.

4. *Appropriate Sized Units of Subject Matter.*   People vary considerably in the amount of subject matter that can be grasped in a given amount of time. Programmers have demonstrated that most people can learn almost anything if it is broken into small enough units and the student can take time to become informed about each unit before proceeding to the next. Any program of study therefore should provide each student an opportunity to adjust the size of the unit to his own ability to assimilate the information, so that those who can absorb large quantities of information may do so in an unrestricted fashion, whereas others who must proceed more slowly are permitted to do so. The audio-tutorial system allows the student to proceed at his own pace and to break the subject matter into units commensurate with his ability.

5. *Adapt the Nature of the Communication Vehicle to the Nature of the Objective.*   It is logical that no simple vehicle such as lecturing or a textbook can achieve the full spectrum of objectives for a complex subject. The student's experiences should not be confined to any particular vehicle as film, audio tape, textbook, or a lecture. In cases where the development of a procedural skill is necessary, there is no substitute for the student doing this procedure himself. A properly structured course, therefore, would carefully define objectives and not try to mold objectives to fit a favorite medium (lecture, for example) but instead would use the medium best adapted to the nature of the objective.

6. *The Use of Multi-Media.*   Individuals differ in their responsiveness to different kinds of communication devices. Some people learn well through reading, some can learn best by auditory communication, and others can learn best by literally handling specimens and performing experiments. The audio-tutorial system thus provides an opportunity for subject matter to be covered in a great variety of ways with the student exploiting the medium which communicates most directly and effectively for him.

7. *Finally, and Most Important, the Integration of Learning Activities and Situations.*   It stands to reason that if learning events are to be complementary and to have some relationship, they should be brought into close proximity and properly sequenced. The conventional structuring of a lecture, recitation, and laboratory does not take this into consideration but rather may expose a student on Monday to a lecture concerning a given subject; perhaps on Wednesday the student does experiments related to that subject; on Friday a recitation will involve the student in some exposure to the subject; and then on Sunday night, late, the student may read on this

subject from text. The audio-tutorial system permits the student to bring all of these learning experiences into an integrated sequence so that each learning event may enhance or complement the adjacent ones and thus result in a synergistic effect. One might compare this analogously to an orchestra. Many musical instruments making sounds in a random fashion result in noise or cacophony; however, these same sounds, if given timing and placed in an appropriate sequence or relationship one to another form a melody. I am suggesting that there is a melody of learning and that teaching is, indeed, an art. It is the art of sequencing learning events into a meaningful experience for students.

Education is a science so that one must define the problem first and then go about logically developing a procedure which permits a student to engage in those activities which result in learning. It may require a total restructuring of courses and reorganization of approaches. Teaching is an art but the artistry comes not through the use of the teacher as a communication device but rather in his skill in determining objectives and developing the materials and sequences which will enable the student to achieve those objectives in the most efficient and effective manner.

Many of us find this approach to education a little difficult. Teachers and educators are the most tradition-bound group of individuals I know. This happened in a logical evolutionary sequence, the explanation of which is relatively simple. In the days of Aristotle, the source of information was the scholar and he was the communication vehicle. It was logical that contact between the student and the educator was through lecturing. It is amazing that many of us still teach in this fashion feeling that our contribution is to expose the student to our knowledge of the subject matter, and many people who want to become teachers do so merely because the lecture is an ego-inflating device. We find it an exhilarating experience to stand before a group of people and to mystify them with our great knowledge of a given subject. In this age there are many communication devices more effective than the human being and ego-inflation of scholars is not a worthy objective for an educational system.

We have come to the point where instructors consider it a promotion when they are given the best students in the university or high school. I am suggesting to you that this is not a professional attitude. What would you think of a doctor who wished to take only those cases which could be cured by merely dispensing aspirin? Most of us would say that this is non-professional, and we would not want a doctor of this kind. We want cases and those cases which are challenging. If this be true, and teaching is a profession, a professional attitude would demand that we too would find the hard-to-get-well cases most challenging. Humbling as it may be, self-examination may be in order for us to determine whether we really and truly fulfill our role in the educational process. Are we succumbing to the ego-inflating exercises which display our great knowledge of the subject matter, or are we willing to accept that it is our responsibility to provide the facilities, provide the guidance and direction, and provide motivation to help students learn?

INDEPENDENT STUDY SESSION: EXCERPTS FROM A WEEK'S UNIT OF STUDY

S. N. Postlethwait
J. Novak
H. T. Murray, Jr.

TAPE COMMENTARY

There are some compounds which are known to affect growth and development, two of which are gibberellic acid and coumarin. The effect of these two compounds on Grand Rapids lettuce seed germination is illustrated by the experi- ment set up for Exercise 4. Will you turn off the tape player, collect the data, and make your conclusions for Exercise 4, please.— Music. (See objective 3d in Fig. 26-1.)

The student would turn off the tape player and do Exercise 4. The data he collected would show gibberellic acid stimulated germination and coumarin inhibited it. He would complete the exercise and return to the tape.

From these data it is clear that gibberellic acid can in some way substitute for the action induced by red light. It is also clear that certain substances such as coumarin can block this action. Now will you turn to pages 165 and 166 in your textbook and study the

SOURCE: These excerpts are drawn from *The Audio-Tutorial Approach to Learning* (2nd Ed.; Minneapolis: Burgess Publishing Co., 1969), a complete handbook illustrating the mechanics as well as the philosophy of the instructional system developed at Purdue University. Reprinted by permission of the authors and publisher.

figs. 11-44, 11-45, and 11-46. Turn off the tape now please, and read your text.—Music.

The student would turn off the tape and study the text to reinforce and elaborate what he had learned from the previous study. He would then return to the tape.

Now will you turn please to pages 8 and 9 in the *Scientific American* article "Light and Development."—Music.

The student turns off the tape and finds the appropriate article. He returns to the tape.

In the *Scientific American* article on pages 8 and 9 you will notice that germination was high in those petri dishes receiving a final exposure to red light and low in those petri dishes receiving a final exposure to far-red light. In other words, those seeds exposed to red light will germinate but if the exposure to red light is followed by exposure to far-red, these seeds will not germinate. These exposures may alternated back and forth and in each case

WEEK'S SUBJECT MATTER   BIOLOGY 108   WEEK II

Numbers in parentheses indicate related problems in Murray's *Manual*. The student should be able to apply information obtained from his study to solve the assigned problems in Murray's *Manual*.

MAJOR OBJECTIVES: PLANT GROWTH AND DEVELOPMENT (continued)

3. *Light and Growth*
    a. Be able to describe the effects of light on lettuce seed germination describing specifically how the experiment was set up, a statement of the hypothesis it was attempting to clarify, and state two justifiable conclusions.
    b. Be able to discuss the results of the experiment in Exercise 2 page 9 in the study guide and relate them to the hypothesis in Exercise 1.
    c. Be able to describe the experiment demonstrating the relationship between inhibiting wavelengths and promoting wavelengths on lettuce seed germination.
    d. Be able to describe the interactions between light and gibberellic acid and between light and coumarin with respect to the effects on lettuce seed germination. (3-2)
    e. Be able to describe the effects of etiolation on plants in terms of gross morphology. Suggest four physiological factors such as changes in photosynthesis, growth hormone distribution, etc. which account for these effects.
    f. Be able to associate particular light quality specifically involved in changes which occur during plant growth and development such as chlorophyll production, lignin formation, hypocotyl unhooking, hypocotyl elongation, anthocyanin production, and leaf expansion. (21-1)
    g. Be able to state which wavelengths of light are involved in producing the effects of etiolation.
    h. Be able to explain (in terms of the changes in phytochrome) the red, far-red pigment system.
    i. Be able to explain (in terms of the changes in phytochrome) the effects of red and far-red light in the following processes: seed germination, leaf expansion, opening of the hypocotyl hook, normal internode length, anthocyanin formation, lignin formation, coleoptile elongation, and flowering. (21-2, 3)

4. *Photoperiod and Temperature*
    j. Be able to define the terms long-day, short-day, and day neutral in terms of the critical period.
    k. Using data such as those on page 13 of the Study Guide, be able to state whether a given plant is long-day, short-day, or day neutral.
    l. Be able to identify the plants on display as to whether they are all long-day, short-day, or day neutral, and point out the relative critical period. (Note: Can all the plants be classified into one of the three categories? Can any of the plants "fit" into more than one category?)
    m. Be able to describe how one could determine whether a plant is a long-day, a short-day plant, or a day neutral plant and how the critical point can be determined. (22-1, 2)
    n. Describe the interacting effects of light and temperature on the growth and flowering of *Guar* plants.
    o. Using the graph on demonstration, be able to explain thermoperiodism as applied to growth of the tomato plant.

FIGURE 26-1

A MIMEOGRAPHED HANDOUT LISTING THE OBJECTIVES FOR THE WEEK

the seeds will respond to the last exposure whether it be red or far-red wavelengths. It is important to note that in some instances certain growth substances such as gibberellins may be substituted and eliminate this light requirement, while coumarin may act as an inhibitor.

Now let us look again at our hypothesis. "There are pigments in plants which affect physiological phenomena in addition to the chlorophyll pigment." The phenomenon affected may be some phenomenon other than photosynthesis. Our answer thus far is "yes, there is another pigment called phytochrome, and a phenomenon germination which is affected by red wavelengths of light and far-red wavelengths of light." One might then hypothesize still further that there are other pigments and other phenomena affected by light.

Earlier in the semester you viewed two films on germination, one on the germination and development of the bean seedling and one on the germination and development of the corn seedling. I'd like you to view these films again and see if you can identify a growth phenomenon affected by light that we have not discussed yet. Will you turn off the tape now please, and view the films.— Music.

The student would turn off the tape and view the films, then return to the tape.

To confirm, or modify, the conclusions you made while observing the films concerning growth responses, turn to page 11 in the study guide and do Exercise 5 (Figure 26-2). Once again we have grown the plants under the conditions required to facilitate and expedite your collection of data. Will you go to the center table and collect data for Exercise 5? Turn off the tape and do this.— Music.

The student would turn off the tape and collect data from the materials set up for Exercise 5. On completion of the study he would return to the tape.

Now, let us see how keen you were in making observations. Let us consider the bean plant first. The bean plant grown in the dark was taller than the one grown in the light. The bean leaves on the plant grown in the dark were smaller than the leaves on the bean plant grown in the light. The bean plant grown in the dark was yellowish to white, whereas the bean plant grown in the light was green. The top of the bean plant grown in the dark was curved toward the ground, whereas the bean plant grown in the light was erect. Now, consider the corn seedlings grown in the dark versus

the corn seedlings grown in the light. Again the plant grown in the dark was yellowish, whereas the one grown in the light was green. The plant grown in the dark had long leaves, whereas the plant grown in the light had shorter leaves.

Which of these phenomena can we account for from our previous study? The formation of chlorophyll is dependent on light—so the green in light and the non-green in dark is likely correlated with the chlorophyll pigment system. Last week we concluded that the tropisms were related to a carotenoid system. We have just learned about the phytochrome system—could it account for any of the other phenomena? The experiment set up for Exercise 6 may give some assistance in identifying which of the phenomena is related to the phytochrome system. Turn off the tape player, please, and make your observations for Exercise 6, answering the questions at the bottom of page 11.—Music.

The student would turn off the tape player and do Exercise 6 (Figure 26-2). He would then return to the tape.

How many pigment systems can you identify which are involved in plant responses?

Exercise 5   One group of seedlings has been grown in light and one group grown in darkness during the past 20 days. List the differences you can observe between the two groups.

Light	Dark

Exercise 6   Are all wave lengths of light effective in preventing etiolation? Three groups of seedlings were grown as in Exercise 5 except they were exposed to: A - red light, B - blue light, and C - far-red (this quality of light is obtained by using blue and red cellophane in combination). Use the plants from Exercise 5 as controls. What was the effect of the different light quality?

Seedlings A	Seedlings B	Seedlings C

Which wave lengths allowed expansion of leaves? _____;
straightening of the hypocotyl hook?_____;
and elongation of the hypocotyl?_____.

What pigments were involved in hypocotyl elongation?_____;
straightening of the hypocotyl hook?_____;
expanding of leaves?_____; and food synthesis?
_____.

FIGURE 26-2

PAGE 11 OF THE UNIT ON GROWTH AND DEVELOPMENT IN THE STUDY GUIDE

Chapter 27. INDEPENDENT STUDY IN GEOGRAPHY

THE AUDIO-VISUAL-TUTORIAL METHOD IN GEOGRAPHY INSTRUCTION

Benjamin F. Richason, Jr.

The Audio-Visual-Tutorial (AVT) method in geography instruction was developed at Carroll College, and implemented during the fall semester, 1966. The purposes for inaugurating AVT work were to improve the content of the beginning course in physical geography, to provide flexibility in class scheduling, to promote independent learning, and to provide a course which would allow all students to compete favorably regardless of their high school backgrounds in geography or the earth sciences.

Basic to the AVT course at Carroll College is a series of 15 independent study carrels, each of which is permanently equipped with a 35 mm. slide projector and a tape transport unit. Extra visual materials are supplied as needed for the exercises. Furthermore, the AVT laboratory area is supplied with a demonstration area in which items and experiments not suited to the booths are placed. Single-concept, continuous-loop films and rear-projection,

SOURCE: This paper was originally presented at the Audiotutorial Conference, Purdue University, October, 1969. Reprinted by permission of author and publisher.

sound-synchronized units are utilized to expand and reinforce the content material presented via tapes, slides, and extra visual materials in the booths. Laboratory work is integrated with the discussion on the tape, and is not an appendage to the course as is frequently the case in the traditionally presented lecture-discussion-laboratory course.

The distinctiveness of the AVT method at Carroll College lies in the fact that the introductory geography course is totally committed to independent audio-visual learning. The entire course presentation is contained on the tape, slides, and in the demonstration area. The student comes to the AVT laboratory on an unscheduled basis at those times and remains during those intervals which he finds most convenient in terms of his own schedule, alertness, and attention span. All of the materials necessary to study and understand the assignments are either present in the study carrels or on the demonstration table when the student arrives in the laboratory.

No textbook is used in this course; however, multiple copies of the major physical geography texts are placed on closed reserve in the college library for those students who feel more comfortable with a book. Assigned readings are made in *Scientific American* Offprints, Bobbs-Merrill Reprints in Geography, and in other selected sources. A dictionary of geographical terms and the college outline series in geography are available for purchase in the college bookstore. All students are required to bring an assigned atlas with them to each independent study session.

A laboratory assistant is on duty at all times during which the laboratory is open. His functions are to check students in and out of booths, to reset tape players and slide projectors, to re-stock booths with expendable supplies, and to aid students with their work if necessary.

Each student is assigned to a weekly, 50-minute discussion session. Although attendance at these sessions is not required, the instructor is present at this time to meet with students face-to-face, to answer questions, and to expand ideas.

The AVT system makes possible the repetition and review of all material. Each step of the work is illustrated by slides, which also serve the purposes of chalkboard work and laboratory demonstrations previously performed in the classroom. Emphasis is placed on the self-reliance of the student to learn independently by repeating those portions of the tapes, slides, and movies until he understands the material. If the student has questions on course content he may take them to the laboratory assistant on duty, to the instructor in his office, or to the weekly discussion session.

The two-semester AVT geography course at Carroll College was written to occupy the student for four hours per week. Considering this projected time requirement and the different speeds at which students perform laboratory assignments, it is estimated that one booth will accommodate with ease 10 students per week. The 15 booths at Carroll College, therefore, should serve

150 students, but uncontrolled enrollment in the course has been as high as 182 students.

Examinations are the only scheduled portions of the course. These are given on every third Monday morning, and they cover three units of work. Students punch their answers to multiple choice questions on IBM cards specially designed for the course. These cards are graded by the IBM 1130 computer, which also provides an item analysis. The time that students spend in the study booths is correlated with examination scores. Such evaluations have served to identify those portions of the course which cause trouble and to aid the instructor in modifying both course content and examination procedures to better meet the requirements of students and teacher.

The results of the AVT laboratory at Carroll College have been analyzed for a period of 12 semesters. The results of this analysis show that about 40 percent more material is being presented than in the course as formerly taught; that students spend an average of 3 hours 32 minutes per week in the independent study booths; and that scores on examinations have increased by 28.75 per cent. During the past six semesters, students scoring "A" on examinations spent an average of 3 hours 48 minutes per week in the AVT laboratory; students scoring "B" on examinations spent an average of 3 hours 40 minutes per week in the study carrels; while students scoring "C" grades on examinations spent 3 hours 21 minutes per week in the AVT laboratory; "D" students, 3 hours 07 minutes, and students who failed examinations spent 2 hours 38 minutes per week in the independent study booths.

Student opinions have been very favorable to the AVT geography course. More than 48 percent have indicated that it was either the best course they had taken in college, or that it was among the best three courses taken. Over 79 percent of those enrolled in the AVT course felt that the method of instruction was superior to the traditional lecture-laboratory course, and more than 88 percent indicated that the discussions on the tape were well organized and well presented, that slides and extra visuals aided their interpretation of facts and concepts, and that the discussion and laboratory work were well integrated. Almost two-thirds of the classes felt that there was no loss of personal contact with the professor.

1. 35 mm slide projector with 3″ lens.
2. Mat white screen, vinyl base (15″ x 15″).
3. Pegboard for displaying materials.
4. Ventilating fan.
5. Map rail.
6. Permanently mounted world relief map.
7. Glass shelf. (Others may be added.)
8. Alphabetical list of place locations discussed on tape.
9. Student identification card indicating times booth was used.
10. Alphabetical list of new terms discussed on tape.
11. Formica laboratory deck (48″ x 32″).
12. Electrical outlets.
13. Laboratory deck light.
14. Forward and reverse buttons for projector.
15. Projector switch. (Automatically shuts off overhead light and turns on deck light when projector is turned on.)
16. Switch for occupancy lights; occupied —red, unoccupied —green. (Lights are located at end of bank of ten booths.)
17. Ventilating fan switch.
18. Guest jack for instructor.
19. Earphone jack.
20. Tape player switch; volume and tone control.
21. Earphones.
22. Laboratory exercise; correlated with tape.
23. Laboratory work sheets.
24. Tape player with footage counter.
25. Fast forward and reverse for tape player.
26. Tape play control.
27. Storage drawers for laboratory equipment.
28. Recessed overhead lighting.

FIGURE 27-1

AUDIO-VISUAL-TUTORIAL LABORATORY GEOGRAPHY DEPARTMENT

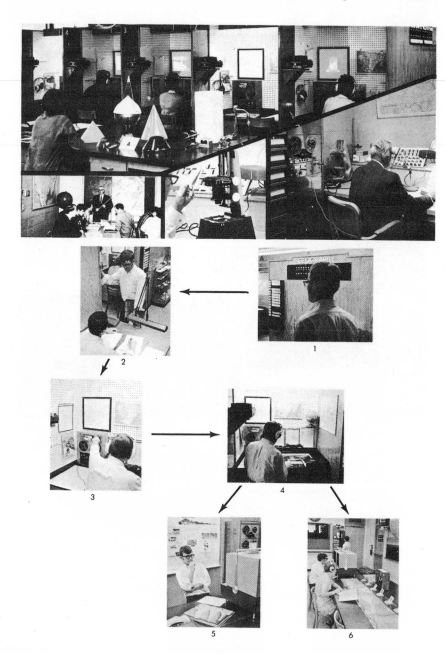

FIGURE 27-2
THE AUDIO-VISUAL-TUTORIAL METHOD IN GEOGRAPHY

REFERENCES

RICHASON, B. F., JR. "The Audio-Visual-Tutorial Method," *The Journal of Geography,* April, 1967, pp. 155-57.

RICHASON, B. F., JR. "The Audio-Visual-Tutorial Method in Geography " (with A. J. Wilner), *Methods of Geographic Instruction* (ed. John W. Morris). Waltham, Mass.: Blaisdell-Ginn, 1968, Chap. 9.

RICHASON, B. F., JR. *Geography Via the Audio-Visual-Tutorial Method,* How-To-Do-It Series, No. 8, National Council for Geographic Education, Chicago, Illinois, November, 1969.

Chapter 28. **INDEPENDENT STUDY IN TEACHER EDUCATION**

THE INDIVIDUALIZED SECONDARY
TEACHER EDUCATION PROGRAM
AT BRIGHAM YOUNG UNIVERSITY

J. Hugh Baird
W. Dwayne Belt
Lyal Holder

PROGRAM RATIONALE

In an age of education characterized by innovations, research in learning and teaching, changing roles for the teachers, and teachers demanding more voice in the educational enterprise, the professional certification program for secondary teachers is yet often based upon the taking of a series of required education courses.

SOURCE: Adapted from *The Individualized Secondary Teacher Education Program at Brigham Young University,* M-Step Monograph 2, Utah State Board of Education, no date. An additional citation is *Teacher Education in Transition,* Vol. I, p. 201. Reprinted by permission of the senior author.

332

The faculty members associated with the Secondary Experimental Program at Brigham Young University are convinced that certification based on a series of courses and credits is no longer desirable. They feel that the ability to perform certain specified behaviors is a more rational basis on which to certify individuals to teach in the secondary schools. The innovations of team teaching, continuous progress education, non-graded schools, and the expanding use of technology in our schools have helped change the role of the teacher to an identifier of learning problems and a director of learning activities rather than a presenter of information. More and more teachers are being given opportunities to assume the responsibility for individualizing instruction, for counseling students, for curriculum changing and curriculum writing, instruction through diverse methods, for emphasizing the processes of inquiry and discovery, for cooperating in planning the presentation of programs, for guiding students in the process of self-direction, and for identifying learning activities which are appropriate and effective in large group instruction, small group instruction and independent study situations.

During the spring semester, 1965, an experiment was conducted at Brigham Young University in a beginning methods class to determine if there was a significant difference in learning between students who complete the course in a self-paced mode and those who complete the same course in the traditional lecture discussion mode.[1] The results of this research seemed to justify moving even further into an examination of our conventional teacher education program.

Specifying behavioral objectives for prospective secondary teachers was one of the first steps taken in preparing the experimental program. Approximately 60 were originally written. The research on effective teaching and learning provided essential teacher behaviors from which we began our list. Analysis of communication problems between teachers and parents, pupils, and administration provided additional behavior. Some of the objectives came as a result of our personal experiences as teachers and supervisors of teachers. Data about students—their similarities, differences, needs, abilities, development patterns, and styles of learning provided the basis for other objectives. A portion of these objectives is shown below for illustrative purposes.

UNIT 8:   LEARNING

8.10   Cognitive Learning Sequence

1. For all assigned lesson plans and curriculum units, the preservice teacher will prepare learning activities to do the following:

    a) Focus the attention of the learners on the referent for each major concept.

b) Provide for conceptualization of each major concept at *and* above the lowest cognitive level .

c) Make provisions for application of each major concept by the learners.

2.   Upon being given a specific teaching-learning situation, the preservice teacher will be able to differentiate between appropriate sequential teaching procedures for cognitive learning by specifically outlining during a timed, open book test, those appropriate teaching procedures to achieve the intended objective.

To be acceptable, the three steps in the learning sequence must occur in the order listed above.

8.20   Psychomotor Learning Sequence

1.   For all psychomotor lesson plans prepared, and all psychomotor skills included to be taught as part of assigned curriculum units, the preservice teacher will prepare and use learning activities to do the following:

a) Help the learner "preview" the psychomotor activities.

b) Provide for exploratory effort and guided practice until the learner performs the act correctly.

c) Provide for repetitive practice sessions which are appropriate in terms of deviation and frequency.

d) Provide for "transfer" of the psychomotor activities to other subsequent behaviors.

2.   Upon being given a specific teaching-learning situation, the preservice teacher will be able to differentiate between appropriate sequential teaching procedures for psychomotor skills by specifically outlining during a timed, open book test, those appropriate teaching procedures to achieve the intended objective.

To be acceptable, the four steps in the learning sequence must occur in the order listed above.

8.30   Learning Styles

The pre-service teacher will individualize the instruction for which he is responsible in student teaching to accommodate the possible differences in learning styles of (at least one of) his students, by preparing special materials or using special teaching methods as appropriate to the needs of the students.

8.40   Transfer and Retention of Learning

Given a variety of teaching method alternatives for concepts, skills, attitudes, facts, etc., in an objective test situation, the preservice teacher will identify those methods leading to greater transfer and retention and identify or state the underlying theoretical basis for his choice. Minimal test performance is 70%.

8.50   Learning Symbols

The preservice teacher will write learning activities for all lesson and unit plans so that symbols unfamiliar to the learner are not taught until the referent of the symbol has been perceived.

8.60   Process of Learning

The student will differentiate between teaching procedures which would facilitate learning based upon insight and understanding (as described under Gestalt psychology) and learning based upon role or mechanical responses (as described under operant conditioning) as follows:

1. When given a typical classroom learning situation on an essay test, outline the precise steps by which a teacher would proceed to promote each type of learning, and

2. Plan and conduct conditioning of a desired behavior in the classroom setting.

8.70   Programmed Material

Having written a behavioral objective, the preservice teacher will prepare programmed material for teaching at least one concept requisite to performance of the objective such that the student can use the materials entirely independent of the teacher.

ORGANIZATION FOR INSTRUCTION

The second step, which proceeded concurrently with the identification of behavioral objectives, was the organizing of learning experiences both varied and comprehensive enough to help prospective secondary school teachers attain the objectives. Just as persons from different institutions would undoubtedly create differing lists of behavioral objectives for a teacher training program, so might the means to accomplish objectives differ widely from one institution to another. The experimental certification program at Brigham Young University is *one* attempt to accomplish a given set of objectives. The program consists of two sequential phases. Phase I, Academic Preparation, consists of instructional activities designed to develop in the trainee capabilities necessary for effective performance in curriculum planning and teaching. Phase II, Student Teaching, provides opportunity for the trainee to use the instructional materials prepared in Phase I in an actual classroom situation.

Phase I Academic Preparation

Phase I is a non-coursed, integrated presentation of academic content presently lasting one semester. (See Figure 28-1.) Eventually, semester bounds will disappear and students will be allowed to progress at their own individual rates through the program whether it takes one semester or more—hence the term continuous progress. Instead of requiring trainees to complete a given number of semester hours of class work, they are required to achieve the behavioral objectives of the program. These behaviors are arranged into 11 units. (See Figure 28-2.) No formal classes are held. Figure 28-3 shows how a student might achieve an objective. At the beginning of each unit, the student is given a syllabus containing the behavioral objectives for the unit and, for some objectives, a pretest designed to assess his mastery of prerequisite behaviors, as well as the degree to which he can already exhibit the performance specified for the objective. Following the pretest or upon receiving the unit where pretests are not applicable or are not yet available, the student counsels with one of a team of instructors assigned to the program and together they select from the syllabus those learning activities which will help the student exhibit terminal performance. If the pretest shows that the student can already demonstrate the terminal behaviors, he will be allowed to omit it and concentrate on those he cannot demonstrate.

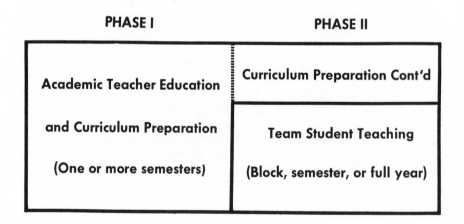

FIGURE 28-1

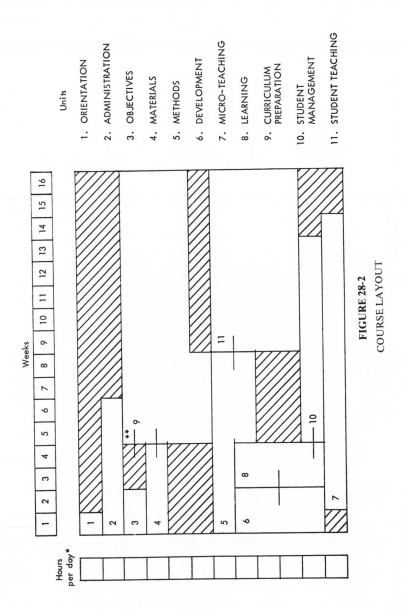

FIGURE 28-2
COURSE LAYOUT

Weeks

| 1 | 2 | 3 | 4 | 5 | 6 | 7 | 8 | 9 | 10 | 11 | 12 | 13 | 14 | 15 | 16 |

Units

1. ORIENTATION
2. ADMINISTRATION
3. OBJECTIVES
4. MATERIALS
5. METHODS
6. DEVELOPMENT
7. MICRO-TEACHING
8. LEARNING
9. CURRICULUM PREPARATION
10. STUDENT MANAGEMENT
11. STUDENT TEACHING

Hours per day*

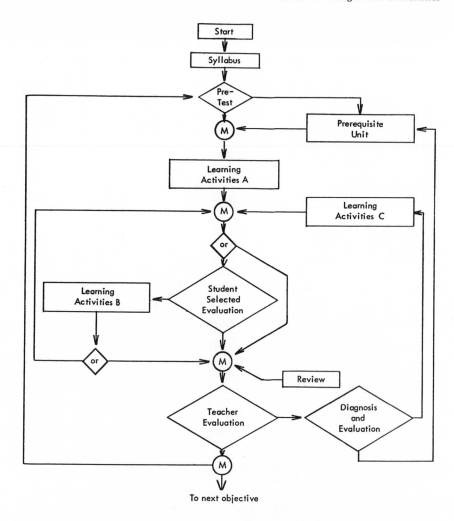

FIGURE 28-3

Students work through suggested learning activities individually or in small groups. The learning activities for a given objective are those which most effectively promote the specified behavior of the objective and are therefore appropriately diverse. For example, learning activities include observations in elementary, secondary, and special education classrooms. Single-concept lessons are micro-taught both with and without video tape recording playback. Interaction analysis of the student's own and other teachers' classroom behavior is required. The use of a Remote Information Retrieval System allows our trainees to hear recorded audio tapes with or without accompanying visual materials. Straight-text and programmed reading materials are assigned and lectures are scheduled when necessary.

When the student finishes the required learning activities for a given objective, he is given a test designed to assess his attainment of the objective. These tests include a wide variety of activities and formats as required by the objective, and are not limited to paper-and-pencil devices. If the student's performance is satisfactory, he moves to the next objective. If his performance is not satisfactory, he meets with one of the faculty members to identify additional learning experiences. A trainee may not certify until he accomplishes all objectives according to the established criteria.

While mastering the objectives which are necessary for effective instruction, the trainee is teamed with one or two other students in his subject matter specialty, and together they prepare curriculum materials to be used when they student teach. (See Figure 28-1.) Their overall objective here is to prepare materials which will allow them to individualize instruction. They write behavioral objectives, design and prepare learning activities, and pre- and post-test instruments. Some of the materials are completely programmed. During the preparation of curriculum materials, observations are made in the classroom in which the team will student teach and materials are pretested with secondary students.

Phase II Student Teaching

In phase two (see Figure 28-1) trainees are assigned as a team to a cooperating teacher in the public schools for the student teaching experience. Our students presently spend one-half day for eight weeks. We anticipate a future arrangement where both the kind and duration of student teaching assignment could be individualized with alternatives such as full or part year internships, teaching in multiple kinds of classrooms in either rural or urban schools.

Curriculum materials used in student teaching are those previously prepared by the team. The same college instructors who supervised Phase I supervise the student teaching experience. Students continue to prepare and revise curriculum materials as they use them in the classroom. Students also micro-teach before video-recorders to improve needed teaching behaviors.

In summary, the experimental program at B.Y.U. has been in operation for four semesters, during which time we have trained more than 60 secondary teachers. Approximately one-half are presently teaching in the public schools, the other half (not drop outs) are continuing graduate work. We have not yet collected follow-up data on our graduates except through interview with them and their employers. As a result of these data and observations we have made, the following strengths of the program seem apparent to us.

The main advantage this program has over others, as we perceive it, is in that it has forced us to practice what we have been teaching. It has forced us to individualize our instruction; to analyze, using the tools available, our teacher-pupil interaction and to do something about it; to concern ourselves with the self concepts of our students.

We have summarized some of the strengths of our program in the following list:

1. The program combines theory and practice.

2. Recommendation for certification is based on ability to perform specified behaviors.

3. Students accept more responsibility for their work in this kind of a program.

4. The program combines and is using many of the best methods for teaching of teacher training, such as inquiry training, interaction analysis, microteaching, curriculum design.

5. The program takes into account individual differences allowing the students to progress at their own best pace.

6. Students are team taught and they work as a team giving them opportunity to teach in large and small groups and to individualize as they student teach.

7. Areas of unnecessary overlap in the professional sequence of courses have been eliminated.

8. The program requires and results in an effective in-service training program for the cooperating teachers with whom we work.

9. Team student teaching, by decreasing the number of classroom stations, allows us to be more selective in assigning classrooms and in assigning the very best cooperating teachers.

10. Activities such as micro-teaching, interaction analysis, and team student teaching reduce the possibility of a student teacher learning from one poor teacher model thus perpetuating the weaknesses of our present education system.

11. The graduates seem to differ in their positive attitude toward themselves as teachers and toward the profession of teaching.

NOTES

[1]Clark Webb and Hugh Baird, "Learning Differences Resulting from Teacher and Student-Centered Teaching Methods," paper presented at American Educational Research Association Annual Meeting, February 16-18, 1967, New York. Victor Bunderson has since conducted similar research to verify these data.

Victor Bunderson, "Computer-Assisted Instruction in Self-Paced Teacher Education," paper presented at American Educational Research Association Annual Meeting, Chicago, February, 1968.

Part E

Individualized Learning:
The Future of
Education

Introduction

In Chapter 29, John Goodlad, for years a leading innovator and a proponent of nongraded programs in our educational institutions, has undertaken a thoughtful analysis of education as it could be by the year 2000. It is his concern that we keep in clear perspective the *human* needs of learning as we shape the instructional environment of the future. Schools of the future, according to Dr. Goodlad, will be radically altered and technology will play an important, though still undefined, role. His paper strongly suggests that the best way to promote humanistic values is through a clear delineation of society's goals and specification of how they are to be achieved through the educational enterprise. Individualized learning will certainly be a key to achieving those goals.

Chapter 29. CHANGING PATTERNS AND CAPABILITIES IN EDUCATION

THE FUTURE OF LEARNING AND TEACHING

John I. Goodlad

One of the reasons that providing instructional leadership will be so difficult in the future is that our concepts of schooling and teaching must change fundamentally. Just a few observations serve to give substance to this generalization.

First, what the school does in educating the young appears to be less or, at best, no more potent than other factors determining what the child learns and becomes. What the child brings to school from his own home and what he encounters there from other homes seem to add more to learning than what the school itself puts in. Second, the incidence of nonpromotion, dropouts, alienation, and minimal learning in school is such that one is led to conclude that today's schools are obsolescent. They were designed for a different culture, a different conception of learners and of learning, and a

SOURCE: Reprinted from *Audiovisual Communications Review*, Vol. 16, No. 1 (1968), pp. 5-15, by permission of author and publisher. It is based on Dr. Goodlad's address at the inauguration of Sam M. Lambert, executive secretary of the National Education Association, Washington, D.C., October 20, 1967.

different clientele. We do not plan for and deal with our clientele nearly as well as the Cadillac agent plans for and deals with his. Third, success in school, as measured by grades, appears to bear little relationship to good citizenship, good work habits, compassion, happiness, or other significant values in the larger human sphere. Fourth, a relatively new medium—television—has entered into the business of transmitting a major segment of our culture to the young. If the years before beginning school are taken into account, television occupies more hours than schooling during the eighteen years from birth to completion of high school. There are few signs that school and television are about to enter into a jointly planned enterprise for instruction of the young.

One could go on and on in this vein, but there is little point. The central problem, it seems to me, is that the intensity of the school must be enormously increased. Each of us is convinced that education is a powerful force for the improvement of man and of mankind. But to assume that school, as it now exists, maintains the central thrust in changing human behavior is to be misled.

I do not know how successful we will be in increasing the intensity of the school. I *do* know, however, that instruction will go on: in the home, in the peer group, through television, and in new institutions to be created. The failure to increase the intensity of the school may very well determine the nature, number, and variety of other institutions to be created and, in fact, the future of the school.

My purpose now is to portray instruction that is to come. We live in a time when one era of instruction is in full bloom; another is well begun; and a third is embryonic. Let us take a look at all three.

HUMAN TEACHERS

The era that is in full bloom and is about to fade is human-to-human instruction. The prime exhibit of this era is the human-based school. Here, we like to believe, children and youth are inducted into their culture; individual potentialities are identified and developed; individuals take on a sense of identity and ultimately transcend themselves; and the young are inculcated in those values that make for the ideal adult. Increasingly, however, we are becoming aware of the myth along with the fact. For a large segment of our population, instruction in school merely increases the gap between the "have's" and the "have-not's."

Nonetheless, we are in an inventive period, and old ways of doing things are tumbling before the drive to increase the intensity of the school. We have not yet eliminated track systems of grouping with their self-fulfilling prophecies; nor have we broken down the grade barriers with their nefarious adjustment mechanism of nonpromotion; nor have we removed classroom walls in all of our new building designs; nor have we learned to teach inductively, with the child learning for himself the skills of inquiry. But we have caught the spirit of these things. Few of our schools are nongraded, team taught, or organized around basic curricular concepts, skills, and values. But the arguments against these advances are few. Today's teachers want to know how to bring them about; and a few courageous souls are even talking about eliminating September madness in the kindergarten and bringing in children during the year when they are five, each on his birthday.

The kinds of innovations in human-based instruction in our schools this past decade or so have been relatively few. And they will be even fewer in number during the next decade or so. The challenge is much less one of inventing than of implementing the several of power and viability that have appeared during recent years. There will not be a revolution in human-based instruction in the schools during the next fifteen years; nor has there been one during the past fifteen years. There will be an accelerating evolution in curriculum, school organization, and instructional practices, while *non*human-based instruction will loom ever larger on the horizon.

HUMANS AND MACHINES IN TEACHING

The era of instruction that will supersede the era of human-based instruction is to be one of man-machine interaction. And the machine is the computer. We have lived in the shadow of the computer long enough now but used it so little in instructional affairs that we may be inclined to believe its future and our own to be things apart. Nothing could be farther from the truth.

The computer will march relentlessly into our instructional lives. Whether or not it will come into the school building is another matter. There is no reason to believe that it will not. The cost of a computer console for each elementary school classroom, I am told, is now about two thousand dollars. If we should decide to put one in every classroom, competition undoubtedly would push the cost down to one thousand dollars. At the first figure, we could equip every elementary school classroom in the United States with a computer at a cost of one billion dollars. If this amount were spread over a ten-year period, it certainly does not appear to be an outrageous figure.

There are problems involved, especially in hooking up the consoles to the computer-instructional system at some remote point. But this can be solved with improved communications connections or by moving small computers closer. One company has built a small computer-based instructional system which can be moved about and which is surprisingly inexpensive. Should development in computers be anything like development in television and in air-conditioning, the technical problems need not trouble us for long.

Already, computers are demonstrating their usefulness in teaching spelling, mathematics, reading, and a host of cognitive skills. Tapes, screens, records, and other audio-visual devices, coupled with the computer, make possible a unique instructional system of sight, sound, and touch.

Current writing on computer-assisted instruction portrays a picture of great instructional efficiency and the freeing of human teachers to do those instructional things that are truly human. But what are these truly human instructional tasks? And have teachers been prepared to engage in them? I have my doubts.

The provision of programed sequences by way of computer offers us efficient means of communicating educational lore and should be welcomed. But we know precious little about the productive interaction of human beings for the achievement of mankind's ends. The computer offers an intense learning environment. But it does not offer an intense *human* environment. I am inclined to believe that it is this lack of an intense human environment that explains why the school today seems not to be a highly significant factor in educating the environmentally deprived.

If the organized teaching profession behaves with respect to the computers as it has behaved with respect to some other innovations, it will reject "the great metallic beast . . . the genie we have raised to rule the earth." But what the teaching profession ultimately must do is to legitimatize the computer as instructor in those basic learnings that can be carefully programed. Then the profession must explore the questions of how computers and people are to live together productively in the instructional situation. By legitimatizing the computer as man's companion in a teaching program, it will be possible to work out who will do what and when in an environment influenced by the teaching profession. If the computer is not legitimatized by the teaching profession, however, it will go its own way as went television. The computer will go its own way to some extent in any case, but the important element is that it join the human teacher in a planned process of inducting the young into their culture.

An important focal point for the teaching profession now is the humanization of the means of instruction. We have reiterated truly human ends for education but have not done too well by the means. Two opportunities lie open to us. The first is the humanization of content. The second is the humanization of the entire instructional environment.

The average high school senior graduating this past June has viewed fifteen thousand hours of television in addition to many hundreds of hours of public movies. These hours and many more spent with newspapers and magazines exposed him to a formidable display of violence, cruelty, dishonesty, and inhumanity to man. I do not believe that his twelve thousand hours in school exposed him to anything like an antidote. And school intensity throughout was low. We appear loath to portray the other side of the coin through the substance of schooling. Could we not mount a program in the social studies and in the humanities designed to portray the best in men and in mankind? We have the tools and the creative minds. Do we not care enough, or have we simply resigned ourselves to inevitable folly in man?

Similarly, we need to design every phase of the human relationship in learning in order to make the total impact more intensely human. We complain about students' relationships to one another and to adults. We set up petty rules to be broken. Clearly, however, persistence in these attitudes and behaviors is indicative of an inadequate educative process. In my 1966 general session address to the Association for Supervision and Curriculum Development of the NEA, I spoke of a humanistic curriculum which I hoped might become a central concern for at least the two concluding decades of this century. Some thought I was too pessimistic and that what I called for might be attained much sooner. What I meant by a humanistic curriculum was emphasis on our very best human values in the substance of the curriculum, and concern for both the human individual and mankind in the environment surrounding instruction and learning.

I believe these tasks to be so formidable and their import to be of such magnitude that I welcome the computer into the instructional process and charge it with teaching some of those basic skills and concepts which are only the beginning in educating the compassionate, rational man. I do not see the computer as the human teacher's competitor. Not at all! I see it rather as replacing the teacher for many instructional tasks which the computer should do and, indeed, can do better. The notion that the computer should replace the teacher for a substantial segment of instruction will not be popular within some segments of the teaching profession.

In the past and in the present, we have viewed the individual teacher as master of instruction in a school setting. We have introduced audio-visual aids into the process but have stressed very carefully that these are to be merely an extension of the teacher. The teacher is to be coordinator of an arsenal of instructional resources. Sensitive to the goals of instruction and aware of resources compatible with these goals, the teacher is supposed to select carefully from film, filmstrip, record, and book. The process has not worked very well. It is complex, and the demands are many. The concept is legitimate for a team of teachers, each individual in the team performing his unique function. But we have been slow to move into the ideal organization of teachers that would permit appraising and using the full instructional arsenal.

I submit that the computer can and will do certain instructional tasks better than any human teacher can perform them. The research challenge is to catalogue those aspects of instruction that are most appropriate for the machine teacher, on one hand, and for the human teacher, on the other. We must *not* make the human teacher a supervisor or coordinator of the computer or he will become its servant. The teacher may very well contribute to programing, but the interface should be between student and machine. For us to take our traditional position with respect to this electronic teacher is to delay advance in the instructional process and, in the long run, to endanger the highly relevant role of the human teacher.

There is, indeed, a significant task for human teachers, one which may very well be accomplished better if we turn over some of the other tasks to the untiring machine. Simply to say that the advent of the computer will leave the more sensitive and significant teaching tasks to human teachers is not enough. The process of humanizing instruction will not occur by chance.

DIFFUSED LEARNING AND TEACHING

To recap briefly, we are still in a traditional era of human-based instruction. Most of the innovations needed to refine human-based instruction so that it will be much more effective than it has been are now with us. Few additional inventions are likely to appear during the next decade. But we have quite enough to occupy us well into the 1980's.

The era of human and machine-based instruction is soon to be upon us. If we turn our backs on the computer, we may delay computerized instruction a little. But we may destroy the school and the influence of the education profession in the process. It is imperative that we explore the most appropriate roles of man and machine and that we legitimatize them.

A third era, only dimly visible at this point, is much more hazy in its outlines, and we can only speculate as to its characteristics, assets, and liabilities. The computer will do much to accelerate its coming, too.

Were we to decide now to put a computer console in every elementary school classroom during the next ten years, the cost would be cut in half very soon and, perhaps, in half again before the decade ended. But supposing we were to accelerate production of software so as to program computers for home use. Clearly, the cost of a computer console would diminish to the point where it would be as accessible to the average family as a television set is today. Begin to think just a little of the potential power inherent in that eventuality!

Now, let me approach the proposition from the vantage point of the school. Most of our schools are anachronisms. If we rethink them well in advance of laying a cornerstone, we may never lay that cornerstone. Let me illustrate.

More than a year ago, a creative, imaginative school superintendent in California came to visit me. He was excited, as he should have been, about his notion of creating a true laboratory school in the public school setting. He wanted to begin with none of the old assumptions; to start from the very beginning. After he had talked a while and I was sharing his enthusiasm, I began to ask some specific questions.

When was the school to open? More than a year hence. Had anything been done about employing teachers? Yes, a principal had been selected and employment was proceeding. How many teachers were to be employed? The answer worked out to a figure of one teacher for every twenty-eight pupils, or approximately twenty teachers. I asked, "Why twenty? Why not five, or seven, or ten?" My visitor became a little irritated. I pushed on. "How large is the school to be?" The answer indicated that there were to be rooms or open flexible spaces for nearly six hundred pupils. I then asked why the school was not being designed for half this number. Now my visitor was very irritated. He thought I was playing a sadistic game.

Of course, I was not. The point I was making is that we effect our major decisions by tradition before getting to the few things we change. We assume that there will be X number of qualified teachers for Y number of children. And we assume that we will construct a school building large enough for all of the children to be housed. But there is no reason at all that we could not employ half the usual quota of fully qualified teachers, using the balance of our money for part-time specialists and a host of instructional aids. And there is no reason at all that we could not plan an educational program requiring only half a school building, with the balance of the money going to trips, special projects, and individualized activities supervised by the staff or even programed by a computer.

Every single decision governing a school was at one time or another made by man. At the time the decisions were made which today govern the schools, less data were available. The men who made these decisions were no brighter than schoolmen today, and they were less well educated. Therefore, it behooves us to reexamine every decision about schooling: size of building and whether we want one at all; numbers of teachers and whether we need a fully certified teacher for every twenty-eight and a half children; whether there is to be a library that houses real books or whether the library is to be a computerized box. A fully automated library with no books but only microfiche is now out of the realm of science fiction and into the actuality of college and university planning in the United States.

A school is not necessary to learning and instruction. We do not need a school to guide children and youth in seeking to grasp their culture. And, certainly, we do not need a school to teach fundamentals of reading, writing, and arithmetic. But we do need formal processes of instruction with the most able members of our society giving their time to it in planning and programing instructional materials, in computerizing varied programs for learning, and in interacting with other humans in the delightful business of learning from one another.

The computer which we must legitimatize for learning and teaching in an imminent era probably will contribute significantly in a still later era to the demise of what we now call school. We shall regard this as a bad thing only if we lack faith in the ability of man to fashion a world better than the one in which we now live.

In viewing learning and teaching for the year 2000 and beyond, it is easier to predict what will not be than what will be. A prescribed age for beginning would be meaningless. The computer console with an array of stimuli and feedback devices will be as natural for the child of 2000-plus as television is for today's two-year-old. Teaching and learning will not be marked by a standard day of from nine to three; nor a standard year from September to June; nor a year for a grade of carefully packaged material. Age will be meaningless as a criterion for determining what a child is to learn. Will learning be any less because there will be no periods, no Carnegie units, no ringing of bells, no jostling of pupils from class to class? What will the school principal and his administrative associates do when it is no longer necessary to schedule teachers so as to produce a balanced diet of subjects? The student will be free to concentrate exclusively on a given field for weeks or months or to divide his time among several fields. It must be remembered that the touch of his fingers and the variability and comprehensiveness of programed learning sequences, not the availability or energies of human teachers, will control a significant portion of his curriculum.

Clearly, the role of human teachers will change markedly. Hundreds of hours of their time will go into what will occupy each student for an hour or two. But because thousands, or even millions, of students might at some time select this hour, preparation time will be well spent. And quality will be vastly improved.

School, as we now know it—whether egg crate or flexible space—will have been replaced by a diversified learning environment involving homes, parks, public buildings, museums, and guidance centers. It is quite conceivable that each community will have a learning center and that homes will contain an electronic console connected to this central generating unit. This learning center will provide not only a computer-controlled videotape, microfiche, and record library, but also access to state and national educational television networks. It is even possible that advanced technology will return the family to center stage as the basic learning unit.

The most controversial issues of the twenty-first century will pertain to the ends and means of modifying human behavior and who shall determine them. The first educational question will not be, "What knowledge is of most worth?" but, "What kinds of human beings do we wish to produce?" The possibilities virtually defy our imagination.

The nerve cells of the brain, far more than muscles or any other organs, are highly sensitive to small electric currents, to a variety of chemicals, and to changes in blood supply and its accompanying nourishment. Sedatives, barbiturates, tranquilizers, and various psychedelics (LSD, for example) provide powerful ways of controlling behavior by direct action on the brain. Similarly, behavior can be manipulated by applying electric currents to regions of the brain. Experiments are now underway with drugs and brain extracts designed to enhance learning or memory. Aldous Huxley long ago introduced us to the possibilities of genetic selectivity through the availability of sperm and ovum banks. The means of drastically altering the course of human development through artificial semination, chemical treatment, and electric manipulation are with us. We are already tampering with human evolution. The possibilities for further doing so will be enormously enhanced and refined as we move into the twenty-first century.

IN CONCLUSION

At least one message should come through in what I have said: Education and instruction are much bigger than schools. Schools are only a convenient means to more important ends, means that may no longer be relevant several decades from now.

As a profession, we have tended to be bogged down in the narrow details of our calling, details pertaining primarily to means: the means of buildings, classrooms, books, and all of these together. As a consequence, we have failed to provide the leadership necessary to raising the minds of our people beyond these trivialities.

As individual leaders, we must assert by our very competence that we know how to manage the means. Our constituencies lose faith in our competence when we hesitate, falter, and in desperation turn to the community for guidance in technique. The intrusion of state legislatures into instructional decision-making processes must be attributed at least in some degree to our failure to grasp the individual opportunity for leadership.

But the charge to the organized profession is a much larger one. We must raise the level of the dialogue to the truly significant questions of educational ends, and we must be as diligent as our lay citizens in laying bare instructional deficiencies in the pursuit of these ends.

As to ends, let me put them as questions to ask about the educational enterprise:

1. To what extent are our young people coming into critical possession of their culture?

2. To what extent is each individual being provided with his unique opportunities to develop potentialities to the maximum?

3. To what extent is each individual developing a deep sense of personal worth, the sense of selfhood that is prerequisite to self-transcendence?

4. To what extent are our people developing truly mankind values, values that transcend all men in all times and in all places?

A fifth question is the most important, challenging, and frightening of all, now that men possess such manipulative powers. As citizen and educator, I cherish the right to participate in the dialogue about it: What kinds of human beings do we wish to produce?

Name Index

355

Subject Index

357

teacher education,
  academic preparation in, 336-339
  student teaching in, 339-340
  through individualization, 85-90,
  332-340
teacher's role,17, 83-90, 157-161, 184,
  197, 199-200, 240, 244, 248-249, 281-
  289, 291-292, 349-350
teachers,
  preparation of, 17-18, 22, 85-90,
  122-123, 164-168, 332-340
teaching process,
  change in the, 160, 193, 352
team planning, 261-262, 284-289
traditional teaching characterized,
  205
Trenton School System, New Jersey,
  162

Union High School District No. 5,
  Oregon, 232
UNIPAC,
  bank concept, 174-182
  defined, 171, 177
  workshops, 179-181

units and unit teams,
  organizational, 240
Universal School, Mississippi, 303-306
University of Chicago High School, 6
University of Hawaii Communications
  Center, 314
University of Pittsburgh, 92, 101,
  103, 115, 130, 158, 162-163

Valley High School, Nevada, 171,
  183, 184, 187

Washington Elementary School, New
  Jersey, 129
Wechsler Intelligence Scale for Chil-
  dren (W.I.S.C.), 266
West Elementary School, Delaware, 129
Westbrook Elementary School, Missis-
  sippi, 301, 303-304
Westinghouse Learning Corporation, 2,
  3, 54, 83
Wilson School, Minnesota, 172, 257-262
Winnetka Public Schools, Illinois, 6
work stations, 79-80